# KYOTO
## A Contemplative Guide

24 September 1967

To Mr. and Mrs. Hendrick,

Welcome to Japan and our
warm wishes for a
wonderful visit.

Affectionately,

D. Lee and John Rich

# KYOTO
## A Contemplative Guide

by Gouverneur Mosher

CHARLES E. TUTTLE COMPANY: PUBLISHERS
Rutland, Vermont & Tokyo, Japan

REPRESENTATIVES
For Continental Europe:
BOXERBOOKS, INC., Zurich
For the British Isles:
PRENTICE–HALL INTERNATIONAL, INC., London
For Australasia:
PAUL FLESCH & CO., PTY. LTD., Melbourne

Published by the
Charles E. Tuttle Company
of Rutland, Vermont & Tokyo, Japan
with editorial offices at
No. 15 Edogawa-cho, Bunkyo-ku, Tokyo

Copyright in Japan, 1964
by Charles E. Tuttle Company
All rights reserved

Library of Congress Catalog
Card No. 64-24951

First printing, 1964

Book design and typography by Kaoru Ogimi
PRINTED IN JAPAN

*This book is dedicated to the
happy memory of my parents
Rebecca Williams Mosher
and
John Stewart Mosher.*

*They thought it was a good idea.*

# Table of Contents

# Contents

## PART THREE: Getting There and Back

# Contents

Appendices

# List of Illustrations

Plates

## Maps

# List of Illustrations

# Kyoto Streetcar System

Map at left shows routes and numbers. If there is a number common to your present location and your destination, you can get there without changing cars. Otherwise, follow numbers until they meet and change there. Many lines start at Kyoto Station. On map at right, streets are in large capitals, streetcar stops in ordinary type, representative sights and train stations in small capitals.

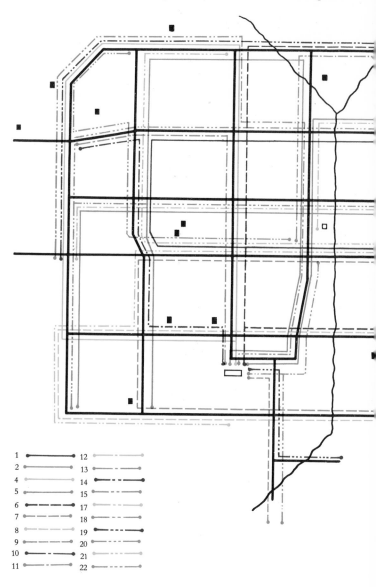

| 1 | 12 |
| 2 | 13 |
| 4 | 14 |
| 5 | 15 |
| 6 | 17 |
| 7 | 18 |
| 8 | 19 |
| 9 | 20 |
| 10 | 21 |
| 11 | 22 |

# Introduction

IN PRESENTING this book I hope to fill a gap that exists in the present body of literature about Kyoto, between superficial travel pamphlets and scholarly, annotated reference works. I found when I went to Kyoto myself that there was no single book between these areas which answered my questions about the temples and other historic buildings I saw; nor was there a book to help me select which among the thousands of sights to see. I hope the present volume will help solve these and other problems for visitors to Kyoto.

The places presented here I chose primarily for their ability to fascinate, whether by a colorful history, a beautiful garden, or a wealth of fine buildings. Lesser considerations were geographical location and ease of access by public transportation. Public transportation is excellent in Kyoto, and by using it one learns much more about the city and its geography than he can from the inside of a speeding taxi.

I hope that the visitor who sees these places will be encouraged to see more of Kyoto, and that their historic and geographic spread will provide him with enough information about the city and its history that visits to places not included in the book will be more interesting than they might be otherwise.

The book falls into three parts. The first part is a series of commentaries on the places selected. The commentaries set each place in historical perspective—something that could not be accomplished in a formal guide. Individually these commentaries will give the reader a better idea of the places he decides to visit, while together they present a general picture of Kyoto's history. If the second part of the book provides factual data, this first part offers some coloring for it.

The second part is a guide which examines each place in detail, and I hope it will enable the reader to do the same without the need to secure a human guide or additional literature. It is intended to answer as many factual questions about these places as a book can. By limiting the number of places considered, I have been able to present a maximum amount of information about each one.

The third and last part of the book is a practical section: how to get to a place (and back), what to take along, what day to go there, how long it will take. This part will please streetcar buffs, picnic nuts, timetable collectors. It may even help the taxi addict out of a jam some day when he's miles from home with no taxi in sight.

Some specific notes about the arrangement of the book may be helpful. The names at the heads of chapters in the first part are of those people who are principals in the story that follows, people whose names will come up frequently and to whom the reader may want to refer more than once. In the second part of the book, paragraphs in finer print present information of a detailed nature, which can be passed over if necessary. Also in the second part many place and temple names are followed by their equivalents in Japanese characters and, where it is possible, an English translation of the name. For the most part these translations are literal renderings made to satisfy the reader's curiosity only, and they have no official significance. I do not wish to attach English names to these Japanese places but thought the reader would like some idea of what the Japanese names indicate.

Before closing this introduction, I wish to mention briefly some of the places not selected for the book. Some were omitted simply because it was only reasonable to include one of their kind: I think of the great Zen temples, like Myoshin-ji, Nanzen-ji, Ninna-ji, Tenryu-ji, and Tofuku-ji. All are worthy rivals for Daitoku-ji, and I hope my material on the latter will add to the pleasure of seeing the others.

Certain other temples—Shisen-do and Saiho-ji, for example—have a special charm which is perhaps just too special to make them indispensable for a book of this kind. For my tastes, the famous Sanjusangen-do is also "too special": interesting to see after one has seen more orthodox Buddhist temples, but likely to bore if seen earlier. In addition, the aura of tourism there discouraged me.

There are three places in Kyoto which are controlled by the

Imperial Household Agency: the Imperial Palace, and Katsura and Shugaku-in villas. At one time I had decided to omit all three, because the restrictions enforced by the Household Agency seemed to spoil the pleasure of seeing them. The visitor has to get permission, meet an appointment, and allow himself to be herded through by a guide. This was particularly damaging to a visit to the "old" Imperial Palace (better "former," because here "old" now only means a hundred years), where there was little enough to see and most of that was boarded up and hidden as one was whisked on a pointless twenty-minute stroll through the grounds. The insignificant history of the present palace and the restrictions on seeing it combine to make it a poor place to see.

Katsura, on the other hand, while being an admirable place, attracts excessive crowds, so that it is difficult to enjoy seeing it. As it is also one place in Kyoto which already has its own ample body of English literature, I decided not to include it in this book. While encouraging the reader to see Katsura, I would warn him that the conditions under which he will see it are not ideal.

Shugaku-in, however, proved to be a different case. It is generally ignored by foreign visitors, and therefore is less crowded and more pleasant to visit. The official restrictions there are fewer and less annoying. The Shugaku-in gardens are good examples of the refined imperial taste since an emperor, not a professional artist, was their chief designer; and they are so beautiful that I decided to include them. I regret that there are restrictions upon seeing Shugaku-in, but its beauty and lack of popularity tend to push them into the background.

In general, it will be a happier day when these three imperial places are opened freely to the public. As a foreigner, I have many times apologized to my Japanese friends for the way foreigners are given preference over Japanese people by the Imperial Household Agency, and for the rudeness that agency displays towards its own citizens. It seems as if the officials there are trying to preserve the feudalism of the past. It is a sad fact that the easiest way for a Japanese person to see these treasures of his nation is not by himself, but by posing as a guide for a foreign friend. Perhaps it will help matters if the agency learns that its rudeness towards its own people has not gone unnoticed by one foreigner whom it treated courteously.

To those who wish I had included the Gold Pavilion I recommend the Silver Pavilion, Ginkaku-ji. At one time I might have chosen the former, but it burned in 1950; so now, when choosing between the two, one must consider their respective dates: Gold, 1955 (and it looks it); Silver, 1483. It is unlikely that the reader would thank me if I sent him to the gold one the day the silver one burned down! And, once again, the slightly lesser popularity of the latter, as well as its unmatched garden, make it the more interesting place of the two to see.

The Heian Shrine is another place which is just too new: in a city that started rising in the eighth century, one should not spend his limited time seeing a shrine that dates from 1895, even if it is a replica of the old imperial palace buildings. In addition, like most Shinto shrines, the Heian offers surprisingly little of cultural interest.

The reader will note that Shinto is largely ignored by this book. It is not a prejudice of my own but the pattern of Kyoto's history that has caused this. The Buddhist sects which emerged at the time of Kyoto's founding suppressed Shinto, and Buddhism dominated political, cultural, and religious affairs during the centuries that Kyoto was capital. Thus Kyoto's period of greatness coincided with Shinto's nadir; only when the capital was moved to Tokyo in 1868 was Shinto revived, purified, and restored to an independent position. For this reason one does not find pure Shinto in Kyoto: this is a city dominated by Buddhism.

Among the Shinto shrines that do stand in Kyoto, Kamigamo and Shimogamo rank high, while the Inari Shrine presents one with an unexcelled myriad of torii and bronze foxes, as well as a history more than 1250 years old.

Finally, I wish to mention two places that could as well be in this book as out of it. My "second volume" would be headed by Nishi Hongan-ji, one of Kyoto's truly great temples. Another is Chion-in, the headquarters of the Jodo sect.

The list of fine places in Kyoto is endless. This book only scratches the surface, but it tries to scratch the best surface available and to do it effectively.

In closing, I regret that there is a certain amount of repetition between Parts I and II. I have tried to keep it to a minimum, but some is necessary so the reader, when visiting a given place, will not find it necessary to skip back and forth between the commentary and the guide.

I have many acknowledgments to make for help in preparing this book, both to living persons and printed works, and they are made on their own page at the back of the book.

GOUVERNEUR MOSHER

# PART ONE
Perspectives and Places

# 1 | Kyoto and Its Beginnings: Shinsen-en

"Ceaselessly the river flows, and yet the water is never the same, while in the still pools the shifting foam gathers and is gone, never staying for a moment."    *Hojo-ki*

KAMMU (737–806), fiftieth emperor of Japan (781–806), founder of Kyoto.

JAPANESE recorded history, despite legends to the contrary, probably began about two thousand years ago. In its early centuries Japan was strongly influenced by its neighbors, especially China. It was only about a thousand years ago that Japan began to crystallize as a country whose culture, arts, and philosophies flourished independent of those of neighboring countries. By the time this process began, Kyoto was the national capital, which it remained until 1868.

Kyoto thus stood at the center of the most interesting and important periods of Japanese history and today presents one with an incomparable cross section of the country's past. While other Japanese cities are famous for their connections with single periods, Kyoto influenced all periods after its founding and dominated most of them. Even today, although it is no longer the country's political capital, Kyoto remains the spiritual capital of Japan. It ruled the country too long to be forgotten by the Japanese people, and so long that no foreigner who cares about understanding Japan's rich past can claim to have seen the nation until he has been to Kyoto.

Kyoto is many cities: there has never been a "perfect" Kyoto. The fragility of the traditional Japanese building made it impossible for a single, durable Kyoto to be built; instead, the city had to be rebuilt over and over again. It rose and fell continuously. Its history is a record of a continuous frenzy of building, burning, repairing, looting, rebuilding, moving, destroying— rebuilding and burning again thousands of wooden buildings, by their very nature built, moved, raided, destroyed, and burned with ease.

Like fishes, Kyoto buildings depended on heavy production to offset a high mortality rate. Politics, wars, natural disasters, and pure chance determined which ones would survive. As the cycle progressed, each era left in its wake a few structures which would somehow make it into the twentieth century, and today they stand here and there about Kyoto, the silent representatives of thousands of less fortunate coevals. Within a single temple yard the buildings of the twentieth century may have among them one from the tenth, an ancestor whose age is not apparent to the casual observer. Today that building stands alone; once there were hundreds like it—enough to make a whole city.

Although haphazard decided which buildings survived, the city as a whole presents today a definite geographical pattern. Its flat center, untouched by World War II but razed in virtually every war previous, is the modern Kyoto. Here alone one finds the big movie houses, the occasional night clubs and myriad small bars, the modernistic buildings that speak of the postwar period. Here too stands most of the city's older Western construction—the homely edifices that rose in Japan's Victorian period. The center of Kyoto has little that antedates the seventeenth century. The same can be said for the southern outskirts, the city's only flat suburb, which have apparently been abandoned to industry.

It is the hilly suburbs to the west, north, east, and southeast of Kyoto that are the repositories of its oldest treasures. Here, in the hidden valleys and hillsides that almost ring the city, one finds ancient retreats and temples that have escaped the wars which tore at Kyoto's center. The farther back one delves into the city's past, the farther outside the city he is drawn, to villages like Uji, Arashiyama, and Ohara.

Kyoto, then, has a thriving modern heart, ringed on three sides by relics of its colorful, venerable past.

KYOTO'S TEMPERAMENT

Kyoto today is a cheerful, unhurried city that is delightful to visit. It is quiet and easy to find one's way about. Although it is large, there is an intimacy about it in which the stranger quickly feels at home. In these pleasant surroundings he savors the city's finest quality, its unending store of carefully hidden and protected gems from the past—gardens, parks, temples, villas. The city continually rewards the visitor who looks at it closely; wherever he goes, he finds endless series of surprises. In its beauty and diversity Kyoto stands today among the few great cities of the world.

Strange, then, that one begins to notice a definite negativism that seems to be part of this place. It manifests itself in various and unexpected ways. A beautiful stand of maples, seen at the height of the fall season, seems to excite admiration not only because its beauty exists but, more than that, because its beauty *must end*. One looks at the straining cherry blossoms in spring and reflects that they will soon be blown away to die. The sad fleeting quality of the moment is savored just as fully as the moment itself.

Similarly one time and again encounters a tale of a hero of Kyoto's past in which it seems that no matter how glorious his early life, it was only the prelude to a more important time when his happiness was shattered and his hopes were swiftly felled. The success story familiar to Westerners does not occur in Kyoto without its sequel of failure, frustration, and—incidentally— death. Death was understandably welcome at the end of these men's lives.

These negative attitudes are part of the city's heritage. Kyoto's past was an unhappy one. Politically, it was marked by powerless and poverty-ridden emperors who were shoved aside by ruthless military dictators. Ironically, this city so closely associated with the Emperor of Japan was the scene of his steady decline as the true ruler of his people. Between two great rulers— Kammu, 50th in the line and founder of the city, and Meiji, the 122nd, under whom the capital was removed to Tokyo in 1868 —only one or two of the long succession of Kyoto emperors even attempted to govern his country. The rest filled purely ceremonial positions and rarely became involved in active politics beyond the petty intrigues of their courts. The real political power was not with them but lay in the hands of their ministers, military and civilian, who gained office as often by violence as they did by legitimate appointment.

Thus if the emperor's residence in Kyoto for eleven centuries is cited as evidence of permanence and hallowed tradition, it must be balanced against the continuous unrest and numberless political changes—many of them abrupt and incredible—that occurred behind the scenes. The emperor weaves a steady thread through Kyoto's history, but it is a weak thread, not the dynamic one which held together the hard core of important events. The true government of Kyoto's Japan was of other men, for whom war and mass death were the only route to personal power and survival.

Kyoto's religious history was similarly dominated by a predatory group: the Buddhist priesthood. It was in Kyoto that these men reached the zenith of their temporal power. It had been thought that they could be checked by being ordered to build their monasteries in the mountains, but the monasteries grew to enormous size away from the city's watchful eye, attaining an independence and strength that could not be controlled. Shinto, the native religion, was quickly eliminated as a rival by the well-organized Buddhists, who simply absorbed it. By swallowing Shinto whole, the Buddhists emerged as Japan's sole religious power. Thereafter Kyoto witnessed centuries of internal wars between the various Buddhist sects. Sect battled sect, and new sects flaked off the old ones. As these wars were bloody and continuous, it may well be said that Buddhism did not retard war but rather promoted it.

Caught in the wars of rival governments and Buddhist sects, the ordinary man found that his only motive in life became one of escape. Some, like the man who wrote the words at the head of this chapter, withdrew from Kyoto and spent their days in an introspection which only drove them deeper into the abyss of gloom. Others struggled on at their posts but without any real hope of glory. Individual accomplishment was held in such low esteem that in fields like painting a great work often outlived the name of its creator simply because he saw no point in signing it. Few attempted and none were able to dispel the torments of daily existence—these were accepted as irremediable. Those few who did enjoy luxury and ease were villains, ruthless lords who did not mind that luxury for one man could only be pressed from the backs of thousands.

Under these circumstances it is not surprising that Kyoto's

past is heavily dotted with stories of suicide, of defeat, of reclusion and retreat; or that it is embedded with an air of sadness which penetrated into the homes of humblest and highest alike —no one group has a greater share of dismal tales behind it than the long line of emperors themselves. When one looks back over Kyoto's history, the heroes he sees are not benefactors, reformers, or liberators. They are hermits, exiled emperors, martyrs, and other tragic individuals or families whose relatively short periods of prosperity always preceded some ghastly inevitable doom.

In the seventeenth and eighteenth centuries conditions improved to the point where people could lead happy lives and feel the material desires of this world; but by this time the focus of national attention had left Kyoto and moved east to Edo (Tokyo), leaving the aged capital contemplating a past heavily caked with physical poverty and spiritual magnificence. Bound up in its memories to an extent unequaled by any other city, Kyoto is perhaps alone in retaining so many vestiges of the philosophical pessimism that formerly dominated Japan. This atmosphere is one of the numberless relics of the past which Kyoto preserves for the modern visitor.

### THE FIRST KYOTO

In Japan's early history the capital city was moved and built anew with the passing of each emperor. It was an act of purification to abandon the capital used by the divine ruler who had just died. These temporary capitals were built here and there in central Japan. Gradually, however, the court and administrative populations grew larger and more cumbersome, and each move became increasingly difficult. The distance of the moves became smaller and smaller as the imperial court spiraled slowly about a valley south of present-day Kyoto; then it finally staggered to a halt at Nara and settled down to spend most of the eighth century there. Nara became Japan's first "permanent" capital.

In Nara, Buddhism, which had by now been in Japan for about two hundred years, grew to surprising strength. Taking advantage of the permanence of the capital, the Buddhists consolidated their position by building huge and numerous temples. As their power increased, they infiltrated the political affairs of

1. "The pond is what remains of Shinsen-en. Scarcely recognizable, this acre or two of the imperial garden has survived for almost twelve centuries right in the heart of the city. . . ." Courtesy of the Asahi Shimbunsha.

the government. Buddhist priests became influential figures: one even attempted to become emperor. The imperial line was saved from this threat, but it is said that the increasing size and power of Buddhism was what persuaded the Emperor Kammu to abandon Nara in the year 784. Since the big temples could not be moved, the emperor simply stepped out from under them, leaving them masters of a city now suddenly insignificant.

Kammu went north to a place called Nagaoka and set up his capital there. The move to Nagaoka was a financial setback, but despite the poor state of his treasury, for reasons that are not clear Kammu decided at the end of ten years to move his capital again. This time he chose a site a little east of Nagaoka which he named Heian-kyo. The city which was later called Kyoto[1] thus housed its first emperor in the year 794. Only 1074 years and seventy-two emperors later did a ruler of Japan remove his capital from this city which Kammu founded.

Kammu's new capital of 794 was a magnificent city in those days, distinguished as it still is by its orderly block plan, an arrangement which the Japanese borrowed from China.[2] Within the new city's rectangular boundary great avenues crossed each other and were interspersed with smaller streets.

One broad avenue split the city into halves called the East and West, or Left and Right Capitals. At its head stood the palace enclosure, a large walled area embedded in the north-central part of the city. The palace looked out on the city to the east, south, and west, while its north side formed part of the city limit. On the left of the great enclosure spread the Left Capital, and on the right the Right, and within each of them avenues, streets, and lanes carefully delineated the blocks and sub-blocks, thousands of which made up what was probably at that time one of the finest cities of the world.

SHINSEN-EN

When Kammu built his great palace in Heian-kyo, he attached a pleasure garden to the main enclosure, stretching south into the city for about thirty-three acres. Like the city itself, this garden

1. Heian-kyo: "peaceful, tranquil capital." Kyoto: "capital city."
2. It measured 5,312 meters (N-S) by 4,569 meters (E-W). The main avenue was 89 meters broad—primarily as a defense against fire.

was designed in Chinese style. Pleasure pavilions for such pastimes as moon-viewing, fishing, and waterfall contemplation hung out over ponds in appropriate places. Other pavilions were scattered about the grounds for parties who attended the dinners, dancing exhibitions, wrestling matches, poetry contests, and countless other entertainments arranged for the distraction of the emperor and his court. The buildings were coated with red lacquer, and the larger ones were connected to the smaller by elaborate wings. Finally, the entire garden was walled off from the city.

This garden was called Shinsen-en, or Sacred Spring Garden. Part of it survived everything around it, including the old Imperial Palace, and still exists today.

The original Shinsen-en was maintained in good order and used by the emperors for about three centuries after Kammu first visited it in the year 800. But even during this initial period of prosperity it was a neighbor to disaster, for the Imperial Palace, dogged by bad luck, was more often down than up. Fire and earthquake constantly visited the palace grounds, where no ordinary mortal was allowed. Between the eighth and thirteenth centuries the emperor's quarters had to be rebuilt seventeen times, including one disastrous stretch of 122 years in which they burned down fourteen times. At first, because the imperial name still had political power, these rebuildings were speedily accomplished. Gradually, however, the power diminished and the process slowed down until finally, in 1227, the but partially reconstructed palace burned for the last time. It was never rebuilt after that, and the site was eventually abandoned.

Shinsen-en lost its purpose when the palace was gone. By the thirteenth century, with imperial funds diverted in more necessary directions, the garden had lain unused for a century or more. Now the palace was gone completely and the garden was left an orphan, a state in which it remained for about four hundred years. In the seventeenth century its grounds were given to To-ji, a temple of the Shingon sect. By that time long neglect had allowed most of the garden's original acres to dissipate. Streets and houses had encroached on the grounds from three sides, and Nijo Castle had just been built on the fourth. To-ji took over what remained of the garden and has held it ever since.

Today the large area that was covered by Kammu's Imperial Palace is a teeming section of modern Kyoto jammed with small houses and shops. Of the old palace and its grounds not a trace remains. It is seven centuries since they were abandoned and their remains began vanishing under the changing city.

Today a small pond with dusty dirt banks stands just south of Nijo Castle. There are three tiny Shinto shrines about it, and off in one corner is a Buddhist temple, but none of these buildings is very important. In the afternoons small boys on their way home from school come by this place and stop for a while. They scramble about on the wooden fences which hold off the dwellings crowding in on both sides, and they walk along the dusty banks of the pond and throw stones in the shallow water. For them this place is a kind of playground.

The pond is what remains of Shinsen-en. Scarcely recognizable, this acre or two of the imperial garden has survived for almost twelve centuries right in the heart of the city, a scene of continual war and destruction. Somehow it escaped the fate of the rest of the garden, which today lies under a tangle of inns, houses, and schools, and a section of Nijo Castle.

The small pond that survives can hardly be called more than a faint reminder of the magnificent garden that once stretched north and south from this spot. It probably lasted only because its water was useful for fighting fires and irrigating fields. If one goes to the Byodo-in at Uji,[3] he may get some idea of the appearance of the original Shinsen-en, but here on the site itself it is difficult to conjure up the past from the muddy pond, tiny shrines, and stone-throwing schoolboys of the present.

Today's Shinsen-en is the only token left of Kammu's original capital. It is little more than a starting-point, a place where the modern visitor can go to orient himself, to learn how far in the past lie Kyoto's beginnings. It reminds one of that happy moment when Kyoto was first laid out, when Kammu made it the national capital, and when it optimistically entered the turbulent, strenuous, and painfully long future that lay before it.

3. See chapter 4.

# 2 The Mountain Monastery of the Tendai: Enryaku-ji

"If I do not take them away now, this great trouble will be everlasting. Moreover, these priests violate their vows: they eat fish and stinking vegetables, keep concubines, and never unroll the sacred books. How can they be vigilant against evil, or maintain the right? Surround their dens and burn them, and suffer none within them to live!" ODA NOBUNAGA

SAICHO (767–822), priest, founder of the Tendai sect in Japan and of Enryaku-ji, posthumously named Dengyo Daishi.

ODA NOBUNAGA (1534–82), general, who unified Japan after more than a century of civil war.

I FIRST came to Sakamoto on a quiet, mid-winter morning whose low sun was badly weakened by the haze over Lake Biwa. The stucco cable-car station there stood alone above the town in a small, tree-lined pocket under the rising wall of Mt. Hiei. It was warm there, because wooded banks and hills and the mountain itself formed a windless trap that caught and held the meagre sunlight. The station was deserted, but from it poured the music and noise of a turned-up radio. About a hundred yards away there sat a large Buddhist hall, silent and inconspicuous in the woods, watching this access to the great mountain monastery.

At departure time alarm bells and gongs began sounding with splendid formality. Some minutes passed, and a man with a briefcase puffed around the bend in answer to this summons. Amid crescendo alarms the conductor emerged in full uniform from behind the ticket window and examined the tickets he had just sold us and punched them as we passed through the wicket to the cable car. He joined us in the car, where buzzing noises and lights created a sense of imminence. A final loud alarm superimposed on the piercing hour-tone of the radio was succeeded by a silent click, and the car pulled up the mountain.

As we rose, the hazy lake and plain fell steadily away; then the car entered a tunnel, and when it came out again the view was

37

blocked by a hill and by woods that were patched with snow. Soon the snow was piled high along the track. Distant reaches of the lake began reappearing far below; then the car reached the upper station and stopped.

At the wicket the conductor examined our tickets again and kept them. The air was cool and fresh. Out in the modest station yard between the terminal and the sheer drop of the mountain the ground was muddy under the now warm sun. An old woman was sweeping water and shale ice into a sort of dustpan she had put in one of the shallow pools there.

I followed the track away from the station. It passed through tall trees, and on one side the mountain dropped off steeply and I could see fragmentary vistas of Lake Biwa through the tops of the trees. Nothing stirred here atop the mountain. There was no breeze, no bird's song—just the tall trees, the muddy track, the snow and the sun, and, ahead, a vague awareness of ramps and buildings.

The single muffled boom of a huge temple bell went by, expanding slowly into the space high over Lake Biwa.

Soon I ascended a narrow ramp and found myself among the holy buildings of the old monastery, Enryaku-ji. They stood on various levels among towering dark trees. One great red and black hall was almost underneath me, down in a hollow, facing steep stone steps to a smaller red building. Above it stood the belfry, where an occasional passer-by would toll the huge bell, and beyond that was a flat space where the Great Lecture Hall had stood and burned. This was the only clearing in sight: it was covered with snow, and the sun poured in on it and rebounded brilliantly into the sky.

As I passed this clearing another red building appeared among the trees on its own, higher plateau. The trees had a way of unfolding to reveal the buildings and then closing in again to hide them. Despite their nearness, the buildings I had seen first were already lost in the forest behind me. The feeling of isolation was heightened by the absence of people. Now and then a monk walked by, crunching the snow under his wooden *geta*, but that was all.

Enryaku-ji sat as it had for centuries near the edge of a steep, wooded drop as if listening for faint sounds to come up from below. Now and then it answered with the deep thud of its bell.

I followed some narrow steps cut out of the snow. They rose in a long flight, at the top of which the sky opened out, but then a dark crowd of pilgrims suddenly appeared against it and began helping one another in huddled groups down the icy steps. Slowly the old people worked their way past, and then I went up again. A bronze fireball appeared in the sky, then under it a rooftree, and as I neared the top a large temple building rose up ahead of me. The snow was deep around it and the sun—refreshing after the raw winter dampness in Kyoto—filled the open sky. From the black insides of the temple a gold statue of the Buddha Amida gazed out at the daylight and open space behind me. I turned to see what he saw.

Amida looked out over the whole eastern precinct of Enryaku-ji, out over Lake Biwa and its flat far shore, out across the distant reaches to the northeast. He saw the plains, the first foothills of the Japanese Alps—the rugged, snow-deep peaks themselves. He was looking at a famous view, famous not only for its beauty but also for the important part it played in Enryaku-ji's history.

### QUIS CUSTODIET IPSOS CUSTODES?

From ancient times, from the time when Nagaoka was still the capital and this monastery was but a small collection of crude, temporary shelters, a priest stood atop Mt. Hiei and watched the northeast quarter day and night, fair weather or foul, under imperial orders. The beauty of the view may at times have made this task easier, but it was hardly the reason why these monks had been ordered to build their huts and stand their watch on the mountain's top. They were searching the picturesque northeast horizon for evil spirits that would come from there to threaten the capital, for in those days it had been determined that all such spirits came from the northeast quarter.

Why this quarter was the evil one is not entirely clear. Perhaps the idea, antedating formal religion in Japan, first sprang from native superstition, or from the early, and presumably unpleasant, contacts between the settlers of western Japan and the ferocious Ainu aborigines who lived in the north. For centuries the early Japanese tried to conquer the Ainu, but even at the time of Kyoto's founding these primitive people were still unsubdued.

39

Whatever its origins, fear of the northeast quarter was very real at the time when Kammu contrived his new capital Heian-kyo. Mt. Hiei, one of the highest mountains about, lay between the site of the new city and the evil direction. For this reason Kammu ordered a priest named Saicho to ascend it and to establish a temple at its top for the protection of his new capital. The priests there were to maintain a day and night watch for the dread evil spirits, upon sight of which they were to ward them off by incantations and loud noises—the ringing of gongs, the beating of drums.

The year was 788. Saicho ascended the mountain and began carving his first image of the Buddha Yakushi Nyorai, in the majestic isolation of Mt. Hiei's cryptomeria forest. Whatever the evils that the Emperor Kammu expected him to ward off, Saicho's northeast quarter did become a source of real trouble for Kyoto—trouble, however, which could hardly be laid to evil spirits or Ainu aborigines.[1]

The most consistent source of trouble was Enryaku-ji itself. Despite its mission of protection and its remote mountain location—or perhaps because of these things—the monastery grew to great power, and for centuries it warred with and carried the day against any and all foes, whether they were political, religious, or imperial.

One of Enryaku-ji's early rivals was the Shinto religion. As the national religion, Shinto had to be respected, but the Buddhists wanted its position for themselves. Shinto was not only the religion of the country but it was also a key to the emperor, for he was a descendant of the Shinto gods.

As a way of infiltrating peacefully, Saicho and his followers claimed to "find" Shinto gods on Mt. Hiei, and then, by identifying these gods with Buddhist deities and doctrines, they revealed that Shinto was "actually" a primitive form of Buddhism. They built shrines to the gods and worshiped them, but they spoke for them too: these Shinto gods were really hostages.

In this way Buddhism appointed itself a kind of protector for Shinto. Shinto lost its independence and came under powerful Buddhist influences. And the emperor, divine descendant that

1. The Ainu were finally defeated not long after Kyoto's founding by armies under Saka-no-ue Tamuramaro (q.v.).

he was, had to acknowledge Buddhism as an influence on him too. Thus Buddhism and particularly Enryaku-ji managed to establish a very real spiritual ascendancy over the emperors.

Time passed and this ascendancy became temporal as well as spiritual. As its sacred mountaintop denied admission to women and constables, Enryaku-ji was an ideal refuge for criminals and social outcasts. Professing religious intentions, they came in increasing numbers until the thirty-sixth bishop of the monastery, Kakujin (1012–81), decreed that the monastery would form its own army, "to put down rebels and rid the temple and its estates of thieves and robbers." Unquestionably the very people whom the army was meant to drive out made up its backbone, and it was not long before the army forgot about internal affairs and busied itself in campaigns elsewhere.

The usual enemies were other Buddhist factions. Even before it had an army, Enryaku-ji often fought the old Nara temples, spiritually defunct but quick to provide opposition where a good religious issue could be found. Then, in the tenth century, the Tendai sect itself underwent a schism, as a result of which a group of monks was driven off Mt. Hiei and forced to establish a separate branch of the sect at a temple called Onjo-ji, or Mii-dera, which stood below the mountain in the plain near Otsu. Their defeat did not prevent these monks from raising an army of their own, and it was not long before Enryaku-ji found Mii-dera added to its enemies in Nara. Thereafter, during political wars, it was customary for the monks of Mii-dera and the Nara temples to support one side, and those of Enryaku-ji the other. If there was no outside war to support, the two Tendai temples fought among themselves: in one $2\frac{1}{2}$-century period Enryaku-ji's monks burned Mii-dera to the ground nine times.

In the meantime Enryaku-ji kept the emperor at its mercy. Whenever the monks disagreed with him, they scrambled en masse down their mountain, stopped at Sakamoto to pick up the sacred palanquin of the Shinto god Sanno, and marched on Kyoto with this holy relic in their van. For centuries these invasions were successful, not only because the monk army was strong, but also because no one dared to obstruct or damage the palanquin sacred to the imperial ancestor, Sanno. The emperor—and Kyoto—remained in constant fear of Enryaku-ji's assaults. The threat from the northeast quarter, which Enryaku-ji had been assigned to repel, had become Enryaku-ji itself.

Between the eleventh and fifteenth centuries Enryaku-ji's army was one of the most powerful in Japan. No force existed that could defeat it. Imperial assaults were thrown back down the mountain, and imperial reprimands were burned. If the monastery supported an emperor in war, he was safe from any force that could be mounted against him; if it withheld its support, as often as not he was doomed.[2] The famous statement attributed to the Emperor Shirakawa (1056–1129) could have been made by any emperor during this time:

"There are three things which I cannot bring under obedience," Shirakawa said, "the waters of the Kamo River, the dice of the *sugoroku* game, and the bonzes on the mountain."

New Buddhist sects found the monastery uncontrollable too. In the twelfth and thirteenth centuries Japanese Buddhism underwent a sudden upheaval, and several new sects were founded. All of the important new sects had founders who had studied on Mt. Hiei, and some of them were based directly on parts of the Tendai doctrine, but Enryaku-ji's army raided their temples impartially, killed their priests, and burned their literature.[3] For centuries the monastery suppressed its new rivals by warfare: for example, as late as 1536 it forced the Nichiren sect out of Kyoto by razing all twenty-one of its temples and slaughtering most of its priests—3,000 of them in the final temple. Thereafter the Nichiren sect was for a long time eliminated from Kyoto, where it has never since been a major force.

Similar events marked the history of each new sect that tried to enter Kyoto. As much as any one force could, Enryaku-ji controlled the religious and political affairs of the capital.

2. The monastery supported the Emperor Go-Daigo (1287—1339) during the dynastic wars of the fourteenth century and twice repulsed attacks on him by the regular national army. On the other hand, it refused to support the retired Emperor Go-Toba (1179-1239) in another war, and Go-Toba was defeated the same year and with two sons and a grandson, emperors all, sent into exile. (The prefix "Go" indicates that an emperor was the second to hold his name; thus these two were "Daigo II" and "Toba II." No imperial name has been used more than twice.)

3. By continually burning both new editions and carved printing blocks, Enryaku-ji's monks suppressed *Senchakushu,* the major work of Honen, founder of the Jodo sect, through several editions over a period of about 300 years.

2. "...a vague awareness of ramps and buildings." Enryaku-ji's new lecture hall and the temple offices, seen from near the cable-car station. Courtesy of Okamoto Ryu-en.

3. "...the holy buildings of the old monastery, Enryaku-ji. They stood on various levels among towering dark trees." Enryaku-ji's Kompon-chu-do. Courtesy of the Asahi Shimbunsha.

4. "Here, in the depths of the mountaintop, is Saicho's tomb, standing alone with graceful dignity in a quiet, hidden hollow." Enryakuji's Jodo-in, site of Saicho's tomb. Courtesy of Okamoto Ryu-en.

5. "... some narrow steps cut out of the snow. ...
A bronze fireball appeared in the sky." Enryaku-ji's
Amida-do.
6. "... the belfry, where an occasional passer-by
would toll the huge bell. ... This was the only clearing in sight. ..." Enryaku-ji's belfry.

RETRIBUTION

By 1536 Enryaku-ji's time was growing short. Hardened by age and blinded by success, the monastery had been entering wars when it should have stayed away. During the fifteenth and sixteenth centuries the famous raids on Kyoto were often repulsed, and attacks on Mt. Hiei by others sometimes met with success. At the height of Enryaku-ji's power there were more than 3,000 temples on the mountain, but now when one of them burned it was not always rebuilt. Nevertheless, the old monastery continued to enter wars such as that last great offensive against the Nichiren temples.

Finally, in 1571, Enryaku-ji sided against the wrong man. Oda Nobunaga was the general who succeeded in ending more than a century of civil war and bringing the whole country under his sway. Enryaku-ji had fought against him, and now in the fall of 1571 Nobunaga placed his army at the foot of Mt. Hiei and determined to annihilate his foe. He stormed the mountain, burned its temples, killed its priests, and left behind him in charred ruins one of the most venerable and powerful monasteries in the history of Japan. The buildings, records, and treasures of eight centuries had all been destroyed, but in Nobunaga's mind this was nothing when compared with the end of the monk-army whose penchant for lawless war had harassed Kyoto for centuries.

For some years after that there was no Enryaku-ji, but only the charred head of Mt. Hiei, the ruins of its stately trees and ancient halls a black reminder to those who might fail to obey the will of Oda Nobunaga. For once, it seemed, the old rival Mii-dera—which had of course supported Nobunaga—had gained the upper hand. But this ascendance was only to last for the brief remainder of Nobunaga's lifetime. When he was assassinated in 1582, Toyotomi Hideyoshi succeeded to power, in the process working his own destruction on Mii-dera. Eventually Hideyoshi would authorize Enryaku-ji to rebuild—and even to use the few remaining buildings of Mii-dera as a start.

Thanks to Hideyoshi, Enryaku-ji came back to life, and new buildings began to rise in a new forest of growing trees. A wary government limited the new monastery to 125 temples, less than a twentieth its former size. Today Enryaku-ji has that

47

many temples and a few more, but even in this heavily reduced state it remains one of the largest monasteries in Japan, as anyone who walks over the mountain will realize. Its buildings cover the mountain and the surrounding plain and house religious pursuits that are peaceful.

SPRINGTIME

The little two-car train that runs from Otsu to Sakamoto makes an early stop at a small station called Mii-dera. It is little more than a pair of sheds, one on each side, and not much else can be seen in the vicinity. Nevertheless, near here stand the battered remains of the famous Mii-dera temple, and from here one may look up Mt. Hiei, which is beginning to loom overhead now, and try to picture the horde of armed monks scrambling down the mountain to bring war and fire to their ancient foe. In the shadow of Enryaku-ji for centuries until Nobunaga delivered it, Mii-dera must have lived through an uncomfortable history.

After Mii-dera the train pulls out along straight track through rolling, open plains that slope ever so gradually down toward the flats by Lake Biwa, eventually merging with the lake at its rim. In the springtime these plains are squared off and filled with crops, distinctive among them the yellow mustard plants; in olden times it was here that the Mii-dera monks, hastily armed, rushed out to meet their enemy and defend their temple. The train is crossing no man's land now; soon it will enter Enryaku-ji territory.

The track runs out at Sakamoto. This beautiful little town is the lowland headquarters of the monastery, today as it always has been. It was spring when I came here for the last time. Our party was five; like all others, it had grown since the winter when I made my solitary trips. Atop Mt. Hiei the bell tolled swiftly now, and from buses parked in ranks at the formerly deserted landing place crowds poured in and milled about the precinct, pressing around the open shops, standing in long lines before the Fundamental Central Hall, in large groups with identifying paper flowers climbing the long flight of wide stone steps to the high Amida-do. The air on the mountain was pleasantly cool, in contrast to the heat collecting on the flat lands below. The almost orderly repetition of the deep bell's toll—coming so

48

often, it lost the solemnity of its solitary winter strokes—the steady toll testified to the ability of Enryaku-ji to attract visitors, few of whom were pilgrims. Many of them stood in the wide, incongruously open space which had once been filled by the Great Lecture Hall—the former rallying point for the temple's monk army was now an empty field.

In the warm seasons the eastern precinct is always crowded like this. It is strange then, especially in a country that loves hiking as much as does Japan, that one can leave this precinct, set out along the path to the other two, and find himself virtually alone. Yet a mere hundred yards beyond the Amida-do one's only companions are the silent, towering trees and occasional holy places along the way—a stone Jizo, a small Shinto shrine.

It is in the western precinct, and in the third one, called Yo-kawa, that one harks back to the austere origins of Enryaku-ji, so often lost among the colorful memories of the monastery's military days. Here, in the depths of the mountain top, is Saicho's tomb, standing alone with graceful dignity in a quiet, hidden hollow. An incense pattern burns before it; the smoke rises straight up among the trees into the sunlight above. Beyond is the dark forest in which stand single temple buildings forgotten by all but the monks themselves. Each shelters a different deity, awaits a different rite, offers a different salvation.

In the springtime one shares the western precinct with singing birds and silent passing monks. We had lunch that last day at the twin temples near the Shaka-do. Behind us the mountain sloped off down its western wall to Yasé, a rural village in the valley north of Kyoto. Ahead the trail re-entered the dark glades and wound off towards remote Yokawa. Inside one temple next to us, Fugen Bosatsu sat alone in the cool darkness, astride his mythical elephant; from the other Amida stared out of an empty room at the path to the eastern precinct. Below us, inside the ancient Shaka-do, three sacred lamps pushed back the darkness, but not for the venerable Shaka, hidden in his sealed box from the intrusion of mortal eyes, protected from unwelcome spirits by the four Deva kings who stood about the hall in the gloomy lamplight. As for us, we picnicked in the sun, listened to the birds, peered inside the halls at gods seated in darkness. We were in no hurry to return to the teeming eastern precinct, where

49

surely the bell still tolled without cease, as if counting the money they offered who tolled it.

In this century the glories of Enryaku-ji and the Tendai sect lie in the distant past; the new sects, none defeated, have surged on by; the emperor has left Kyoto, and gone too is the time when he could be controlled by a single temple, when it was important to control him at all. There are no worlds to conquer now, and the thousands of warm-weather visitors are curiosity-seekers, not pilgrims. Like an aging gentleman who has outlived the excesses of his youth, Enryaku-ji stays here on its mountain, aware that its great days are over yet still gazing out over Lake Biwa to the northeast reaches of Japan, still imagining itself as the bastion between Kyoto and her ancient spiritual enemies.

# 3 Small Country Temples and Popular Buddhism: Sanzen-in

"When a pious person dies, the Buddha appears before him. The Lord of Compassion (Kannon), one of his great Bodhisattvas, brings a lotus flower to carry the pious soul, and the Lord of Might (Seishi) reaches him welcoming hands, while other saints and angels innumerable in number sing hymns in praise and welcome of the pious."  ESHIN SOZU, in his *Ojo-yoshu*[1]

ESHIN SOZU (942–1017), or Genshin, priest of the second rank *(Sozu)*, author of *Ojo-yoshu*, and one of the best sculptors and painters of his time.

ALTHOUGH Enryaku-ji was a fine example of a great Heian monastery, such monasteries were few and exceptional. The more usual center of Buddhist worship was the small temple distinguished as much by its modesty as were the monasteries by their grandeur. This temple would consist of two or three buildings—or only one—and would be maintained by a single priest who might have assistants or novices under him. Although this priest would have come from one of the great monasteries, he did not try to reproduce the imposing range of worship he had been taught there, a worship involving a vast array of deities most of whom were installed in individual temples. At the small temple there were neither priests nor buildings enough to pursue such a worship. Therefore, the priests of small temples tended to specialize in the worship of a single deity, devoting their whole effort to but one phase of the mother sect's diverse religious objectives.

Buddhist temples of this sort did not flourish in the cities, where the great metropolitan temples held sway, but sprang up most often in isolated areas, sometimes in the vicinity of a small village or hamlet. In many cases, a village grew up in a lonely spot only after a temple had been founded there.

1. Anesaki Masaharu, *History of Japanese Religion,* London, 1930 (reprinted, Tokyo and Rutland, Vermont, 1963), page 152.

It was in these small temples that movements first appeared to simplify drastically the complex forms of Heian Buddhism. This had to be done if Buddhism was ever going to reach and influence the great masses of poorer people, but it was something the monasteries could not accomplish. Their rituals were directed at their own monks and at urban lords and patrons, people who neither required nor wanted a simplified form of worship. On the other hand, the small, isolated temple that had few well-educated or wealthy parishioners was an ideal place for the growth of efforts to simplify Buddhism. Its priest was surrounded by people who could not understand his teachings, while he was removed from the esoteric ways of the city and the complex rites of the monastery. His temple's size had forced an initial step toward simplification by preventing him from focusing on more than one or two facets of his many-sided religion. This same priest thus became the logical man to begin evolving a doctrine which the common people around him could understand.

The origins of popular Buddhism go back to the priest Ennin (794–864), a famous follower of Saicho.[2] Like his master, Ennin studied for many years in China, and returned to Mt. Hiei with new religious knowledge. This included a new concept of a practice known as Nembutsu, or "invoking Buddha's sacred name," a Tendai sect practice which had previously been little understood in Japan. In the Nembutsu the worshiper repeated the phrase *Namu Amida Butsu* ("Save me, Amida Buddha") while meditating upon Amida and the Western Paradise into which that deity received the souls of the deserving dead. Under Ennin this practice became a songlike, musical chant intoned by the monks as they filed about the image of Amida. Ennin was responsible for building the first hall on Mt. Hiei in which the Nembutsu was regularly practiced, and eventually each of Enryaku-ji's three precincts had such a hall.

In Ennin's time, however, the Nembutsu was but one of the many holy rites performed by the monks of the Tendai sect. It

2. Both were honored posthumously with the title *Daishi* (大師 great teacher). Saicho became Dengyo Daishi; Ennin, Jikaku Daishi. The titles were conferred in 866, after Ennin had died. The two priests are usually referred to by their posthumous names today.

was the later priest, Eshin, who freeded it from other practices and gave it independent value. In doing this, Eshin did not turn his back on the complex practices of his own Tendai sect, but he pointed out that these, while highly desirable, were beyond the understanding of ordinary men and were therefore useful only to priests and other intellectuals.

For most people, Eshin pronounced the Nembutsu *sufficient in itself* to assure one of attaining *Ojo,* or entry into Amida's Western Paradise after death. The Nembutsu would enable the dying man to attain Ojo even if he only said it once, as long as he did so with complete sincerity, Eshin claimed. In his autobiography Eshin noted that he himself relied solely upon the Nembutsu; his most famous work, *Ojo-yoshu,* explained his theories in great detail. It is said that when *Ojo-yoshu* was sent to the Chinese headquarters of the sect at Mt. T'ien-t'ai, it won about 500 converts there.

Thus there was created for the first time a form of Buddhist worship simple enough to be performed by anyone yet valuable enough to promise salvation. With the elimination of complexities, the emphasis shifted from understanding to faith: a man could attain Ojo regardless of his ability to understand the inner workings of his sect, if only he called upon Amida with the earnest desire to be saved. By granting the Nembutsu independence within the Tendai sect, Eshin laid the groundwork for later priests who would eventually extract it altogether and use it as a sole basis for new sects of their own.

One result of these attempts to make Buddhism available to a wider group of people was an increased emphasis on the concrete, visual images needed to hold the mind of the worshiper, to assist his concentration and to remind him of the glory of his aspirations. Visions of the afterlife and other Buddhist glories, until this time vague and unreal, were made tangible by priests who wanted to convey them to less educated people and used painting and sculpture to do it. Where the older halls had contained but a single image of Amida, in the new ones of the eleventh century he became the center of a glorious panoply of Paradise which covered walls, pillars, ceilings, and all other interior surfaces with depictions of his heavenly retinue, hosts of lesser deities, angelic women, spiraling colored clouds, and anything else the worshiper might hope to find in his own world-after-death.

As it did in iconography, the emphasis in writings and discussion too centered on the actual appearance of the other world. Eshin's own description of it appears at the head of this chapter; consider also the following section of a thirteenth-century sermon:

" ' . . . and so the lotus pond of that Land of Bliss whose waters are blessed with the properties of the eight virtues, is as full of blooming lotus flowers as there are diligent Nembutsu devotees here. The three Holy Ones (Amida, Kannon, and Seishi) are kept so busy welcoming newcomers, that they have hardly time to set down the lotus stands on which they bear each to his proper flower in the pond, before another arrives to be conducted in like manner. So we see that our neglect to call on the sacred name means a desolate pond there, and indifference to Ojo will bring the land itself to ruin.' "[3]

The effect of these promised glories upon the common man must have been great indeed. With death, he was told, he would easily shake off the desperate circumstances that had hounded him every day of his mortal life. Amida himself would remove the believer from this humility and deprivation and place his soul with those of all pious men on its own lotus stem in Amida's own paradisiacal garden. There was no place more beautiful, no place more serene. Even the luxuries with which the wealthiest and most powerful lords of this world surrounded themselves would pale and wither before the glories of Amida's Western Paradise.

It is small wonder, then, that the practice of the Nembutsu and the worship of Amida, reduced by Eshin and his successors to these simple and attractive terms, swept through the ranks of the Japanese people. Amida held hope for something in death which was beyond the scope of any man, let alone the poor one, in mortal life. So strong was this hope and their own mortal despair that men embraced death gladly when it came, and even sought it out by suicide.

---

3. H. H. Coates and R. Ishizuka, translators, *Honen the Buddhist Saint*, Kyoto, 1949, page 627.

7. "The Hon-do ... belies its age in the arch of its fat shingle roof. The building under this roof is modest and plain...." Sanzen-in's Hon-do. Courtesy of Sanzen-in.

8. "In front of him kneel his two attendants, Seishi and Kannon. . . . They are sensuous, gold, and close." Kannon in Sanzen-in's Hon-do (Amida in background). Courtesy of Sanzen-in.

SANZEN-IN

Sanzen-in, a small temple of the Tendai sect which stands near the village of Ohara, a few miles north of Kyoto, is undoubtedly the finest remaining example of a temple devoted to early Nembutsu worship. This is so not only because the temple's ancient Amida hall stands virtually as it did in the tenth century, but also because the man who built this hall and sculptured its image of Amida was none other than Eshin himself.

Eshin built the Ojo-gokuraku-in (Temple of Rebirth in Paradise) in 985, the same year in which he finished writing his *Ojo-yoshu*. The selection of Ohara as the site is perhaps best explained not in light of its remoteness from Kyoto but rather by its nearness to Yokawa, the northern precinct of Enryaku-ji. Eshin had retired to Yokawa about the year 970—when he was not yet thirty—and had spent fifteen years there studying Buddhist scriptures and writing works and commentaries of his own. Now, when he considered building a hall to Amida, the site fell to nearby Ohara.

In those days Ohara was considered to be very remote from Kyoto. It was in many ways the "end of the line"—the last of the little villages that strung out up the valley to the north of the city, a place that was mentioned only when one wished to imply a cold climate, deep frost, loneliness, or even exile. Perhaps Ohara would not have been thought of so bleakly if it had been on the way to some larger town, but it was not, and it must have been only rarely visited, by occasional fugitives and other aimless wanderers.

When Eshin built his hall it stood virtually alone on Uo-yama (Fish Mountain). Gradually, however, other temples cropped up in the vicinity. Two or three were built within a little more than a century afterwards, and, as in Eshin's building, the emphasis in them was upon the worship of Amida. Although nominally Tendai, in their concentration upon Amida and their emphasis on the Nembutsu the temples of Fish Mountain were closer in character to sects which came after them—sects devoted to Amida to the exclusion of everything else. Thanks to them, Ohara was from the beginning a center of the Amidist movement that produced these sects.

In modern times its fine condition alone makes Sanzen-in pre-eminent among the old temples of Fish Mountain, for it offers the visitor a trip straight into the unspoiled past. In addition, the continuing rural nature of the long valley between Ohara and Kyoto allows one to approach the temple through surroundings which must be little changed, even from Eshin's time.

The present road to Ohara is probably the original one—hemmed in by hills and a river, it could not very well have been elsewhere. The bus follows the Takano River north out of Kyoto and works up into a narrow valley. Between small villages fields spread out across the valley bottom and terrace up into the hill-sides as far as they can go. On one side of the road, the river drops in flat, clear falls from ledge to ledge, traversing silently the transparent pools between. Gravel is piled out along its edge, waiting to be hauled away, and in the empty cones it has left behind are deep water and silent fish. On the other side of the road rise the foothills of Mt. Hiei, pushing in towards the mountain that looms beyond them. This is the kind of country which the bus crosses bumpily, until eventually it reaches Ohara.

At Ohara one leaves the dirt highroad and follows a small path that takes him quickly deeper into the past. Because the way up the hill is too narrow for an automobile, one climbs to Sanzen-in as visitors always have done, on foot. The left side of the path is lined with thatch-roofed farmhouses, built among bamboo groves. On the right, a short retaining wall drops into a small cascading stream. Near the bottom of the path this stream turns a moss-laden water wheel which, if one did not know better, he might easily suppose to date from the time of Eshin himself.

Climbing uphill along the stream, which gets larger above the occasional irrigation sluices that sap its strength, one reaches a crosspath that goes off to the left through a tunnel of cherry trees. This is the beginning of Sanzen-in : the path and the stream continue uphill to another of Ohara's small, old temples, while the famous tunnel of cherries leads one away to the temple of Eshin.

Ojo-gokuraku-in, now mercifully abbreviated to Hon-do (Main Hall), is the innermost building at Sanzen-in. It is shielded from the outside world by a ring of younger buildings and stone walls that reflect the increased importance and independence of the temple since Eshin's time. Passing through these halls, one comes out on a wide, even lawn of cedar moss broken only by occasional camellia, maple, and cryptomeria trees. The outer buildings face in on this lawn, and a single path crosses it, along which cryptomerias form a simple colonnade. The lawn is almost unruffled by the plain, straight trunks that emerge neatly from it. At the end of the path stands the old Hon-do. A tall Jizo in stone stands weightless on the calm sea of moss, brooding over this still scene and the arrival of the traveler whom he protected on his way.

No matter what the season, this place is calm and beautiful. It is famous for its maple leaves, whose flames shoot up against the steady evergreens in the fall, but even on a rainy day, when these same leaves cover the cedar moss like patches of blood-red stickers, one is struck by the natural beauty which brought Eshin here. Its remoteness and tranquillity, and the reverence given nature almost to the exclusion of the creations of man, are indications of Eshin's reasons for choosing this site for his temple, for they are a perfect introduction to the Paradise which awaits inside the hall.

The Hon-do, perched on a stone foundation, belies its age in the arch of its fat shingle roof. The building under this roof is modest and plain, its weathered wood surfaces blending easily into the natural background behind them. It is very dark and very small inside. Momentarily one senses only the darkness; this room is the tight interior of the building, of the temple itself. It is chopped down even smaller by the partition that shields the holy images. But on the other side of the partition the darkness is firmly thrust aside by Amida and his two attendants. Gorgeous and serene, as unreal as the world outside is real, they fill the inside of the crowded little building with their deep golden radiance.

Eshin was not a great sculptor or painter, but he was among the best of his time, and perhaps there is strength to be found in the imperfections of his work. Amida is stern and stiff, but his restrained manner and the finality of his seated position suggest a serenity and detachment befitting such a deity. He is not the benevolent, almost human Buddha that later sculptors would have had him, but for this reason he may be more awesome and other-worldly than the more mortal portrayals that followed Eshin's time. He is not particularly large, but in the crowded interior of the Hon-do, surrounded by smaller and even miniature subordinates, he appears much larger than he is.

In front of him kneel his two attendants, Seishi and Kannon, the one praying for the soul of the dying believer, the other about to receive it on a lotus blossom. They are sensuous, gold, and close. On the walls of the little hall hang fragmentary remains of the *mandala* paintings which once covered them with a heavenly host of thousands. On the old, rough-hewn pillars are traces of the many-colored intricate patterns that made them columns of heavenly cloud and fire, and behind Amida a halo of golden clouds and lesser Buddhas gilds the sky. Above him, at one time, were heavenly maidens and Bodhisattvas, posed in the blue sky of the famous boat-shaped ceiling. Of all these accoutrements only the last is now gone without a trace. What remains gives a clear idea of the very material persuasion that was brought to bear on the simple pilgrim by this portrayal of Amida's Paradise.

When a common pilgrim came here in Eshin's time he left behind him the hardship, hunger, disease, sewage, filth, and uncertain reward of his daily life; he escaped his paper house that let in every winter breeze, his paper master whose head might roll in the street tomorrow. If life on earth held rewards, it had not seen fit to bestow them on this man.

Here in Ohara clear streams, tall trees, and fine gardens spoke of a different world. Here noise gave way to silence, conflict to peace. This was the unreal edge of the human world, the threshold to Paradise, and when the pilgrim entered the hall he suddenly found himself very near Amida's realm. It was a world of golden Buddhas hovering in a sky of every color through which floated angels and gliding saintly gods. On all sides were thousands of those who inhabited this Paradise, yet the hall did not seem crowded. Candlelight flickered quietly across the face of Amida, and perhaps it flicked the pilgrim out of his daze and reminded him that the glory of this Paradise, surely only hinted at here, depended upon the devotion and faith of all men, including those who were poor like himself. Never before had a Buddha called upon one of such a low station to uphold his Paradise. It was an awesome and unusual responsibility, but a joyous one. This wretched man needed only to repeat the Nembutsu. Who could refuse to do this for Amida, for *himself?* Who could be surprised at how hard this man prayed?

# 4 The Fujiwara: Byodo-in

FUJIWARA MICHINAGA (966–1027), the greatest of the Fujiwara civilian ministers.

FUJIWARA YORIMICHI (992–1074), his son, founder of the Byodo-in.

IT IS a steaming hot summer's day in Uji. The bumpy horseback ride over the hills from Kyoto, even though accomplished the day before, has left its mark and you are tired, for by horseback or palanquin this trip is no pleasure excursion. In this year 1067 it is rather an ordeal, but also a privilege and gladly borne.

At the invitation of Fujiwara Yorimichi, the emperor's first minister, you, a lord of high station but infinitely inferior to your host, have come to see his great temple-villa, only recently completed. Already it is rumored in the city that the place will be visited by no less than the emperor himself during the coming autumn. The honor to you is doubly great, should this report be true.

The climax of your visit is about to take place. Under the baking sun you, your host, and a small retinue most carefully selected for this moment are walking along a path which leads through the numberless buildings of the great villa and temple to the Amida-do, Yorimichi's private chapel and paradise, rumored to be of pearl and gold inside, with angels flying about overhead. No less could be expected of the temple in which this great minister communicates with those who rule other and far greater worlds.

As the party comes out from behind a building, you walk into the full glare of the sun. It bounces off the pond into your eyes; for a moment the glare blinds you and you glance off to one side at the river nearby.

Now you have followed your host around the bank of the pond to a place between it and the river, and he has stopped. The Amida-do stands opposite you now, on the other side of the lotus pond, and you dare to look across at its island, up to the building itself. It hovers there like a giant bird that has just dropped out of the sky. What words will convey properly your admiration and humility in this moment? Your host seems to understand your problem—perhaps he has seen it before, in others. Encouraged by his apparent understanding, you look again.

Truly this is a building with wings, lighter than the air in which it floats. It is the earthly incarnation of the King of Birds, worthy to bear Amida Buddha into this world, or Yorimichi out of it.

You notice the grillwork in the central door, and now you look at it more closely—through the round window in the grill, into the darkness inside. Slowly your eyes, narrowed by the brilliant sunlight, cautiously open themselves and draw outlines from the shadowy black interior....

It is the face of Amida! *He* is there inside this magical, floating building, looking in upon himself—not out through the window through which you gaze, not out across the pond to such unworthy beings as Yorimichi's guests. His eyes are downcast, saved for evening, for Yorimichi. While he waits it is for you an untold privilege merely to gaze across the still water and in through the window at his silent contemplation. And his house —that floats in the air and hovers over the island, about to but never quite settling onto the ground below—his house is reflected exactly on the calm surface of its pond.

What shall you say to your host? What words can express your gratitude, your overwhelming humility in this delicate moment? Beads of sweat sprout eagerly from your brow as you grope to arrive at the proper words. But we shall leave you with your problem and skip, as is our privilege, to some other century and some other year—it could be any of several, but let us say the year is now 1817.

You are a different man now, a poor man, a beggar and wanderer, who in this depressing vale of unending want makes his body drag out its pointless aging process only by instinct. It is a never ending search for food, which, they say, in the old days used to be plentiful, but it is hard come by now for the likes of you. The rags you wear—they are more like rough places on the skin, so long have they been there. Their color? They have no color, unless dirt has color.

They said it would be better away from the city, but it didn't seem so today. For Uji is no better off in these times than any other country town, except perhaps for the tea merchants—but what would tea merchants have to do with the likes of you?

The sun is gone now—it is time to find a place to stop for the night. You wander forward through an unkempt field.

Here is a large building with a porch, standing alone in the field. You look it over, but it is bolted and shuttered, so you wander on. The river—you hear the river over the bank on your left.

Out of the gloom comes another place, standing next to a dirty pool. Smoke rises out of it—a strange, smoking house on stilts! Has one ever seen the like? You come closer and look more carefully through the dull remaining light of evening. The smoke rises from the center of the building, but there are strange high sheds on either side—what could they possibly be for? Too low, that roof, for a man to stand up under it. Warehouses? But how does one get up there? No ladder, and yet those stilts! It is almost laughable.

The building is dark, obviously abandoned. You climb up to the middle part. Inside it you find an old woman, squatting before a small fire. There are two or three other people lying off in a dark far corner, apparently asleep. It is a small room, but it will do. It is open on one side—there is no wall over there—but it is not so cold tonight, anyway.

"What is this place, woman?" you ask.

"It was once Amida's Paradise," she replies, "but now it is only a temple, yet Amida stays on to remind us that all men will be saved."

What rubbish! But you had not noticed the huge statue sitting in the room—how much space it takes up! Yes, it is another old temple, left over from the days when food was plentiful. Perhaps there is a comfortable place to be found up there on the platform, under the statue. . . .

And in the morning, before you move on, you make some ink and scratch your name on the door, next to Amida's picture. You write out the year—it is Bunka 14, as if that meant anything!

And you leave the Amida-do, or Phoenix Hall, of the old Byodo-in, and wander away.

9. "The small figures are made from single blocks of wood to which the projecting parts have been cleverly joined. . . . Their action postures and lively attitudes are unique among the sculpture of this period. . . ." One of Amida's attendants in Byodo-in's Phoenix Hall. Courtesy of the Asuka-en, Nara.

10. "Truly, this is a building with wings, lighter than the air in which it floats." Byodo-in's Phoenix Hall. Courtesy of the Asuka-en, Nara.

11. "He is there inside this magical, floating building, looking in upon himself." Amida in Byodo-in's Phoenix Hall. Courtesy of the Asuka-en, Nara.

The Byodo-in—the "Hall of Equality": equality between man (Yorimichi) and Buddha (Amida), or, as history has shown, between man (first minister) and man (wandering bum). How the Phoenix Hall has survived the nine hundred years of its neglected existence is a matter of mystery, but luckily it has, for it stands today not only as the finest relic of Kyoto's golden eleventh century, but as perhaps the greatest architectural relic of any era in Japan. Certainly today it is the most famous one.

The Byodo-in was originally a private temple which had seven pagodas and twenty-six other buildings. It benefited from the protection of the great Fujiwara house while they held power, but it also suffered greatly without their protection when they were gone, replaced by the more powerful regimes of other families. For this place grew and prospered as a family temple—specifically the private villa and worshiping place of Fujiwara Yorimichi, the last of the great Fujiwara ministers and the son of the greatest. In those days the Fujiwara family owed allegiance to no man save the emperor, and their temple did not require the protection of any monastery. Through its owners it had the allegiance of the nation—that was enough. Nominally, the Phoenix Hall was attached to the Tendai sect; actually, it was the house of Yorimichi's personal Amida, ruler of the Western Paradise, and when Yorimichi died, and after him, like drifting leaves, his sons and grandsons gradually left the scene, the temple was left alone to stand the tests of time and history as best it could.

Now, eight centuries after the Fujiwara lost their power, there remains none of the seven pagodas and twenty-six halls that originally comprised the Byodo-in—with the exception of the Phoenix Hall. When one considers that for centuries at a time this hall stood abandoned, inhabited by wanderers and bums who used its decorative timbers to make their fires on its floor, and sometimes, if they were clever enough, picked out what was left of the inlaid pearl and gold and took it off with them—when one considers this, the Phoenix Hall's survival must be called a miracle. And this miracle continued into the present day, for it is only since the war that any attention has been paid to this building and that it has come under government protection. An old man who visited the Phoenix Hall one morning when I was there said that he was seeing it for the first time in forty-three years, and that he had come just to see if the building still stood. What was it like forty-three years ago? It stood alone and un-cared for in a field overgrown with weeds. Inside, under the altar rail, there was still some of the inlaid pearl that had been put there nine centuries before.

There is no inlaid pearl today. The last bits of it were picked out in our own, the twentieth century.

### THE FUJIWARA

Kyoto was founded in 794; by 850 the Fujiwara family was in firm command of the government. It is true that this family had been influential even before Kyoto was the capital, but it was in the ninth century that they first attained the power that enabled them to control and fill virtually all the important ministerial posts for three hundred years and to establish the custom that only their daughters should become the consorts of an emperor. This last was a wise custom, for emperors were young and ab-dicated early, sometimes even before reaching the exalted age of twenty. Thus it often happened that the Fujiwara minister in power was the father-in-law of the emperor. If the emperor had more than one wife, that usually meant only that he also had more than one Fujiwara father-in-law.

The process of intermarriage became complicated, and the Fujiwara quickly climbed to a zenith of entanglement which meant absolute supremacy. This brings us to the beginning of the eleventh century and the Fujiwara family's greatest and most powerful minister, Michinaga. A man with a natural flair for siring daughters, Michinaga was brought into a world where this act was a virtual guarantee of success. Of his five daughters known to history, four married emperors and the fifth a crown prince who only missed the throne because he turned insane. Like a spider, Michinaga surrounded the imperial house with his web of daughters, and the emperors of the entire eleventh cen-tury—eight of them—were the husbands and descendants of these girls.

The intertwining family trees of Michinaga, his daughters, and the imperial house, shown in the accompanying chart, re-veal some strange relationships. Three emperors married their

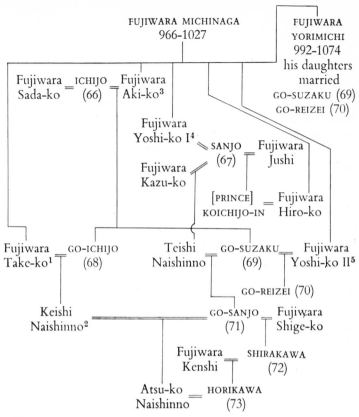

CAPITALS: men     Regular print: women
Emperors are numbered according to their
  position in the line of succession.
"Naishinno": princess.
N.B.: Only Michinaga's eldest son is shown.

1. or *Ishi*, 999–1036.
2. or *Kaoru-ko*.
3. 988–1074, later *Joto-mon-in*.
4. or *Kenshi*, 994–1027.
5. died young.

own aunts, another his cousin. Michinaga, father-in-law to four
emperors, was grandfather of two more, great-grandfather of
another, and great-great-grandfather to still another; but he was
also the grandfather of two of his sons-in-law, great-grandfather
to one grandson, and great-great-grandfather to one great-
grandson.

Michinaga also had sons, the eldest of whom was Yorimichi,
who reaped the glories of his father and who rebuilt his father's
Uji villa into the magnificent Byodo-in. Yorimichi was the
most powerful figure in the nation from the time of his father's
death until the time of his own, a period of nearly fifty years. His
daughters, too, married emperors, although not in such great

numbers, and on one occasion he entertained his son-in-law and nephew, the Emperor Go-Reizei, at the new villa in Uji. In those days a visit by the emperor to the residence of a subject, even a Fujiwara, was an unheard-of honor, but such was the power of Yorimichi that he not only governed for nearly thirty years from his Uji villa but induced the emperor to visit him there.

The year after that visit Yorimichi retired and passed his titles on to his youngest brother Norimichi, while in the same year Go-Reizei died at the age of forty-four and was succeeded by the Emperor Go-Sanjo. These two events marked the beginning of the end of the Fujiwara power, for Go-Sanjo, virtually alone among all the emperors who reigned while Kyoto was capital, determined to govern the country by himself and successfully shunted aside the ministrations of the Fujiwara and their family relationship. For four brilliant years the country was actually governed by this emperor, who ranks among the very few great ones. He abdicated in 1072, intending to continue his rule through his successor, but before he could do this, within a year of his retirement he was dead at the untimely age of forty. It was a great setback for the fortunes of the imperial house.

Nevertheless the zenith of the Fujiwara era had been reached and passed. The paradise on earth that Yorimichi had created in the Phoenix Hall was hardly built too soon, for already the military clans of the Taira and Minamoto were gaining strength, while at court the Fujiwara sealed their own doom by cultivating the arts of poetry, dancing, and court music—but neglecting the art of warfare. Before long they would be depending on these military clans to keep order for them, and by the end of the next century (the twelfth) the Taira clan would already have usurped the power of its masters, and a long age of schism, warfare, and violence would have been ushered in to Japan.

The Phoenix Hall was visited by the Emperor of Japan in 1067. Less than a year later, through the person of Go-Sanjo, the Fujiwara were visibly weakened; less than a century later their role in directing the government was eliminated completely, and the Phoenix Hall was left to weather the centuries as best it could. Were its beauty not enough, the fact that this wooden building has stood since the days of William the Conqueror is sufficient reason to admire it.

# 5 The Rise of the Taira and the Battles of Uji Bridge

TAIRA KIYOMORI (1118–81), lay priest chancellor of Japan.

MINAMOTO YORIMASA (1106–80), warrior, longtime ally of the Taira clan.

MINAMOTO YOSHINAKA (1154–84), distant relative of the above and conqueror of Kyoto.

TOMOE GOZEN, Yoshinaka's fellow warrior and beautiful wife.

The Minamoto brothers, first cousins of Yoshinaka:

YORITOMO (1147–99), leader of his clan;

NORIYORI (1156–93); and

YOSHITSUNE (1159–89), one of the most famous warriors in Japanese history.

TOKIWA GOZEN, their mother.

WHEN the Fujiwara government began to show signs of real weakness in the twelfth century, its civilian ministers depended increasingly upon the two military clans, the Taira in the west and the Minamoto in the east, to maintain order for them. For a while these clans did as they were told, suppressing unrest and obeying the orders of the Fujiwara ministers. But as the military clans themselves grew more powerful, it became evident that their obedience was unenforceable—the aesthete lord had no power over his generals. Soon it was only a matter of time until both clans, or one of them, should decide to push the Fujiwara family aside and to govern Japan by themselves.

At first this event was delayed because the two clans opposed each other, creating a stalemate neither could break. The clans also feuded within themselves, so that often they were unable to act in concert when an opportunity arose. Thus the powerless Fujiwara government hung on, and the years moved past 1150.

In 1153 Taira Kiyomori succeeded as chieftain of his clan, and under him its star began to rise. Overt actions between various factions of the Taira and Minamoto became frequent, and finally, when a coup was attempted against him, Kiyomori marched on

12-14. "It was the scene of great battles. . . ." Three prints by Kuniyoshi (19th century): 12. Minamoto Yorimasa prepares for suicide after defeat at Uji Bridge, 1180. 13. The Awazu Battle, 1184: at center, Yoshinaka dies, struck by arrow of Ishida Jiro (extreme right); at left, Tomoe Gozen wields a tree, while Wada Yoshinori comes from right to seize her. 14. Battle of 1180: Tsutsui Jomyo and Ichirai Hoshi defend Uji Bridge. Courtesy of B. W. Robinson, from his *Kuniyoshi*.

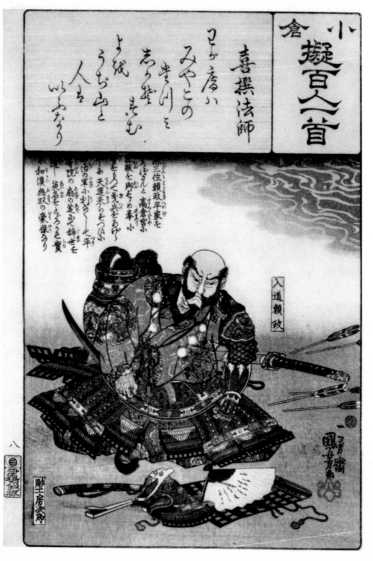

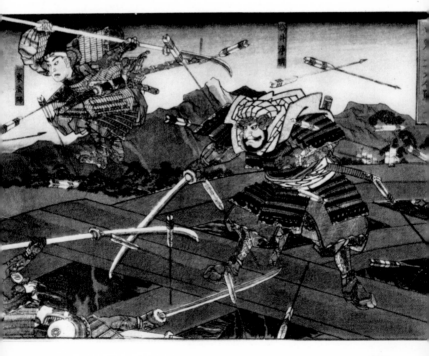

75

Kyoto and crushed the opposition, emerging suddenly in 1160 as the supreme and undisputed master of Japan.

The Minamoto leader, Yoshitomo, was killed in the fighting with some of his many sons, but at least three of the younger sons survived. Kiyomori spared the thirteen-year-old, Yoritomo, because he said he desired to pray for the souls of his massacred family. A five-year-old, Noriyori, was also spared; and the youngest, Yoshitsune, was saved by his mother, the beautiful Tokiwa Gozen—once a lady of the Emperor Konoe's court and later Yoshitomo's concubine—who offered herself to the eager Kiyomori on the condition that Yoshitsune be allowed to enter a monastery. This deal was consummated—eventually Tokiwa Gozen presented Kiyomori with a daughter—but in allowing the Minamoto children to live Kiyomori had shown a weakness which would in later years haunt and destroy the rest of his clan.[1]

Nevertheless Kiyomori held the state in a very firm grip. Aided by a band of three hundred youthful red-robed spies who patrolled the streets of the capital, he eliminated all opposition to his rule. He gained control of the emperor by deposing the five-year-old incumbent and replacing him with his eight-year-old uncle, who was afterwards married to Kiyomori's daughter.[2] She was proclaimed empress within a year of the marriage, and Kiyomori sat back and awaited imperial grandchildren.

It was not until several years later that the empress conceived a child. The delivery was awaited with apprehension on all sides, and it was not an easy one. Priests had to be summoned, and when their incantations failed to improve the situation, more priests were called, until the religious strength of the capital had been exhausted to no avail. Now the retired Emperor Go-Shirakawa, himself a priest, appeared and by reciting a sutra was able to eliminate the evil influences that were interfering with the long-awaited birth. The child was a boy, and his grandfather Kiyomori wept with glee.

Bad omens accompanied this birth—in one case a ceremonial announcement that an imperial son had been born went awry and indicated instead that it was a girl, causing people to laugh

1. Tokiwa Gozen later left Kiyomori and completed some sort of cycle by marrying a member of the Fujiwara family.
2. Previous to this, Kiyomori had had her adopted by the retired Emperor Go-Shirakawa so her lineage would be acceptable for the match.

in the streets. But Kiyomori paid the omens no heed—he was already making plans to have this infant, his own grandson, become the Emperor of Japan.

He did not wait long. In 1180, when the boy was only two, the young emperor suddenly decided to abdicate, and his infant son became the Emperor Antoku.

This was the moment when the Taira reached their zenith. For twenty years Kiyomori had controlled the country, and now his own grandson, barely old enough to talk, much less to rule, was its emperor. Kiyomori's sons and other relatives filled all the important government posts, and the Taira power was unequaled in the land. Nevertheless, this culminating event, the accession of Antoku, was itself accompanied by initial signs that all was not well.

### A REBELLION FAILS

Minamoto Yorimasa, a famous warrior of his clan, had sided with the Taira when they rose to power, and for a long time thereafter he was their congenial ally. But when Kiyomori set about placing his own grandson on the imperial throne in 1180, their strained alliance appears to have snapped.

Yorimasa opposed the forced accession of the infant Antoku and formed a secret plot to raise a different prince to the throne. He was backed by Mii-dera and the Nara temples, but any hope they had for success was dashed when word of the plot leaked out to the Taira. With the expected backing of Enryaku-ji, the Taira forces moved quickly to crush Yorimasa's plot.

Yorimasa's protégé was viewing the moon on that May night when he received a message telling him to flee for his life. He escaped from Kyoto disguised as a woman and took refuge at Mii-dera. But "the Prince, seeing that Hieizan had turned against them, and Nara had not yet sent their men, since Mii-dera alone could do nothing, on the 23rd day of the same month left that temple and started for the Southern Capital [Nara]. The Prince had with him two flutes of Chinese bamboo called 'Semi-ori' and 'Koeda.' . . ."[3]

3. Passages in this chapter and the next are quoted from *Heike Monogatari* as translated by A. L. Sadler in *The Ten Foot Square Hut and Tales of the Heike*, Sydney, 1928. I have quoted at some length largely because the translation is so difficult to acquire.

15. "The small parapet near its west end is reputed to mark the spot where the war lord and connoisseur of tea Toyotomi Hideyoshi once dipped water for his brew. A dipping ceremony is held here annually. . . ." Uji Bridge. Courtesy of Foto Kyoto (Oka Keitaro).

16. "The Uji Bridge ... is renowned both for its longevity and for the colorful events connected with it." Courtesy of the Asahi Shimbunsha.

Perhaps Yorimasa had chosen his prince unwisely. In any case
the latter headed first for Uji, a few miles away, where Yorimasa and his forces had encamped. Although he fell from his
horse six times en route, he managed to arrive a little ahead of the
Taira forces, who had already learned of his flight and were
bearing down on Uji from the northwest, from Kyoto. Yorimasa, seeing the situation, sent the prince straight on to the
friendly city of Nara, while he himself with a band of about two
hundred faithful followers determined to hold the Uji Bridge
against the Taira, who are said to have numbered more than
twenty thousand.

At the age of seventy-five and with the balance about a hundred to one against him, Yorimasa knew "in his heart that this
fight would be his last, [and] went forth in a suit of armor in
blue-and-white spots worn over his long-sleeved Court hitatare,
purposely wearing no helmet on his head, while his son Izu-no-
kami Nakatsuna wore a suit of black armor over a hitatare of
red brocade, he also leaving his head bare for greater ease in
drawing the bow."

The defenders tore up the bridge on their side of the river, so
that when the onrushing enemy stormed across, despite their
cries the horsemen in the lead were forced off the edge of the
bridge and drowned in the river. Now the Taira forces drew
back and an archery contest began. Although outnumbered,
Yorimasa's men were not outskilled. One archer killed twelve
of the foe and wounded eleven others, for some reason leaving
the last of his twenty-four arrows in the quiver. He then climbed
up onto the bridge, which was in no man's land, and crossed it
"as one who walks along the street Ichijo or Nijo of the Capital,"
and slew large numbers of the enemy, using his sword "in the
zigzag style, the interlacing, cross, reversed dragonfly, water-
wheel, and eight-sides-at-once styles of fencing."

Others were equally bold, and successful too, but the Taira
cavalry finally determined to ford the river and soon had fought
its way across. There was no hope, of course, for the defenders,
save to give their prince time to escape to Nara. Yorimasa, who
had known this from the start, was finally persuaded by one of
his sons to retire to the Byodo-in, so that he might die peacefully
and by his own hand rather than fall into the hands of the enemy.

His eldest son, grievously wounded, dropped back to the building called Tsuri-dono and killed himself, and they hid his head "under the verandah." A younger son was at the same time in the process of being killed by the overwhelming forces of the enemy.

So Yorimasa retired to the temple and placed his open fan on the ground and sat down upon it. He bade his faithful retainer to strike off his head, but the latter would not do it while his master still lived. So Yorimasa turned to the west, the direction of the Western Paradise of Amida, and composed a short poem—"it was not a time when people usually make poems, but as he had been extremely fond of this pastime from his youth up, so even at the hour of his death he did not forget it"—and then committed suicide. The faithful retainer lopped off his head, and weighting that prize down with stones, "sunk it in a deep part of the Uji River."

One would like to report that the prince made good his escape, but, as he proved on the trip from Mii-dera to Uji, he was no horseman, and besides, the monks of Nara were alerted too late to save him. They rushed out to meet him only to find that they had been anticipated by the cavalry of the Taira, who caught and killed their prey and rode back to Kyoto "in the midst of them a headless corpse in white clothing borne on a shutter. It was the Prince without doubt, for in his girdle was the flute 'Koeda' which he had bidden them bury with him. . . ."

This is a sad tale and a cruel one, but it shows the loyalty and bravery that men preserved in those chaotic, dangerous times. Their monument is a tiny fan-shaped plot of ground near the Tsuri-dono of Byodo-in—the spot where Yorimasa sat on his fan and killed himself.

FIGHT AMONG THE VICTORS

The troubles of the Taira were not over. Although he had failed to place his man on the throne, Yorimasa had led the first of a series of Minamoto rebellions. The leaders of the succeeding ones hovered in the eastern provinces, just out of reach, awaiting their chance to strike. They included the very children Kiyomori had spared in 1160, the oldest of whom—Minamoto Yoritomo—was now a man in his thirties.

Kiyomori himself was not destined to witness their revenge, for in 1181 he became mortally ill; but that he recognized the threat from the east was obvious when they asked what last wishes he had, for he replied:

" 'Since the time of Hogen and Heiji my unworthy house subdued the enemies of the Emperor many times and thereby gained great rewards, for which we are most grateful, and I, having been permitted to become the maternal relation of the Heavenly Sovereign and to reach the office of Prime Minister, am about to hand down my glory to my descendants, wherefore in this world I have nothing else left to desire. The only thing I have to regret is that I cannot see the head of Yoritomo. When I am dead do not perform any Buddhist services or make offerings to me, or build temples or pagodas; only make haste to slay Yoritomo and cut off his head and lay it before my tomb. That will be the best offering you can make me either in this world or the next.' "

Unfortunately for the Taira, this request was never fulfilled. After Kiyomori's death the leadership of the clan passed to his son, but it was greatly weakened, and within two years the whole clan, including the infant Emperor Antoku, had been driven out of Kyoto by a Minamoto army led by Yoritomo's cousin, Yoshinaka.

Yoshinaka—or Kiso Yoshinaka, after the place whence he came—had been steadily increasing his strength in provincial wars, so that when he finally invaded Kyoto, he had little trouble in taking the city. He was thirty years old that year—1183.

At first he got along well with the retired Emperor Go-Shirakawa, who had encouraged his invasion and remained in the city, but before the year was out they were arguing over whom to place on the empty throne. Balked by Yoshinaka, Go-Shirakawa sent secret messages to Minamoto Yoritomo in eastern Japan. The latter obligingly sent an army of 60,000 against his cousin, led by his brothers, Noriyori and the famous Yoshitsune.

There were two bridges between this army and Kyoto: one was at Seta, near Otsu, where the river falls out of Lake Biwa, and the other was Uji Bridge. Kiso Yoshinaka defended them both, from Noriyori at Seta, and from Yoshitsune at Uji. Yoshinaka's forces were small, although he was still accompanied, as he always had been, by the four trusty companions known as his Shi-tenno,[4] and by his beautiful warrior-wife, Tomoe Gozen. This last was one of the truly unusual women in the history of Japan; she had "long black hair and a fair complexion, and her face was very lovely; moreover she was a fearless rider whom neither the fiercest horse nor the roughest ground could dismay, and so dexterously did she handle sword and bow that she was a match for a thousand warriors, and fit to meet either god or devil. Many times she had taken the field, armed at all points, and won matchless renown in encounters with the bravest captains. . . ."

Yoshitsune, with his usual brilliant tactics, forded the river and broke through Yoshinaka's lines at Uji and surged on into Kyoto, leaving the Uji Bridge, which Yoshinaka had destroyed, behind him. It was the 19th of February, 1184. Yoshinaka, who less than two weeks before had had himself appointed the third *sei-i-taishogun* in the history of Japan and had seen his protégé made emperor, now fled for his life. His small band went out toward Seta, but he was cut off there by the forces of Noriyori, who blocked the bridge they had been unable to cross.

"That day Kiso was arrayed in a hitatare of red brocade and a suit of armor laced with Chinese silk; by his side hung a magnificent sword mounted in silver and gold, and his helmet was surmounted by long golden horns. Of his twenty-four eagle-feathered arrows, most had been shot away in the previous fighting, and only a few were left, drawn out high from the quiver, and he grasped his rattan-bound bow by the middle as he sat his famous grey charger, fierce as a devil, on a saddle mounted in gold. Rising high in his stirrups he cried with a loud voice: 'Kiso-no-Kwanja you have often heard of; now you see him before your eyes! Lord of Iyo and Captain of the Guard, Bright Sun General, Minamoto Yoshinaka am I! Come! Kai-no-Ichijo Jiro! Take my head and show it to Hyoye-no-suke Yoritomo!'"

The opposing sides met in battle and fought on until there were only five survivors on Yoshinaka's side, one of whom was Tomoe Gozen. Yoshinaka tried to persuade her to retire from the field, but she would not, and she thought to herself:

4. Named after the "four heavenly kings" of Buddhism that protect Buddha by keeping watch over the four quarters of the compass.

" 'Ah, for some bold warrior to match with, that Kiso might see how fine a death I can die.' And she drew aside her horse and waited. Presently Onda-no-Hachiro Moroshige of Musashi, a strong and valiant samurai, came riding up with thirty followers, and Tomoe, immediately dashing into them, flung herself upon Onda and grappling with him dragged him from his horse, pressed him calmly against the pommel of her saddle and cut off his head. Then stripping off her armor she fled away to the Eastern Provinces."

Soon Yoshinaka had but a single man at his side, and that man persuaded him to retire from the field, so that death might at least come from his own hand. At first Yoshinaka refused, but faced with the inevitability of death for both of them, he eventually consented.

"Yoshinaka rode off alone toward Awazu. . . . It was now nearly dark and all the land was coated with thin ice, so that none could distinguish the deep rice-fields, and he had not gone far before his horse plunged heavily into the muddy ooze beneath. Right up to the neck it floundered, and though Kiso plied whip and spur with might and main, it was all to no purpose, for he could not stir it. Even in this plight he still thought of his retainer, and he was turning to see how it fared with Imai, when Miura-no-Ishida Jiro Tamehisa of Sagami rode up and shot an arrow that struck in the face under his helmet. Then as the stricken warrior fell forward in his saddle so that his crest bowed over his horse's head, two of Ishida's retainers fell upon him and struck off his head."

Thus, on a winter evening, in a thinly frozen rice field shrouded in gathering gloom somewhere upriver from Uji, Minamoto Yoshinaka, *sei-i-taishogun* of Japan for less than two weeks, met his end, but not before he had made his mark on history and paved the way for the eventual conquest of the country by his enemy cousins.

And as for Tomoe Gozen, who was then twenty-eight years old, some say that she did not leave but died in the fighting, others that she survived it and retired, and still others that she was overpowered by the opposing warrior Wada Yoshimori, who made her his mistress and sired on her his famous strongman son, Asahina Saburo.

# 6 The Fall of the Taira: Jakko-in

"Could I e'er have dreamed
That from such a spot as this
I should view the moon—
Then, the stately Palace halls,
Now, this lonely mountain cell."

KENREI-MON-IN

GO-SHIRAKAWA (1127–92), retired emperor become priest.

KENREI-MON-IN (1155–1213), daughter of Taira Kiyomori and widow
of the Emperor Takakura, as well as mother of the infant Emperor
Antoku.[1]

AFTER Yoshinaka's death, the army of Yoshitsune and Nori-yori pursued the Taira clan west. For two years thereafter the fortunes of the Taira dragged out towards an inevitable end. Pressed by the Minamoto army, they dropped back on friendly provinces but failed to find the support they needed to stave off defeat. The poor leadership of the Taira was no match for the brilliant Yoshitsune. The end came in April 1185, when the opposing forces met for the last time, in a naval battle at Dan-no-ura, a bay near the western end of Honshu. Here the Minamoto cut down their foes to a man, and it is said to this day that the strange designs on the faces of the crabs and fishes in that bay are none other than the ghostly faces of the slaughtered Taira clan, who were wiped from Japan's history even more swiftly than they entered it.

As to the infant Emperor Antoku, his grandmother, Kiyomori's widow, seeing that all was lost, leaped into the sea with him in her arms, and they both drowned. The ex-empress, his mother Kenrei-mon-in, also leaped into the sea, but in the mean-

---

1. Her original name was Toku-ko. After the death of Takakura she changed her name to Kenrei-mon-in. Kenrei-mon was the name of the great south gate of the Imperial Palace. For some reason it was usual for imperial widows to take the names of the palace gates, while princes and the like were often named after their palaces.

time their ship had been captured, and the Minamoto soldiers managed to snag her by the hair and pull her out, and she became a lonely survivor on the side of the Taira.

The fate of the young empress dowager was thus postponed.

SOLITUDE

Kenrei-mon-in was brought back to Kyoto, where she went to the temple Choraku-ji and shaved her head and became a nun.

"She was twenty-nine years old this year, and the beauty of her face was not yet dimmed, neither was the elegance of her slender form impaired; but what now availed the loveliness of her hair?"

More or less forgotten by the world, she lived in a small hut that had none of the amenities she had once known as empress; it barely protected her from the weather, and it was empty inside. This was her home for the summer of 1185, but it tumbled down quickly during an earthquake that fall, and Kenrei-mon-in, who had neither the ability nor the wherewithal to reconstruct it, was left homeless.

"Then a certain lady came . . . and said to her: 'There is a place northward from here, in the mountains of Ohara, called Jakko-in, and it is very quiet.'"

Kenrei-mon-in had no choice but to accept the suggestion, little knowing that she would spend the remaining half of her life—almost thirty years—in that distant and lonely nunnery.

"Thus at the end of the ninth month she proceeded to the temple of Jakko-in. As they went along she gazed at the beauty of the autumn tints, while the sun sank gradually behind the mountains. The dreary boom of the evening bell of the wayside temple, and the thick-lying dew on the grass as they passed drew tears from her eyes, while the fierce gale whirled the leaves from the trees in all directions. Suddenly the sky grew dark and the autumn drizzle began to fall; the cry of a deer sounded faintly and the shrilling of the insects was incessant. Nothing was wanting to add to the sum of her afflictions, which seemed indeed such as few have been made to suffer. Even when she was driven from island to island her melancholy was not to be compared to this.

"The place she had chosen to dwell in was ancient and surrounded by mossy rocks; the reeds in the garden were now cov-

17. "A deep ravine that works in through densely overgrown hills crowding close on all sides. On one slope... sits the little Tendai nunnery called Jakko-in." Jakko-in's entrance. Courtesy of Asano Kiichi.

18. "The mood of the whole garden, in keeping with the tale of Kenrei-mon-in, is a melancholy one." Section of Jakko-in's garden. Courtesy of the Asahi Shimbunsha.

ered with hoar-frost instead of dew, and when she gazed on the faded hue of the withered chrysanthemums by the wall, she could hardly fail to be reminded of her own condition. Entering before the Buddha she prayed: 'For the Sacred Spirit of the Emperor, that it may attain perfect Buddhahood, and for the departed spirits of all the Heike,[2] that they may quickly enter the Way of Salvation.' But still the image of the late Emperor was impressed on her mind, and wherever she might be, she thought she could never forget it.

"So they built for her a small cell ten feet square beside the Jakko-in, and in it were two rooms, in one of which she put her shrine of Buddha, and in the other she slept; and there she spent her time continually repeating the Nembutsu and performing the Buddhist services, both by night and by day. . . . Formerly she had lived delicately in the Jewel Halls, and couches of brocade had been spread for her in the Golden Palace, but now she dwelt in a hut of brushwood and thatch, and the sleeves of her robe were dishevelled and tear-stained."

In the spring of the following year the old *ho-o,* Go-Shirakawa,[3] decided that he wanted to see Kenrei-mon-in and the place where she had retired. Go-Shirakawa had lived on in Kyoto, a survivor of his own political schemes against Minamoto and Taira alike. As a priest he practiced austerities, but his austerities were not so austere as those undertaken by other priests. For his trip to Ohara, for example, he chose to travel incognito, which for him meant wending his way up the valley accompanied by seventeen courtiers of various ranks and several imperial guards. Nevertheless his arrival came as a surprise to Kenrei-mon-in, who had had no visitor since she had come to the remote little nunnery. She was returning from a flower-picking expedition; her sad appearance moved the *ho-o* and his retinue to wet their sleeves with tears, and Kenrei-mon-in for her part was so ashamed to be seen in her bedraggled clothing and humble state, and so amazed by the sight of Go-Shirakawa

2. The Taira clan was familiarly known as the Heike, just as the Minamoto were called the Genji. These names were often abbreviated to "Hei" and "Gen." They are used today to refer to opposing sides in contests, games, etc.

3. The title *ho-o* was carried by emperors who became priests after abdication. Go-Shirakawa should not be confused with the earlier Emperor Shirakawa, mentioned elsewhere in the chapter and book.

seated there waiting for her, that she stood rooted to the spot, not wanting to come closer, unable to go away.

He visited with her for the entire afternoon. They discussed the vanity of human ambition, and Kenrei-mon-in recalled in touching words her sublime happiness as empress:

" 'Dwelling in the Seiryoden and the Shishinden behind the Jewel Curtain, I gladdened my eyes in spring with the blossoms of the Imperial Cherry Tree. In the hot months of summer I refreshed myself with crystal streams, and in autumn I viewed the moon in the midst of my ladies. In the cold nights of winter soft bed-quilts were heaped up to warm me, and I thought that I had only to wish for the draught of immortality, and the magic potion of eternal life and youth brought from Horai the Elysian isle, for it to be immediately forthcoming. So full was my life of joy and happiness, both by day and by night, that perchance even in heaven nothing could surpass it.' "

This was the life Yoshinaka had ended by driving her clan from Kyoto. Now she told how they fled to the west, ironically driven before armies that Go-Shirakawa himself had spurred on against them. The women were huddled in rolling ships without enough food or water as the clan was forced west. Now Kenrei-mon-in told Go-Shirakawa the terrible saga which had ended in the simultaneous suicide of her mother and son.

" 'My eyes darkened and my heart stood still, and it is a thing I can never forget or bear to think of. And at that moment from all those who still lived there went up so great and terrible a cry, that the shrieks of all the damned burning amid the hottest hell of Avichi could not exceed it.' "

Their talk shifted to Buddhism, and the afternoon passed quickly. When it was time for him to leave, Go-Shirakawa could not hold back his tears, and Kenrei-mon-in cried too as she watched his procession "until she could see it no more."

Now she prayed to the west, towards Amida's Paradise, for she was shifting her thoughts toward death, even though it was not yet near at hand. With Go-Shirakawa's departure her contact with the outside world had ended forever. Just as the dusk settling about her mountain cell was followed by night, so Go-Shirakawa took with him the light of the mortal world and left

Kenrei-mon-in in a dark solitude that would only be broken twenty-seven years later by death.

## JAKKO-IN

West of Ohara there is a small, fertile valley of compactly knit fields and farmhouses that one crosses by narrow paths and single-plank bridges. It ends in a deep ravine that works in through densely overgrown hills crowding close on all sides. On one slope of this tight cluster, hemmed in by a network of hills, sits the little Tendai nunnery called Jakko-in.

The tiny nuns who inhabit Jakko-in seem almost as startled at the arrival of strangers as was Kenrei-mon-in herself when she first saw Go-Shirakawa, even though visitors often come to this place today. The nuns are perplexed by these strangers—they don't quite understand why they come here. Nevertheless, they conduct them about the little nunnery and recite to them the long, sad history of Kenrei-mon-in. The nun-guide tells her story by rote, mechanically, in a formal and archaic tongue that even her Japanese listeners cannot always understand. She is quite unaware of this, and at each stopping place emits a microscopic paragraph of indeterminately mixed prose and poetry that travels uncaught in a thin, unending line past the ears of her listeners. Somehow, she thinks to herself, I am quenching the strange thirst of these people. She does not understand why they ask her to repeat this information which is so familiar to her; she receives their questions with blank and wondering stares, especially when they ask for something she has just finished telling them. Most times, the questions go unanswered. One of Jakko-in's unique characteristics is that it manages to remain a nunnery first and a historic place second—it is a rarity in modern Kyoto to find a temple still better prepared to receive the one who comes to shave his head than the one who now comes to take pictures.

From a corner of the verandah of the little main hall one stops to look out over the tiny, sad garden, made sadder by the presence of the pathetically decayed and carefully fenced off stump of what was once a cherry tree. In her astringent voice the starch little nun reels off a few paragraphs from *Heike Monogatari,* culminating, one may be sure, in the recitation of a poem, for centuries ago when this stump was a tree it was the first thing seen by old Go-Shirakawa when he entered the grounds, and it moved him to poetry:

> Lo! the cherry tree
> Leaning o'er the silent depths
> Of the garden pool
> While the fallen petals float
> On the gently rippling wave!

There are two little ponds in the garden, and a hidden waterfall, and a tree or two in better shape than that old cherry stump. Like everything else here, the garden is small, and it is touched by the aura of sadness that Kenrei-mon-in brought when she came but failed to take away when she died. If it is fair to put words into the mouth of the little nun-guide, she says that Kenrei-mon-in likened the trees "to the Seven Precious Trees of Paradise, and the water that collected in the hollows of the rocks she compared to the Lake of the Eight Virtues in the Pure Land." These comparisons could only have been made by one who was in very unhappy straits indeed.

At the Sho-in, where Kenrei-mon-in lived, the modern nun stands on the verandah and peers through her round, steel-rimmed spectacles down the long, narrow view away from the temple, the single opening in the surrounding hills and trees that shows in the distance a section of the highroad between Ohara and Kyoto. As she gazes, perhaps with curiosity, at the distant road, her mouth emits more pages of miniature prose that are washed away by the breeze: here is where Kenrei-mon-in herself stood that evening, watching the procession of the incognito Go-Shirakawa "until she could see it no more"; here she must have stood many times, looking in vain for a trace of the world to which she had been empress, of the family so totally wiped away as to have become no more than a figment of her imagination. This is Jakko-in's window to the world; it is scenic, but unrevealing.

So the visitor tours the grounds, seeing the rooms where Kenrei-mon-in lived, the artifacts and relics preserved from her time, her statue, her worshiping hall. Yet the most interesting part of this place is probably the little nuns themselves, for without revealing anything of their own persons or thoughts they somehow shed a greater light on the personality and life of Kenrei-mon-in than all the ancient relics combined. Are they happy to see the visitor go? Or are they just relieved, and a little curious? There is no way to tell. In time this will change. It is changing now. But for the moment these nuns live in another world, interesting because it was once the world of Kenrei-mon-in.

EPILOGUE FOR THE TAIRA

Kenrei-mon-in's imperial tomb lies close by Jakko-in. It might be called the last vestige of the ambitions of the Taira, but even so its modest grandeur is only the result of relatively recent attentions by the government. Who could have guessed that the suddenly glorious line of the Taira would end in a nunnery outside the village of Ohara, so far removed from the imperial halls and palaces of Kyoto? One might wonder what would have happened if Kiyomori had killed the Minamoto children, if he had been able to check his lust for the beautiful Tokiwa Gozen.

When one looks back on the meteor-like rise and fall of the Taira clan he notices its apparent dependence upon the one man, Kiyomori, who raised them to a pinnacle of power which they lost as soon as he died. This was an age in which individual men could determine the course of the nation, as Minamoto Yoritomo himself later showed. Clans rose and fell on the shoulders of single men, and for the Taira that man was Kiyomori.

But in the case of Kiyomori, one fact should be mentioned that throws some doubt on the ability of the Taira to have risen at all. Kiyomori's mother was originally a concubine of the retired Emperor Shirakawa; one day the latter presented her to Taira Tadamori in reward for a courageous act. At the time of this presentation, however, it appears that the woman was pregnant, and the child she eventually bore, actually Shirakawa's, became none other than Taira Kiyomori. Thus it may well be argued that this man who led the Taira to their glory was not a Taira at all, but an emperor's son whom his adoptive clan could not replace when he died.

It is probably true that the Taira would have hung on in Kyoto longer had Kiyomori killed the children of the rival clan, but suppose the retired Emperor Shirakawa had not chosen to give away his favorite, pregnant concubine? The short history of the Taira seems to depend so heavily on the whims of the people involved that one can say little more than that it did manage to happen, and as to the fate of Kenrei-mon-in, it hardly seems stranger than do most of the events connected with her unfortunate clan.

# 7 Honen and the Jodo Sect: Anraku-ji and Honen-in

"Do not be troubled about whether your heart is good or bad, or your sin light or grievous. Only determine in your heart that you will be born into the Pure Land, and so repeat the 'Namu Amida Butsu' with your lips, and let the conviction accompany the sound of your voice, that you will of a certainty be born into the Pure Land."                                                        HONEN SHONIN

HONEN SHONIN (1133–1212), Buddhist priest, founder of the Jodo sect of Buddhism.

ANRAKU (?–1207), one of his disciples.

JUREN (1169?–1207), another disciple.

GO-TOBA (1179–1239), 82nd emperor of Japan (1184–98), who later ruled from retirement.

BETWEEN the time of Kyoto's founding and the twelfth century two Buddhist sects, the Shingon and the Tendai, had a virtual monopoly on the city's Buddhism. But by the twelfth and thirteenth centuries these sects had begun to show their age, and suddenly several new ones were founded and joined them. This was the single great revision of Japanese Buddhism between the ninth century and the present day. The Zen sect became the last one to cross from China, but significantly the other new sects of this time had their origins right in Japan. Devised by Japanese minds, they were bound to have a strong persuasion on the country, which until now had attempted to adapt itself to the Buddhism of China.

The most important sects to be founded at this time were the Nichiren, Jodo, Zen, and Shin. All of them had to struggle against Enryaku-ji for survival in Kyoto. The Nichiren and Shin sects were the most heavily persecuted, and the former never flourished in Kyoto as a result. Its success has been concentrated in other parts of Japan. The Shin was kept out of Kyoto for nearly two centuries, but eventually it grew so large that it had to be let back in. It was a child of the Jodo: as the Jodo simplified

Tendai doctrine, the Shin simplified that of the Jodo. The result was a sect with an appeal so broad that it is today the largest in Japan.

The Jodo sect is discussed in this chapter; the Zen, in chapter 8.

### SHISHI-GA-TANI

Shishi-ga-tani is a suburb of Kyoto that until very recently was unsettled and decidedly rural. It lies off the northeast corner of the city, between a small river called Shirakawa and the first thickly wooded slopes of Higashiyama. For centuries this shallow valley was farmer's land, interrupted only occasionally by a small temple or country villa.

Recently—ten or fifteen years ago—houses began rising in the northeastern sector of the city, and a wave of them swept out of it toward Shishi-ga-tani, crossing the valley and the little Shirakawa. Strangely, this was just a continuation of Kyoto's historical tendency to move to the north and east, a tendency which from the time of the city's founding had left its southwest quarter an abandoned area, as in many respects it remains today. Since the city came there, Shishi-ga-tani's farming has been confined to tiny backyard gardens, although occasionally one still sees an old farmhouse among the rising stucco homes.

The back line of Shishi-ga-tani, where Higashiyama begins to get steep, is held by a string of old temples. Some, like Ginkaku-ji, are famous; others are virtually unknown.

Anraku-ji belongs to the latter group. Its entrance is so modest as to be invisible. Inside the gate there is not a great deal, either. The temple consists of a single hall that hardly rises above the hedges around it. There are two small paths which cross at right angles near the center of the grounds. Where they cross, there stands a stone marker. "Anraku, Juren," the marker says, pointing to the visitor's right. "Suzumushi, Matsumushi," it says, pointing straight ahead.

The story of these four people, who lived and died before the temple was founded, and of the famous priest Honen, is the story of this small, forgotten temple called Anraku-ji.

### HONEN, ANRAKU, AND JUREN

He was born in 1133, and at the age of fifteen was sent to Mt.

19. "Inside the gate one passes two large oblong mounds of sand. . . .
They have designs raked in them. . . ." Honen-in's entrance. Courtesy of the Asahi Shimbunsha.

20. " 'I send you herewith an image of the great and revered Monju.' " The boy Honen arrives on Mt. Hiei to study for the priesthood. From the scroll *Honen Shonin Eden* (Biography of St. Honen). Courtesy of Chion-in, Kyoto.

21. "Anraku was taken off to the execution ground on the flat gravel bed of the Kamo River at Rokujo-kawara...." From the scroll *Honen Shonin Eden* (Biography of St. Honen). Courtesy of Chion-in, Kyoto.

22. "The Hon-do deserves careful inspection. . . . it gives one a good picture of the fast-disappearing small country temple." Anraku-ji's Hon-do.

23. ". . . when the sun is high, visitors begin to come, to walk in the graveyard, to ponder the garden, to pray." View of Honen-in's gate.

Hiei to study for the priesthood, bearing a note to deliver when he got there. It is said that on his way to the mountain his path crossed that of the imperial regent, who was so impressed by the boy's countenance that he stopped his carriage and saluted him, later explaining to his surprised attendants that the boy was "of no common mould."

At Mt. Hiei the boy delivered the note, which said, "I send you herewith an image of the great and revered Monju." Monju, the god of wisdom. The priest asked to see the promised image, but there was only this boy. At first he was annoyed, later he became incredulous, and finally respectful, for the boy himself was the promised image of Monju.

"If you told him one thing he understood ten"—this was what they said of that boy.

They gave him the best and most challenging masters they could find. Before a year was out he had been ordained a priest of the Tendai sect, in the Kaidan-in of Enryaku-ji. His name as a priest was Genku, but his prodigality brought him the nickname Honembo—"nature's own priest"—which was eventually shortened to Honen.

Honen's career was as illustrious as its beginnings. He accepted Eshin's reliance upon the Nembutsu and eventually decided that the Nembutsu was a religion in itself. Honen then began converting people to a worship which required only faith and the repetition of the holy words, "Namu Amida Butsu." This became the basis for a sect known as the Jodo, and it took hold quickly among the great mass of the people who, unable to understand the complex practices of the established sects, had until now been denied the hope of salvation after death. To Honen, intellectual understanding was commendable but unnecessary— the common man too had a right to be saved, and to this end Honen created a religion based solely on faith.

The infant Jodo sect had to struggle for its life against older, established sects that wanted it suppressed and eliminated. Enryaku-ji, Honen's old monastery, was foremost among these foes. They managed to prevent Jodo from gaining a formal establishment in Japan—even for centuries after Honen had died both the temples and the followers of the Jodo technically belonged to other sects, a bondage unbroken until the seventeenth century. Nevertheless, the faith persisted, and, formal or not, the arrival of the thirteenth century found the Jodo sect very much among the living, despite the persistent opposition of Enryaku-ji, the Nara temples, and other traditionalist foes. To their dismay the new sect spread like wildfire; however, among the many new priests who followed Honen there appeared a dissolute group whose actions provided his enemies with the excuse they needed to promote public persecution.

Official protests against the conduct of Jodo priests were lodged by both Enryaku-ji and Nara's Kofuku-ji. Honen himself tried to counteract these protests by issuing a code of conduct to his priests, but the pressure continued to mount on the retired Emperor Go-Toba—who was the force behind the ruling emperor—to suppress the new sect. Go-Toba might well have done so had he not been faced with pressure from another source. Many members of his own court had been converted to Honen's teachings, and their influence was strong enough to stay Go-Toba's hand. In order to sate Enryaku-ji and Kofuku-ji he punished some acknowledged wrongdoers among Honen's priests, but he refused to extend the punishment to other priests, or to Honen himself.

Toward the end of the year 1206 Go-Toba had occasion to make a pilgrimage to Mt. Kumano, in the hill country north of Kyoto. At the time of this pilgrimage two of Honen's priests, Anraku and Juren by name, happened to be preaching the Nembutsu in Shishi-ga-tani. It was an isolated place in those days—there was the old Tendai temple, Jodo-ji, but very little else there. Anraku and Juren were working among the country people.

It happened that in Go-Toba's absence two women of his court, whom he was said to have favored greatly, went out into the city to pray. Some say that they had already been to Kiyomizu-dera and were on their way home, while others say that they went directly to Shishi-ga-tani—whatever the case, at the latter place they heard the preaching of Anraku and Juren and were deeply moved. How many times these ladies returned to Shishi-ga-tani, and whether they were spellbound by religion or love, no one will ever know, but when Go-Toba finally returned from Mt. Kumano he learned that two of his favorite concubines had left him—they had been admitted as nuns to the new Jodo faith.

It was suggested to Go-Toba that the motives of Anraku and Juren in enrolling his ladies had been somehow less than religious. This stung him personally, the complaints of the older sects came alive again, and the stalemate which had existed between them and the Jodo was suddenly broken. Anraku and Juren had provided Go-Toba with a reason for action.

"The Emperor was very angry with them, and on the ninth of the second month in the second year of Ken-ei (1207), he summoned them to the Court and imposed on them quite a severe penalty."[1]

This is one way of saying that Go-Toba sentenced Anraku and Juren to death. They could have had clemency if they had recanted, but they were defiant in their belief in the Nembutsu, "even if it meant tearing their bodies to pieces." Anraku, for one, was not easily cowed by Go-Toba, and to his face recited the following passage from the writings of Zendo:

" 'When they see others engaged in their religious practices, they verily hate them, and, inspired by bitter enmity, they try by all means in their power to put a stop to it all. Infidels like this, born blind to the truth, who thus would destroy that practice which is the quickest and shortest road to salvation [the Nembutsu], shall themselves utterly perish, and even though they were to try to escape from those three states of misery ordained, and keep on trying for endless dust *kalpas*,[2] they still would never be able to effect their escape.'

"At this, the Emperor became more enraged than ever...."

Anraku was taken off to the execution ground on the flat

1. Passages in this chapter, including the one at its head, are quoted from H. H. Coates and R. Ishizuka, translators, *Honen the Buddhist Saint,* Kyoto, 1949.

2. *Kalpa:* In Buddhism, as explained by Coates and Ishizuka, *op. cit.,* page 367, "the general term for a long period. The length of this period is so great that it can not be defined by months or years. Buddhist scholars have invented such comparisons as the time it would take for a mountain of granite 100 cubic *yojanas* (one *yojana* = 12.12 English miles) to be worn away by an angel flying over it once in a hundred years and touching it gently with its wings; or the time needed for a man of very long life to come once in one hundred years and carry off one seed at a time from a castle full of mustard seeds, whose dimensions are 100 cubic *yojanas.*" There are three great *kalpas* in the Buddhist "eternity." They are divided and subdivided into lesser *kalpas.*

gravel bed of the Kamo River at Rokujo-kawara, and while on-lookers stared in amazement at great purple clouds which were quickly approaching from the west—the direction of Amida's Western Paradise—he calmly explained to the executioner how he wished to be killed.

" 'After I have repeated Amida's sacred name several hundred times,' he said, 'I shall then repeat it separately ten times. Just at the conclusion of the tenth, please let your stroke fall, and you will know that I have attained my long cherished desire for Ojo, when you see me with my hands clasped, inclining to the right.'

"Thus saying he repeated the Nembutsu several hundred times, and then ten times at the end, when the executioner struck him. Everything happened just as he had said, as he fell to the right with his hands firmly clasped together. Many there were among the spectators, who, with tears of joy streaming down their cheeks, joined the cult of the Nembutsu."

Of the fates of Juren and the two court ladies less is known, except that most stories of Juren end in his death at one of various execution grounds, and it has been suggested that, upon learning what had happened, the two court ladies killed themselves.

Go-Toba was still dissatisfied and now turned his attention to Honen. Since Honen was a venerable priest in his seventies, Go-Toba could not deal with him in exactly the same manner as he had dealt with the younger men; besides, there were public opinion and the Jodo faction at court to consider. Nevertheless he had Honen defrocked and sent into exile, to the distant province of Tosa. Undoubtedly it was expected that the old man would never return; Honen's disciples were alarmed by this possibility, but Honen calmed them by pointing out that his exile was also an opportunity.

" 'The fact is,' he said, 'I have labored here in the capital these many years for the spread of the Nembutsu, and so I have long wished to get away into the country to preach to those on field and plain, but the time never came for the fulfillment of my wish. Now, however, by the august favor of His Majesty, circumstances have combined to enable me to do so.' "

With this attitude Honen went into exile and converted folk wherever he went. In Kyoto his departure was followed by a persecution in which several of his followers were either exiled or beheaded, and for a time the opponents of the Jodo were satisfied. To them the whole proceeding was an orderly application of justice. One court official, for instance, wrote in his diary:

" 'Genku Shonin (otherwise called Honembo) was banished to Tosa for his dissemination of the Nembutsu doctrine. His disciples these days fill the city and the country, and under the name of Nembutsu give themselves up to fornication and immoral association with the wives and daughters of good families. They set at naught all the laws of the Buddhas and the State, and daily practice shameful deeds. So the Government has ordered the proper officials to arrest them, and mete out suitable penalties, whether of imprisonment or execution, the women too being punished as they severally deserve. These punishments are inflicted, on the ground of due accusations by the priests of the established sects.' "

Honen lived in exile for four years, and at various times his sentence was diminished so that he was permitted to come closer to Kyoto but not to enter it. Eventually he settled in Settsu (Osaka), where, as everywhere, he preached his doctrines and won new converts for his faith.

Then in 1211 Go-Toba heard an oracle which was interpreted to him as calling for Honen's return. He took no action, but in the seventh month of the same year he had a nightmare: "He thought he was visiting the Rengeo-in Temple, where a venerable-looking priest shabbily dressed drew near him and said: 'Honembo was a religious teacher who administered the perfect commandments to the late Emperors Go-Shirakawa and Takakura. His virtue is like that of the wisest and holiest of old, and his influence felt everywhere. Your Majesty has taken away his priestly rank, and sentenced to exile this veritable incarnation of the Buddha. The five deadly sins are no worse offence than this. Do you not dread the retribution sure to come?' He awoke in great fright. . . ."[3]

The nightmare persuaded Go-Toba to pardon the old priest,

3. The promised retribution did apparently come, for in 1221, when a plot of his failed for lacking the support of Enryaku-ji, Go-Toba himself was sent into exile, where he eventually died.

and a messenger was sent off to Settsu to inform Honen that "the feathers on the crow's head had changed" to white—that is, that he could now re-enter Kyoto.

It was a triumphal return for the old man, whom none in the capital had ever expected to see again. On all sides he was received by friends who flocked to pay him homage. He settled down for the winter, but as it arrived and he entered his eightieth year he took sick, and early in 1212, surrounded—as he reported clearly to his disciples—by Amida and the entire heavenly host, Honen died and his soul was borne off to Amida's Western Paradise.

### ANRAKU-JI AND HONEN-IN

The old housekeeper at Anraku-ji welcomes the rare visitor to her temple enthusiastically, for she has a fine story to tell, and the opportunity to tell it comes seldom indeed.

Actually, she says, it was Honen that the ladies had gone out to hear preach, and they were "possessed by him and experienced much pain." In those days, she says, women were not free and could not do what they wanted to; so these two reflected on their unhappy lives and decided to go back to hear Honen again. This time Anraku and Juren were there, and when the ladies became nuns it was Anraku and Juren who shaved their heads.

No, they did not fall in love with the two priests, the housekeeper insists—it was a religious thing that they did. But the retired emperor did love them very much, and because this made him angry, those connected with the act had to be punished, including Anraku and Juren. So Juren was taken to a place called Mabuchi, where he was killed "by the cutting of the neck by an officer," while Anraku was taken to Rokujo-kawara and killed by the cutting of his neck at the execution ground there. And the two newly made nuns escaped to Kokawa, where they heard the news and killed themselves.

And as to this temple, the housekeeper continues, it was built by Honen himself when he returned from exile, to the memory of his two priests, on the very spot where they had been preaching.

As she talks, one looks about the hall. All the statues are there —Anraku, Juren, the two nun-ladies, and Honen. It is as if all the actors had been asked to sit quietly here while the housekeeper told their story.

She steps to the back of the hall to unlock a sliding door so the sunlight will shine in on the temple's Amida. Oh yes, there are Kannon and Seishi, and even Jizo back there too. She shakes the door, and a small lizard drops from the top of it and lies still on the floor, waiting for those who have disturbed him to go away.

Outside in the sunlight, the stone marker at the path crossing points toward the tombs of the priests and the concubine-nuns, set at opposite ends of the grounds, as if those who put them here wanted there to be no mistaking the sanctity of their holy relationship. The respectable distance between them is filled with sunlit shrubs, and camellia trees whose falling carmine flowers are a poignant reminder to all of these martyrs' fallen lives.

Honen-in is a larger Jodo temple that stands hidden away on a wooded promontory about a hundred yards from Anraku-ji. The wood is mostly bamboo, a dark, neat stand of which forms a band between the temple and the outside world. Here and there giant camellias soar up through the bamboos; at their feet lie their beautiful flowers, like loose gems scattered over the ground.

Honen-in has a large graveyard, pleasant for strolling, a place where lovers and daydreamers come to escape the city below. The temple is better known—and hence more used to visitors—than is Anraku-ji. Outside its main hall there is a sign which says:

"Please call me by hitting the board three times.

Please come freely to pray.

There is no fee to see the garden."

Leaning over to punk away at the board after the first three timid whacks have gone unanswerered, one is met by the smell of fresh *tatami*. The board noises bring a courteous young priest, who readily shows one inside.

In the dark main hall, narrow shafts of sunlight cut through the incense and pick out the deep gloss of Amida, the glassy polish of the hardwood floor, the fresh cut flowers scattered across it. The flowers, the priest explains, are the twenty-five Bosatsu, those followers of Amida who are nearing the end of the long climb to Buddhahood. Perhaps this is the only temple where the Bosatsu are represented by fresh flowers spread over the floor at Amida's feet. The way the sunlight picks their colors out of the dark recesses of the hall brings these Bosatsu very much alive.

The priest is asked about Anraku-ji. It is an interesting story, he agrees. Those priests were very handsome, and their prayers had a very nice sound to them. It was just a matter of love at first sight, and when they had reflected on their empty life at court, the two concubines returned and became nuns—to fulfill their love.

As to Anraku-ji, he points out that it belongs to a different wing of the Jodo sect from Honen-in, which adheres to Honen's "main" temple, Chion-in.

He is proud of Honen-in, and he has reason to be. It is a fine and beautiful temple, and its history measures well the value of the sacrifices made by such men as Honen, Anraku, and Juren. In its early days, during the last years of Honen's life, Honen-in was little more than an image of Amida with a roof over its head, hidden uphill from the temple's present site. Even before Honen's exile the shelter was destroyed, leaving only "the people who believed in his goodness" to protect the temple's Amida from the ravages of time, weather, and war.

Like its sect, Honen-in had nothing in the way of buildings until the seventeenth century, when the Jodo was finally patronized, by the Tokugawa, and became a truly independent religious organization. Through the intervening centuries Honen-in had been little more than the Amida and the small cult passing from generation to generation around him. But now they had their hall; now they could scatter flowery Bosatsu at Amida's feet—new ones every day.

Today the Jodo is the second largest sect in Japan—only its own offspring, the Shin sect, is larger. All the others, old and new, have dropped into the wake of these two. Today the farthest reaches of Japan have their Jodo temples, and at Honen-in, every day, the bell tolls to morning prayer at four, and a new set of flower-Bosatsu is laid before Amida, and when the sun is high, visitors begin to come, to walk in the graveyard, to ponder the garden, to pray.

# 8 The Zen Sect: Daitoku-ji

Monk: "Has the dog Buddha-nature or not?"
Master: "Mu!"

DAITO KOKUSHI (1282–1337), Zen sect priest, founder of Daitoku-ji.
HOSOKAWA TADAOKI (1563–1645), a leading general of his time.
HOSOKAWA GRACIA (1563–1600), his wife.

THE HISTORY of the Zen sect in Japan goes back at least as far as the seventh century, when the priest Dosho tried to spread it upon his return from China. He failed, as did a long line of others after him, which points out a great difference between the Japan of their time and the one five centuries later that allowed Eisai, another priest trying to bring the sect from China, to succeed. For the Zen sect in Japan has always been heavily favored by the samurai, or military class, and this class did not emerge until the twelfth century.

When Eisai arrived in 1192, the samurai were still new to power, but already they had control of the state. Eisai spent ten years in Fukuoka, at the western threshold of the country; then he was invited to Kyoto by the shogun, and there he became master of the city's first Zen sect temple, Kennin-ji. Once it was established in Kyoto, the new sect was quickly adopted by the samurai, who protected it from the older sects and promoted its rapid growth there and in the shogun's seat at Kamakura. Early patronage by warriors and even emperors enabled the Zen sect to establish itself more quickly than any of the new sects which appeared at this time; eventually it was so successful that it became the one Chinese sect which Japan imported and improved upon: Zen's ultimate development was achieved in Japan.

It was the only new Japanese sect of that time that came from China and it was the last, a latecomer to a country that was now busy creating sects of its own. In its retinue Zen brought with it its own artistic and architectural conventions, as well as its own system of thought. The former became the major fresh artistic contribution made to Japan by the new religious forces of this period. The latter too was a fresh contribution, but its nature was less easily understood, and it was in this field of doctrine that Zen found its strongest opposition.

The exchange at the head of this chapter is a *ko-an*—a dialogue or statement containing a hard kernel of Zen sect wisdom which the aspiring novice may spend weeks, months, or even years attempting to extract. Of all the *ko-an* this one is perhaps the best known; another famous one is this: "What is the sound of the single hand?"

In the thirteenth and fourteenth centuries it was only natural that the priests of the established sects, which relied for their wisdom upon voluminous and ancient sutras, should view the newly arrived Zen as a fraud and a hoax when they learned that it stored its "doctrines" in such sayings as these. Their opposition took many forms; on one occasion it was a challenge to debate.

"When the day came a scholar of great reputation appeared and opened the forum: 'What is Zen that claims a special transmission outside the scriptural teaching?' To this Daito Kokushi answered, 'An hexagonal grind-stone runs through a vacuity.' The questioner was non-plussed. Another learned doctor came forward with a box. Seeing it, Daito asked, 'What is your box?' The doctor answered, 'This is the box in which the whole universe is packed up.' The Kokushi raised the short stick which was in his hand and struck the box, breaking it to pieces. He said, 'How would it be when the universe is broken up?' The doctor did not know what to do with this Zen monk whose language and behavior were more than they could cope with."[1]

In their actions too, the priests of the Zen sect baffled outsiders. One priest, lacking fuel to heat the bath, stripped his temple until he had it. When the roof leaked, he ordered a receptacle to be brought, and was pleased by the monk who brought a bamboo basket, while he was greatly angered by a second monk who took the time to find a watertight vessel. And when a relative came and offered to underwrite the repairs to his battered temple, this priest's only response was an angry order that the man finish his business and be gone.

1. This quotation and the next are from D. T. Suzuki, *Japanese Buddhism*, Tokyo, 1938, pages 63-65.

While opponents of the Zen sect were continually being reinforced by the actions and words of its priests in the conviction that the sect was a collection of fools, they were bothered by the lingering doubt that total victory was not theirs. By all logical standards the sect should have displayed its emptiness and disappeared, but time passed and it refused to wane. Furthermore, the Zen sect priests by the very consistency of their "meaningless" words and actions displayed an underlying discipline that was disturbing. Was it actually possible that their nonsense was a doctrine of wisdom beyond the reach of ordinary men? These priests were men of iron will, and sometimes even their worst detractors had to admit that the sheer force of that will, shining through apparent nonsense, commanded admiration:

"Daito Kokushi was lame of a leg, and had some difficulty sitting properly cross-legged. When his death approached he mounted a chair in which he wished to sit, but as his leg was not obedient to his will, he forced it with a crack, the blood staining his robe. He said, 'As I have been obedient to you all my life, you obey me in this last moment for once.' He quietly wrote out his farewell poem and passed away."

The suspicion that Zen is a fraud lingers even today, if not in Japan at least in countries where it has recently been introduced. If the sect is indeed a fraud, it is the longest-lived and most strikingly successful one in history. But what belies this possibility is again the consistency of the sect—it is virtually unchanged today, as it has been for centuries.

Why, then, if it has value, does Zen appear so meaningless to the outsider? The answer is that this meaninglessness is confined to the outsider. The sect clearly states that physical manifestations, whether in writing or other forms of expression, of its philosophies are not only meaningless but are also impossible. The repository of Zen sect philosophy is the inner spirit of the Zen man. He carries it within himself and cannot easily convey it to others. Transmission—*satori,* that renowned flash of enlightenment—lurks neither in books about Zen nor up in the eaves of a Zen sect temple. It is an elusive thing that one may—or may not —experience after an arduous apprenticeship has brought him into full rapport with his master. One not so apprenticed is unfit to judge the purpose and value of Zen sayings and deeds. This is something which many of Zen's foreign purveyors are reluctant to advertise.

Despite its elusiveness the Zen sect reveals more about itself through the physical design and arrangement of its temples than many another sect whose objectives are more clearly recorded. It may surprise the man who thinks of Zen as an unruly, intuitive religion to learn that of all the Japanese sects this one presents in its monasteries the most consistent arrangement of a set style of buildings: both the architectural design of these buildings and their geographical plan are predictable with amazing certainty.

The reason for this apparent contradiction lies in the character of the sect itself. While the ultimate objective is for the Zen man to be able to "think simultaneously in all ten directions," as it is sometimes put, this freedom is only achieved by driving that man through the tests of a rigid, arduous apprenticeship. As the scene of that apprenticeship, the Zen monastery reflects the extreme and unvarying disciplines which it entails. That even the physical appearances of the buildings of different monasteries must not vary gives one some idea of the intricacy of Zen's central disciplines and the exactitude with which they are preserved and reproduced.

Thus the central, functioning buildings of the Zen sect monastery reflect the repetition, consistency, persistence, and order of the monastery ritual. The ritual was brought from China; the building styles—almost part of it—came from there too. The Chinese arrangement of the worship halls, with the lecture hall —not the Buddha hall—at their head, is preserved; so too is the architectural style of these halls, including such Chinese elements as swinging doors, solid walls, tiled floors.

Still within the monastery, but outside the central complex of buildings, we find the limit beyond which the Japanese Zen sect did not accept the standards of China, in the living quarters of the monks. These are totally Japanese in style: sliding screens, matted floors, and the sprawling building design of Japan take over here. Apparently the Japanese monks would not go so far as to adopt Chinese methods of eating and sleeping, and conformity in living quarters was unimportant enough so that it could be neglected, despite the hold the sect seizes on every aspect of the apprentice's life. One concludes that while the Japanese

24. "Daitoku-ji is a classic example of a Zen sect monastery. Its gates and halls still follow the Chinese canons of arrangement and design...." Daitoku-ji's Butsu-den. Courtesy of Daitoku-ji.

25, 26. "... a bamboo railing ... the long, narrow walk." Koto-in, Daitoku-ji. Courtesy of Koto-in.

accepted the Chinese heart of the Zen sect, they changed it to suit themselves in peripheral areas.

Now, farther from the center, the influence of Japan becomes complete. This is in the small Zen temples that cluster around the great monasteries and spring up here and there in hidden spots in the country. While the appearance of Zen monasteries is rigidly consistent, that of small Zen temples is exactly the opposite: they show more freedom of design than any other religious buildings in Japan. Once again, to find the reason for this apparent contradiction, we must turn to the character of the sect itself.

The small Zen temple is the center of practice. His monastery training firmly established and tested, the Zen priest carries it within him and is able to practice his religion independent of stereotyped surroundings, scriptures, and images. *The man is the temple;* placing it within him was the achievement of his apprenticeship. The buildings in which he lives are a temple because he is there and because he uses them, but beyond that they are little more than his home. Without the man they would almost be secular. This is why small Zen temples are Japanese in style and show little exterior evidence of their sect: their physical appearance is unimportant. Many are simply private homes or villas that have been transplanted to the monastery grounds and made temples—Zen alone among the sects converts homes into temples without making a major change in them. For similar reasons the physical properties and images of small Zen temples are as likely to differ as to be the same, for this religious process can thrive without images but not without its men.

The primary requirement for a small Zen temple is that its appearance and surroundings should be conducive to contemplation and thought. Such a temple is therefore likely to have good gardens, outbuildings for aesthetic pursuits, uncluttered rooms; but beyond these general characteristics its arrangement is difficult to define.

Zen monasteries and temples do not reveal the inner wisdom of the sect, but they do show eloquently the sect's system of achieving freedom and limitlessness through discipline and inner mastery. At the heart of the monastery stand the orderly, predictable buildings which are the scene of formal apprenticeship. Around its edge cluster the numerous sub-temples, each one possessing a character and individuality of its own, each one, perhaps, more famous to outsiders as a miniature repository of art works and other aesthetic treasures than as a religious building, more famous for its connection to a family of patrons than for those distinctive religious achievements which its abbot cannot transmit to the outside world.

### ROCK GARDENS AND TEAHOUSES

The contrast between restriction and freedom, discipline and intuition which is so much a part of the Zen sect extends to two artistic areas which are particularly associated with Zen in Japan, rock-garden design and ceremonial tea. Both took hold within this sect and achieved an importance independent of its bounds. It should be pointed out that Zen did not create these practices for its own use, but rather that they were born independently and later attached themselves to Zen. A natural kinship to Zen was what caused them to flourish within that sect. As one writer puts it, "the practitioners of these arts found in Zen discipline an aid to the more expert handling of their own art."[2]

The origins of rock gardens seem to be clear: they appeared at a time when black-and-white painting, having been imported to Japan from China, was creating great interest, as was simultaneously the art of "tray landscape" design. The application of these influences to garden design produced gardens in monochromes and in miniature. Because it was meant to be symbolic, a rock garden had to be small, lest its symbolism approach reality too closely and break down. Because it was small, this garden had to be clearly outlined. It was usually placed next to a building, as it tended to get lost in natural surroundings.

Here, then, was a garden limited in size, color, and environment. Usually it consisted of little more than plain rocks set into a bed of white gravel. Its main virtue seemed to be permanence, for such gardens are not easily destroyed, but beyond that the limitations of the form would seem to have been too great to allow any range or depth of expression.

The truth is just the reverse. The symbolism in these gardens is sometimes nearly unlimited, for by their very simplicity and plainness they open themselves up to an endless variety of inter-

2. R. F. Sasaki, *Rinzai Zen Study for Foreigners in Japan*, Kyoto, 1960, page 10.

pretations.[3] Even very complex gardens using a large number of rocks may be limited to a single interpretation but manage by their abstraction to plumb great depths.[4] As abstractions, rock gardens are one ancestor of what we call "modern" painting, and in scope the abstraction of the garden is not hindered just because it is limited to rocks and gravel set into a particular place, any more than the scope of a painting is hampered by the physical limits of canvas and paint.

If the meanings of these gardens are broad and deep, they are also often abstruse. Like Zen *ko-an,* these gardens hide their message from the unreceptive mind, to which they appear as no more than a haphazard scatter of rocks. With contemplation and patience, however, the viewer realizes that the rocks are heavily charged with ideas. As he becomes more familiar with the garden, he finds himself being drawn deeper and deeper into the tangled web of its meanings, which may eventuate in such simple things as color patterns, strange concepts of motion, or the tension of stillness. Often these concepts are inexpressible, and the viewer finds that from such disciplined and basic beginnings he has arrived at a proposition he cannot put into words. One does not have to be a monk of the Zen sect to have this experience, but, having it, he can well understand why these gardens flourished under the aegis of Zen.

It was for similar reasons that the teahouse and tea ceremony, which did not come into their own until the beginning of the sixteenth century, took hold within the confines of Zen Buddhism. It may not be an oversimplification to say that the tea ceremony was intended to create a situation catalytic to thought yet so unobtrusive that it would release one's mind from all distraction, while assisting it to roam at unusual depths in unaccustomed directions. The exacting job of the teahouse was to cleanse the mind and to place it in a neat unfettered suspension where it would be most receptive to the loosening effect of the ceremony.

The teahouse began its work as one approached it. The path, a rough line of stones or a repetition of diamond-pattern slabs,

3. An example is the garden at Ryoan-ji.
4. An example is the garden at Daisen-in, a sub-temple of Daitoku-ji. (See Part II of this book.)

was different from the paths of one's daily life, so that even in this small detail he would be drawn away from his usual, and by their repetition meaningless, patterns of thought. The house itself appeared rustic and impermanent from the outside, so that one might feel he had happened upon it by chance. It had nothing to do with everyday life; indeed, in its frailty it might last only this day.

Inside the teahouse, natural elements were used to create "natural" surroundings. For this purpose, unrefined nature would not do, for its disorder and irritations would intrude on the mind and hold up the process of release. Contrived disorder was the result, disorderly enough to seem uncontrived yet not so much as to annoy. For this, only the simplest reminders of nature were used: the plain limbs of trees, a window grating of latticed twigs, a mud-colored clay wall. Anything more dramatic would deny the building its passive role, as would any unusual view let in from outside. Views were kept small.

Because the teahouse had to be physically perfect in all respects, size was an important consideration. The $4\frac{1}{2}$-mat room became a standard, being accepted by most as the smallest in which men could take tea without feeling crowded.[5] Size and the psychology of interior space were so important that a man much larger than the one for whom a given house was built would have been uncomfortable and therefore out of place inside it. These teahouses were built for sixteenth-century Japanese men, not twentieth-century foreigners; for the latter, presumably, a proper teahouse would have to be erected on a somewhat larger scale.

So delicate was the proposition of the tea ceremony that it is doubtful it survived long with its true meaning intact. It was undoubtedly dealt a crushing blow late in the sixteenth century when the lowborn dictator, Toyotomi Hideyoshi, characteristically held a single tea ceremony for the entire population of Kyoto, and it continues to stagger today before the "tea ceremonies" purveyed to mass gatherings of foreigners in public halls. But it does not take a public hall to throw a tea ceremony

5. An exception was the famous master Sen-no-Rikyu, who perfected the casual and impromptu aspects of the art of tea. Many of his teahouses were made with rooms of three, or even two, mats.

out of balance. Presumably a camera lying on the floor of the tearoom, or even the presence of foreign dress or a foreign mind, introduces an irritant large enough to disturb the delicate suspension created by the little house and the formal preparation of the tea.

From the above one might conclude that the tea ceremony as it was originally conceived has been contaminated by the very passage of time. Nevertheless it is still practiced, and one cannot say that its purpose, so akin to that of Zen Buddhism in attempting to release the mind through a formal exercise, is not still achieved by those who understand it.

Rock gardens must express themselves with black rocks and white gravel, set into a limited shape; the tea ceremony must speak through the formal preparation of a beverage which takes place in a refined, passive little house. Both arts would seem to be overwhelmed by limitations, yet both produce inexpressible thoughts for the receptive mind. The nature of these arts is so close to that of the Zen sect itself, with their limited means and limitless products, that it seems only natural that they should have flourished in the company of Zen, and that their gardens and houses should be today, as in the past, accepted properties of most Zen sect temples.

AT DAITOKU-JI

Daitoku-ji, the temple which the priest Daito Kokushi founded, is a classic example of a Zen sect monastery. Its gates and halls still follow the Chinese canons of arrangement and design, while its abbot's and priests' quarters, rambling and held together more by the wall about them than by their own design, follow the Japanese tendency towards informality. This is the true monastery, the center of training. Around it cluster more than twenty sub-temples, each in its own enclosure, each with its own history, each independent from all the rest despite the ties which bind all to the monastery. The monastery is characterized by the expected; its sub-temples take one by surprise.

I had been in Daitoku-ji all one morning with a girl from the prefectural university. It was in May or June, and we were about to leave the place and return to the city to get our lunch. We had just finished visiting one of the sub-temples, and a lady at its gate urged us to go to another which she favored, called Koto-in. It was true that we had never been to Koto-in, but because of the hour our hunger was stronger than our curiosity. As we walked through the monastery, we fixed on a compromise: we would pass by Koto-in on our way out and have a look at it from the outside. Both of us knew this meant nothing, for one can never see anything of these places from the outside save their walls.

We arrived there in the middle of a heated discussion of the commercialism which seemed to be invading certain Kyoto temples. I deplored the ubiquitous ticket windows and the indiscriminate pasting of cardboard and paper signs, while Atsuko defended the signs as a service to the visitor and the ticket money as a means of support for the temples.

Our argument continued after we stopped at the entrance to Koto-in. There was a bamboo railing there next to the walk, and we sat on it, first testing it to see if it would hold us, and went on talking in the pleasant warmth of the sun. For the moment a decision about Koto-in was postponed and forgotten.

We had been talking thus for several minutes when a shadow crossed our sunlight and stopped over us. I looked up into the face of a portly, elderly priest whose glistening cassock left me with strong impressions of deep purple and shimmering gold—a giant, benevolent beetle. His face was heavy but kindly. He asked us if we were going inside. Perhaps because it seemed impolite to be sitting on the bamboo fence while he stood there before us, we assented almost before recalling where we were. The priest started up the walk, and Atsuko and I followed.

"Who is he?" I asked her, as we followed the sharp turns in the long, narrow walk.

"He is the abbot of this temple," she said.

He seemed pleased that we had followed him inside. For our part, to look through his temple was a small kindness that would not take very long. When we reached Koto-in, the old abbot left us with a plain, middle-aged lady and disappeared into the building. She was spare, and she wore a plain Western dress. It was as if we had surprised her in her home.

The temple was small. It had two or three buildings and a garden that was undisciplined in a pleasant way. One part of the garden was a clean moss lawn, shaded by trees, with a single stone lantern standing in the middle; around the corner it was an easy tangle of shrubs and paths. It was so relaxed that the nearby wall which held it all together did not exist in the on-looker's mind.

The lady led us back to the main altar room and showed us a dark altar crowded with images and memorial plaques. At the center was a small image of Kannon, a foot or so high, enshrined in a miniature gold-leaf temple which had real roof bracketing and real beasts' heads carved on its tiny beam-ends. The gold temple had two double doors, on each panel of which was painted one of the four "heavenly kings" in full color. The gold leaf and the miniature style of the whole thing gave it a somewhat medi-eval appearance. There was no reason one would expect to find Kannon at the center of a Zen altar—there were probably good reasons why a Kannon should *not* be there, and I had the distinct impression, which I am tempted to believe was correct, that this little image had the center of the altar simply because it was the finest and best painted piece of sculpture possessed by Koto-in.

Next to the Kannon was a memorial tablet to the man who originated Kabuki dancing. More conventional images, of Shaka and other Buddhas, were in the dark recesses of the side altars, as were the tablets of the temple's founder and his family.

We stepped off the verandah into small cloth slippers and fol-lowed the lady into the garden, where she began telling us about a branch of the famous Hosokawa family. Hosokawa Tadaoki had established Koto-in in 1601. There were several tombs on the far side of the garden that belonged to him and his family. Tada-oki was a general who had led expeditions for Toyotomi Hide-yoshi into Korea, and later he distinguished himself in all the famous battles that occurred in the beginning of the seventeenth century, unlike most warriors surviving them all and living to a very old age. His wife was a daughter of the man who assassinated Oda Nobunaga, a relationship which had brought her temporary exile at the time that deed was done. She died a year before her husband established Koto-in, a heroic death which she took to avoid becoming a hostage. The most unusual feature of this woman was that she became and remained a Christian, embrac-ing that faith in secret when her husband was away and later winning his full consent and support. She was one of the most prominent converts to Christianity in her time, and her name was Hosokawa Gracia.

This, then, was the first generation of patrons for Koto-in. The temple has been loyally patronized by their descendants in a line unbroken to this day. Hosokawas have left their marks everywhere on the grounds, particularly in the representations of their three family crests that are inlaid, cut out, and placed in relief on the furnishings, walls, gates, and columns of the temple.

On the matted verandah of the second building the lady showed us some rocks that lay in a corner. Two or three of the rocks had shapes resembling the imperial chrysanthemum crest seemingly embedded in their surfaces. These were natural formations, we were told, and these rocks were a hundred million years old. High numbers being what they are, I supposed I had not heard her correctly. I looked at Atsuko. She reassured me— a hundred million. I gave her my pen. She wrote, "100,000,000." Our guide looked on unblinking.

There was also a brown rock there, a later acquisition which had been brought back by an Antarctic expedition. This rock, now the prize of Koto-in's collection, was five hundred million years old. The lady, who knelt next to the rocks in the woman's position, showed us some magazine clippings and other articles about them. Then she stood up and led us into the building, leaving the rocks behind in their sunny corner to grow older.

We were in a small teahouse that had reddish purple walls when the abbot reappeared. He spoke at some length about the teahouse, explaining its features and comparing it to other teahouses he knew. He had a fine old face, and it was a pleasure just to watch him talk. The lady had gone, but she came back and, kneeling down, spread a handful of papers across the shadowy floor. Some of them were color photographs sent the abbot by grateful visitors; there was one in particular of him in which there was snow on the ground. The picture had come out quite blue, making his face appear pale and old, draining it of its character and leaving behind only a very mortal mask—powdery, needing a shave. In the picture the abbot looked like a tired businessman wearing a priest's costume, whereas here in the teahouse he and his vestments were one, he was all priest, all timeless age, all steady wisdom. He obviously treasured the photograph, but it had failed to capture his character.

Back at the main hall, we sat in wicker chairs on the verandah and looked at more photos over some foaming green tea. These were not of the abbot but of the treasures of Koto-in, paintings and ancient bowls. One Kodacolor triptych was devoted to different aspects of the same bowl, *the* bowl, Koto-in's most precious possession, an 800-year-old bowl that had come from Korea. The abbot decided to show this bowl to us. Although I had little genuine interest in ancient bowls, this was a compliment not to be refused. The abbot went off and soon returned with some boxes and a red felt blanket. He spread the blanket in the room next to us, and we went inside. At this point another priest suddenly appeared from around the corner. The two priests greeted each other, and he joined us. His temple, he said, was Koho-an—not the Koho-an here, he hastily added, but one near Otsu, on Lake Biwa. I hoped that the bowl was being shown for him, for the compliment sat heavy on us.

There were three bowls in all. Each one was in a double box that had felt bags and other padding, including a stuffed insert that matched the exact inside shape of its bowl. When the boxes, bags, and inserts were all in their places, there was no way the bowl inside could move. The whole unit was tied with ribbons that were always knotted in exactly the same way—the wrinkles in the ribbons almost tied the knots by themselves.

The priest from Otsu talked to us while Koto-in's abbot unwrapped and rewrapped his treasures, laying them one at a time upon the red felt blanket. The first two were three to four centuries old, and the last was eight. All three of them were very cold. Although Atsuko and I were hard pressed to make appropriate comments as each bowl appeared, the kindness with which they were treated gave them an importance that required no further explanation. They had survived that era when a man destroyed his treasured bowls before he died, and now they were respected members of history.

We left the little temple soon after we had seen the bowls. They urged us to stay, and undoubtedly we could have stayed on much longer, but we thought we had received kindness enough for one afternoon. They stood in the entrance, the two priests and the lady, and we waved to them at the first turn in the path, and then the temple disappeared behind the wall.

It was all out of sight now. I reflected on the strange group of things we had seen. There was the little Kannon in her gold-leaf box and the plaque to the founder of Kabuki. There was Tada-oki's famous Christian wife Gracia and the prehistoric rocks in their sunny corner; the pale photo of the abbot and the aged Korean bowl. Who would have thought to find any of these at the end of that long and crooked path? What had they in common—what had they to do with Zen? What, for that matter, did Koto-in have to do with Zen? There was no manifestation of the sect here except the abbot himself. It was interesting that the character in his face did not transmit to photographic paper. To me, that was like Zen: the moment you went to capture it, it disappeared.

We walked to the street and looked for a restaurant. It was four-thirty when we finally had our lunch that day.

# 9 The Ashikaga: Ginkaku-ji

"Mr. Nikwaido also mentioned that as late as 1887 people had come to the temple, and offered 5 yen to be allowed to beat the statue of Yoshimitsu!"[1]

ASHIKAGA TAKAUJI (1305–58), general, first Ashikaga shogun.

ASHIKAGA YOSHIMITSU (1358–1408), his grandson, third Ashikaga shogun.

ASHIKAGA YOSHIMASA (1435–90), *his* grandson, eighth Ashikaga shogun.

EVEN from the heart of downtown Kyoto one can easily see the bare patch on the little hill under Mt. Hiei, branded with the giant character *dai* (大). When it is set against Hiei this hill appears small, but as you get closer it gets more prominent, and the yellow, bare grass triangle shaved out of its wooded slopes looks large, and naked, and strange. When one walks from the streetcar stop to Ginkaku-ji this naked patch of *dai* seems to hang right over the course of the road, to mark its sure end. As one draws nearer to Ginkaku-ji, the big yellow patch on Dai-monji-san rises and looms, straight ahead, straight over the road, right over the temple.

There is a paved court at the end of this narrow road, beyond which a walk leads into the temple. The court is enclosed on three sides by a plain wall which funnels one's eyes toward the single opening opposite, an opening which promises to reveal the famous Silver Pavilion. Anticipating this sight, one is not likely to notice the plain buildings to either side of the court, and few pause to look at the little temple on the left, almost hidden behind the wall. This may be to that temple's advantage, for what is hidden is not encouraging: a narrow dirt yard squeezed between the temple's single hall and Ginkaku-ji's wall, filled, usually, with the priest's drying laundry.

1. R. A. B. Ponsonby-Fane, *Kyoto, The Old Capital of Japan,* Kyoto, 1956, page 195.

It is unlikely that many would go to visit Jodo-in (for that is the small temple's name) even if the Silver Pavilion were not so close by; as it is, no one goes there. Its single priest, young, interrupted from some other activity, minus his cassock, is startled to find he has visitors. He leads them to a black, charred image of Amida. We cannot tell its exact age, he explains, but it must be about two thousand years old—"a semi-national treasure." Hmmm!

In the early days of that image, about a thousand years ago, Jodo-in was a lot bigger than it is now. It was quite alone, for of course neither the Silver Pavilion nor the crowded houses and shops existed here then. This was countryside, and the large temple known as Jodo-ji covered most of it.[2]

One day in the eighth century there was a great fire, and Jodo-ji burned down. The hall which housed the temple's image of Amida was a total loss, yet the next morning there was a great light on top of the nearby hill, and searchers found the image there, shedding brightness, unharmed by the fire. It had apparently escaped the blaze by itself! They brought it back down the hill and built a new hall for it.

In the year 808 there was plague and famine throughout Kyoto. The emperor was at a loss how to end the sufferings of his people and summoned the famous priest Kukai (Kobo Daishi), who ascended this hill and lit a huge bonfire in the shape of the character *dai* ("great") on the spot where Jodo-ji's Amida had been found. The emperor saw the fire reflected in the ponds of the palace, and all the people of Kyoto saw it too. And this strange supplication worked, for the plague and famine soon subsided. After that a bonfire in the shape of a *dai* was lit on this hill whenever the people suffered from such things as plague, disease, or starvation.

At Jodo-in they have some folders of old postcards left over from more ambitious days. Nowadays the priest gives away as many of these as he can. Inside the folder it tells the story of the charred Buddha, of Kobo Daishi, and of Dai-monji-san. At the end of the story it says, "Later, in the times of the Ashikaga shoguns, [this custom] took on meaning, and the ceremony [of the

2. While *ji* and *in* are both suffixes meaning "temple," the latter often refers to a smaller edifice than the former.

27. "... even today, every year on an evening in August, the people of Kyoto look to the northeast and await the appearance of the huge bonfire *dai*." Ginkaku-ji lies in the darkness at the foot of the mountain. Courtesy of Foto Kyoto (Oka Keitaro).

28, 29. "... the Silver Pavilion stands as the only Ashikaga 'palace' to survive into the present day.... The garden is perhaps the best preserved natural garden of its period." Ginkaku-ji. Courtesy of Asano Kiichi (above) and the Asahi Shimbunsha (below).

bonfire ] flourished more and more." That this is a gentle understatement becomes abundantly clear when one looks at the history of the Ashikaga shoguns.

## THE ASHIKAGA

In the fourteenth century political power lay with the regents of the Hojo family, a kind of leftover from the Kamakura shogunate begun by Minamoto Yoritomo. The Emperor Go-Daigo was determined to restore full authority to himself, and he set about overthrowing the Hojo regents.

War ensued. One of those on the Hojo side was Ashikaga Takauji, whose mother was a Hojo. He fought with the forces opposing Go-Daigo, but later he changed his mind and went over to the side of the emperor. This was a timely move, for Go-Daigo was successful, and upon the defeat of the Hojo he doled out rewards, giving Takauji three provinces in return for his support. The emperor, however, underestimated this man's ambition, for Takauji wanted to be shogun.

Somewhat later there was an uprising of Hojo forces in Kamakura, and Takauji was sent against them. When he had suppressed this uprising, Takauji took over Kamakura and once again deserted his side, declaring himself the shogun and setting up headquarters in the city he had captured. Imperial forces were sent against him, but he managed to defeat them. Now Takauji marched on Kyoto. The emperor fled the city. Takauji met with a series of defeats and successes, but eventually the city was his. He offered his own candidate for emperor, declaring that the absent Go-Daigo had forfeited his right to the throne, and thus threw Japan into a period of more than fifty years during which she had two emperors, a schism that time and again turned peace into war.

Takauji never saw the country settled under his sway. In later years he found his brother and his illegitimate son against him and fought on against them. The struggle was not over when he died, but nevertheless he had managed to launch the Ashikaga line of shoguns.

Ashikaga Yoshimitsu, who became the third in the line at the age of ten, was the first to reveal the aesthete strain in the family that sometimes distracted its members from performing their duties as shoguns. The more interest the Ashikaga shoguns took in the arts, the harder it was on the people. Here is one chronicle of conditions in the time of Yoshimitsu:[3]

(1361–62)... there were nine great shocks of earthquake. Plague was so bad people fell dead in the streets. In the sixth month snow fell, and people were frozen to death.

(1362) There was a great drought and famine all over the country.

(1365) There were many fires, and smallpox was rampant.

(1366) Plague was so bad that people died in the streets.

(1369) There was a bad earthquake.

(1371) There was a bad earthquake.

(1373) Plague was very prevalent during the summer.

(1374) There was an epidemic of smallpox.

(1378) Plague was prevalent.

(1379) Yoshimitsu built the Muromachi-dai.[4] It was called Hana-no-Gosho ("Flower Palace"). There was a famine all over the country.

These were hard times for Kyoto but not for Yoshimitsu. In later years he built a large villa outside the city that included a building covered with gold leaf, he became a priest, and he retired, governing the country through his ten-year-old son from the pleasant surroundings of his Gold Pavilion. He sent missions to China and received in return the acknowledgment that he was "King of Japan." Before he died he was even visited at the Gold Pavilion by the emperor.

The history of the Ashikaga line reads somewhat like that of the Caesars of Suetonius. They followed violent, self-centered careers that ignored a country torn by internal wars and near anarchy. The fourth in the line took the title at the age of ten, and later came out of retirement to succeed his son, who died after only two years in office at the age of nineteen. The sixth was assassinated by a man who learned that the shogun was plotting against him and invited him to a large banquet in the middle of which he had him killed. The seventh became shogun at eight and was killed when he fell from a horse two years later. Then

3. Ponsonby-Fane, *op. cit.,* page 168.
4. It was this place, or rather its location, that gave a name to the whole Ashikaga period, the Muromachi.

his younger brother, at that time himself eight years old, became the shogun: this was Ashikaga Yoshimasa.

Yoshimasa seems to have wanted to fill the role of his grandfather Yoshimitsu. He followed him in his interest in the finer arts, and under Yoshimasa conditions in Kyoto were the same or worse than they had been under his grandfather, as the following chronicle shows:[5]

(1447–48) This autumn mobs of citizens, raising troops, demanded just government.

(1447) There were many earthquakes, and in the 7th month great floods, which washed away the Gojo and Seto Bridges. Many people were drowned.

(1449) Plague was very bad this year till the 7th month (August). At its height more than a thousand people died every day.

(1452) Smallpox was very bad, causing the death of many children.

(1454) Sept. 29: Mobs ringing bells demanded just government. Nov. 21: The capital was in an uproar.

(1457) Bands of citizens rioted.

(1460) There was a great famine, people dying of starvation in the streets. Great mounds were raised in several places where corpses were buried.

(1461) Food was distributed to the poor at the Kennin-ji, the Rokkaku-do, and other places. From the previous winter plague had been rife, and for several years, with famine conditions prevailing all over the country, the people had poured into the capital. Rice and millet were insufficient, and the lanes were piled with corpses; consequently effigies of hunger-appeasing spirits were erected on Shijo and Gojo Bridges.

(1462) A band of citizens revolted. . . . Hasude Hyoye, the leader of the revolt, was arrested, and his head exposed at Yotsuka.

The ceremony of burning the character *dai* must have been performed regularly in those pestilential days. Nevertheless, Yoshimasa did not lag behind the example set by his grandfather, and set about building his own "Flower Palace."

"In 1461 there was a famine and pestilence, and two-thirds of the people were starving; the streets were piled with skeletons, so

5. Ponsonby-Fane, *op. cit.,* page 172.

that passers-by were filled with pity. But in 1459, when conditions were but little better, the then Shogun, Yoshimasa, built the Hana-no-Gosho. He loved this place, and constructed a lovely garden, day by day causing people to bring him rocks, trees, &c., to beautify it, and he cared nothing for the sufferings of the people. The Emperor Hanazono, hearing of this, composed a poem, and sent it to him as a reproof. . . . The Shogun was struck with shame, and gave orders to stop the building. The people were filled with admiration and said: 'If the Sovereign be Sovereign, then are his subjects subjects.' "[6]

Despite the poor condition of the city in the 1460's, Yoshimasa did not hesitate to promote the Onin War;[7] to retire, making his nine-year-old son the shogun; and to begin seeking a place for a retirement villa, even though the war was not over. While he looked for a villa site, Kyoto was destroyed, and the war moved out into the provinces. It reminds one of Nero helping personally to burn the city Rome. Unmindful of his ruined capital, Yoshimasa, about 1480, selected his site outside northeastern Kyoto and made plans to begin the villa. The site was already occupied by part of Jodo-ji, but Yoshimasa had those parts of the temple that were in his way removed. Then, under the direction of the great and versatile architect So-ami, work began on the buildings, gardens, and ponds of Yoshimasa's retreat, which was intended to have one pavilion coated with silver, the final accomplishment to equal those of Yoshimitsu.

In 1483 the villa was ready. Outside its walls Kyoto was a desert where the emperor lived in "a ruined palace"; inside them stood a dozen new buildings designed for tea ceremonies, incense parties, audiences and banquets, tree- and moon-viewing, ball games, and the like. They centered on a garden that contained as fine a wealth of stones as had been gathered in one place up to that time. The pavilion to be coated with silver hovered on the edge of the pond. Most of the buildings faced east, and with his back to the city Yoshimasa gazed at his garden and at the forested flank of Higashiyama, and lived out his retired life indulging in the various arts, surrounded by refined companions.

When he died, he again followed the example of his grand-

6. Ponsonby-Fane, *op. cit.,* page 192, quoting from *Choroku Kanshoki.*
7. See chapter 10.

father and had his country villa converted into a Zen sect temple. Only in his failure ever to coat his pavilion with silver did Yoshimasa not reproduce the pattern set by grandfather Yoshimitsu. Nevertheless the temple, named Jisho-ji, soon came to be called Ginkaku-ji, or "the temple of the silver pavilion," by which name it is known to this day.

### GINKAKU-JI

Ginkaku-ji entered history in little better shape than had the Byodo-in. Both were family temples that had no one else to protect them. While the line of Ashikaga shoguns did continue, it was meaningless, since they were unable to control the country—by now immersed in continuous and total war—and they exerted virtually no power of their own.[8]

The temple suffered badly in the sixteenth century. Armies camped and fought there, and the area was razed by fire several times. One by one the original buildings were destroyed until only two were left, one of them the "silver" pavilion. In the seventeenth century, with peace restored, the garden was saved from oblivion by extensive reconstruction, and the place was put in order, but again it deteriorated, and doubly cursed as it was by connections with both shoguns and Buddhism, Ginkaku-ji was lucky to escape destruction in the imperial restoration of 1868. Perhaps only its secluded location spared it from the vengeance of the imperial side.[9] Nevertheless, its condition was very bad, so much so that a guidebook of the 1890's warned travelers: "The pavilion is so dilapidated as to be no longer worth looking at."

8. The imperial house was also in desperate straits. The Emperor Go-Tsuchimikado, too poor to abdicate, had died in 1500, and his body was not buried for six weeks until money could be found for funeral expenses. His successor, Go-Kashiwabara, ruled for more than twenty years before—near the end of his reign—his enthronement ceremony could be held. On one occasion the shogun ordered funds to be provided by the various barons, but the order was ignored and the ceremony further postponed.

The next emperor, Go-Nara, waited ten years for enthronement and was reduced to supporting himself by selling his autograph.

9. That feeling still ran high against the Ashikaga is indicated by the quotation at the head of this chapter. Not only did people wish to beat the Ashikaga statues at Toji-in, but in 1863 a band of marauders raided the place and decapitated three of them, dumping the heads into the Kamo River.

Now Ginkaku-ji is worth looking at. Since Yoshimitsu's Gold Pavilion burned in 1950, the Silver Pavilion stands as the only Ashikaga "palace" to survive into the present day. The two remaining original buildings are in excellent condition, and others have been reconstructed following the original plans. Although the city of Kyoto has surged out to the very walls of this villa, we are still able to feel the reclusive nature of the original place, thanks to the peculiar plan of the grounds that has the buildings facing east, right into the viewless, rising wall of Higashiyama, instead of west, out over the city as one might have expected. The garden is perhaps the best preserved natural garden of its period, thanks to restorations performed on it in the seventeenth century, without which the wooden pilings of the ponds would have rotted and the pond's shape been lost forever.

To the uninitiated, Ginkaku-ji hardly seems to be the magnificent palace of an unscrupulous war lord. The buildings are so small and frail that it is difficult to convince oneself that they have really stood since before the time of Christopher Columbus. To judge from their size and number, this might be the modest retreat of a religious man. But it must be remembered that there were once many more of them, and that they were built at a time when the rest of the city was a charred ruin. By these standards the place is a palace, and if the buildings do not reveal it, the quality of the garden, with its overpowering wealth of stones, is evidence enough of Yoshimasa's position.

Nevertheless, this is a strange monument to Ashikaga Yoshimasa. His excellent taste is reflected in the architecture of the pavilion, the natural and sand gardens, and in the $4\frac{1}{2}$-mat tearoom which was to set the standard for the teahouses of Japan. Yoshimasa possessed a refinement perhaps unmatched by any lord who ever ruled Japan, and it is all apparent in the remains of his villa. But what does not show here is his great ability to ignore the unmatched sufferings he had helped to wreak on his people, and his distaste for the duties that accompanied his position. In this respect Yoshimasa was overrefined, and placed in the perspective of his times, his finer qualities seem as questionable as in other times they would have been admirable. This was a Japanese Nero who, although more talented than his Roman counterpart, was like him in pursuing his own artistic ambitions to the extent that he ignored, and even assisted in, the destruction of his city and state.

It is ironic that the great shaved Dai-monji-san should hang over Ginkaku-ji, and that the unnoticed Jodo-in should stand by its gate. They are reminders of the plague and starvation with which the country paid for this place, and of the penance which the Ashikaga never performed. Nor are they dead reminders, for even today, every year on an evening in August, the people of Kyoto look to the northeast and await the sudden appearance of the huge bonfire *dai*. When at long last it flares up, a long, soft "oooooh" runs through the city, and a few minutes later the *dai* sputters and is gone. Is it not significant that the one place in the city from which the *dai* cannot be seen is the very precinct of Yoshimasa's villa, which despite its proximity to this great sign of pestilence is cut off from seeing it by an intervening network of hills and trees? This blind spot is the true memorial left behind by Ashikaga Yoshimasa, the aesthete shogun.

# 10  The Onin War and the All-Time Garden: Ryoan-ji

HOSOKAWA KATSUMOTO (1430–73), general, head of his family, high government official.[1]

YAMANA MOCHITOYO (1404–73), father-in-law of the above, baron who became a priest named Sozen, also called "the Red Monk."

SO-AMI (1472–1523), famous architect, painter, and designer of gardens.

HOSOKAWA Katsumoto was born into the fifteenth-century Japan of the Ashikaga shoguns. His family was one of three, the Hosokawa, Hatakeyama, and Shiba, from which the shogun chose his prime minister, the most important position in the land after the emperor and the shogun himself. All of Katsumoto's immediate forebears held this office at one time or another, and Katsumoto himself was first appointed to it when he was only fifteen. Replaced four years later, he began a second term at the age of twenty-two, and eventually he would serve a third.

Katsumoto's father died when his son was twelve years old, leaving him at the head of their powerful family. The Hosokawa had their own army, some sixty thousand men, and a domain including most of the huge island Shikoku. Their young leader, a wry-looking boy with heavy eyelids and large ears, took hold of his responsibilities fast and quickly gained a reputation as a clever politician and strong disciplinarian. Katsumoto is reputed to have maintained the strength of his family by weeding out all factionalism, that poison which throughout Japan's history— especially in this period—decimated the power of clan after clan. Lest one think that a young boy was not capable of such things, it can be added that when Katsumoto was twelve, the shogun was only nine, and the following year his death brought in the Shogun Yoshimasa at the age of eight. The emperor was an old

1. An ancestor of Koto-in's Hosokawa Tadaoki, but in a different branch of their family.

30. "In the meantime, Hosokawa Katsumoto's estate had become a Zen sect temple...." Ryoan-ji about 1500, reproduced from a painting. Courtesy of Nozaki Shigyo.

31. "Ryoan-ji is all paths and trees . . . a pleasant, roaming park. . . ."
Ryoan-ji in winter. Courtesy of Nozaki Shigyo.

32. "... there is a fine life-sized statue of Hosokawa Katsumoto, sitting there looking skeptical and comfortable...." Ryoan-ji. Courtesy of Nozaki Shigyo.

man in his early twenties. It was a time of short lives and early accession to power.

Katsumoto's home in Kyoto was a large estate in the north-western outskirts of the city that had been built in Heian times by the Tokudaiji family. The mark of its age was the beautiful lake on the grounds, of a size and style that had been extinct for four centuries. The buildings stood in a fine location on the south side of a wooded hill that afforded a wide view out over the lake to most of the city and its western environs. It was from here that the Hosokawa family received its direction and it was to here that the shogun turned for support when national affairs escaped his control.

From the time he was thirteen, Katsumoto lived his whole life under a single shogun, the aesthete Yoshimasa. Yoshimasa had succeeded to his post young and apparently disliked the need to govern, so that before he was thirty he was eager to retire, a prospect which made him anxious to find someone to succeed him. As his wife had borne him no son, he had to look elsewhere for an heir, and he set about persuading his brother Yoshimi to abandon the priesthood and "return to the world." The latter finally agreed to do this in 1464, and Yoshimasa quickly adopted him and named him his successor. At the same time he appointed Hosokawa Katsumoto to be Yoshimi's counselor.

Within a year of this arrangement Yoshimasa's wife presented him with a son and with the choice of going back on his word or not having his own son succeed him. The shogun did not hesitate to renege his promise to his brother, but the latter appealed to Hosokawa Katsumoto to support his claim. Yoshimasa brought in Katsumoto's father-in-law, Yamana Sozen ("the Red Monk"), to stand up for his newborn son, and battle lines were drawn. At this time both the Shiba and the Hatakeyama families were internally split, so factions of each quickly fell in on opposite sides of the quarrel. Each side was further reinforced by the support of lesser barons, all of whom found it necessary to take a side in the issue, enlarging it and impelling both sides toward war.

1467, the first year of Onin, found the Red Monk encamped across the southwest corner of Kyoto at the head of 90,000 men, while Katsumoto held the northeast part of the city with a force of 100,000. With the heart of Kyoto thus selected as its battle-ground, the war of succession began.

Gradually Kyoto was laid to waste. Rare is the pre-Onin temple in the city whose records do not mention destruction at the hands of the Onin War. The center of the city was leveled, and whole areas of its outskirts were razed by the war's outreaching fingers.

Both armies entrenched themselves in the center of Kyoto, and neither could dislodge the other. It was a war in which no one got the upper hand. There was no victory, only defeat. There was death, but it led to nothing except the gradual attrition of both sides without advantage to either.

Meanwhile, the issues which had started the war became so muddled that they were shifted back and forth between the two stalled armies. Those who had originally supported Yoshimasa's brother were soon supporting his son, and vice versa. For their own part the parties supported tried to find a difference between the two sides—some indication of strength or weakness that might help them choose the victor—but they found none. Indeed, it made no difference who supported whom, for no one could resolve the war.

The Onin War was in its seventh year when the commanders of the opposing sides, Yamana Sozen and Hosokawa Katsumoto, both died. Their deaths occurred within months of each other. Katsumoto was buried at his estate in western Kyoto, and his monument erected there. As he had directed, his estate became a Zen sect temple. It too, however, was eventually destroyed in the war.

The war, which had long ago outgrown its generals, continued like a headless monster that had Kyoto locked in its grip. When it was in its eighth year, Yoshimasa, as eager as ever to retire and vexed by the war's delayed outcome, passed the shogunate on to his son without disturbing the entrenched armies in the slightest. No one deposed Yoshimasa's son; no one stopped the fighting either. Yoshimasa's brother, who had retired to Enryaku-ji on Mt. Hiei to await the war's end at a safe distance, remained there, now that his claim to the shogunate was ended. As to Yoshimasa himself, he now set about planning his retirement villa in dead earnest, devoting his time to examining sites and studying outstanding gardens.

Nevertheless, the war raged in Kyoto for three more years. The armies fought on, but they were fast approaching a state of total exhaustion. Gains for either side over a ten-year period had been negligible, but attrition in both camps had been great. Supplies were low, and the ravaged countryside could produce no more. What had once been the central issue was now forgotten; other family rivalries now fueled the combat.

At last, in December 1477, the "Yamana" side could take it no longer. One night they simply abandoned their positions and set out for home. The next day the "Hosokawa" side found its opponents gone, but it was too weak and disinterested to set out in pursuit. Instead, its members too abandoned their positions and left Kyoto. Overnight the Onin War vanished, after ten years without a decisive battle. Left behind were a desert where Kyoto had stood and the bodies of thousands of dead. Technically, one of the most pointless wars in history was ended.

Actually it continued, nourishing on other causes as it fanned out into the countryside south of Kyoto. Fought by new armies, it dragged on there almost to the end of the century, and then it began spreading over Japan. The contestants and issues had no relation to those which had touched off the Onin War, but war flickered continuously across the land. Throughout the sixteenth century there was war in Japan, until Oda Nobunaga finally forced peace and unity on the country in the 1570's.

Perhaps the greatest irony in the whole chain of events was that Yoshimasa outlived his son and found it necessary to make a reconciliation with his brother, in order that the latter's son, by becoming shogun, could continue the Ashikaga line.

In the meantime, Hosokawa Katsumoto's former estate had become a Zen sect temple under the guidance of the neighboring monastery Myoshin-ji, whose superior oversaw the beginnings of the new temple and was himself its first abbot. Since both Myoshin-ji and the new temple, Ryoan-ji, had burned in the Onin War, they found themselves with bare grounds and charred foundations, and a major reconstruction job to be done. No one gave either of them great notice while this work was going on, with the result that their history in the latter part of the fifteenth century is largely a blank today.

### A GARDEN APPEARS

Around the year 1500 a garden appeared at Ryoan-ji. Where it came from no one will ever surely know, but a contemporary drawing shows that by the turn of the century the buildings were up again and a rock garden had been added, surrounded by a low wall near the largest building. Because nothing of its history, including the year of its creation, is known with any certainty, no one knows who made this garden. Usually it is attributed to So-ami, a famous painter and designer of gardens and buildings of that time, because it is so fine that many believe only So-ami could have made it. Historians have done their best to read its history through some unexplained markings on one of its rocks, but they have failed.

But the detailed past of this garden is unimportant; what matters is that it existed and that, being made of rock and gravel, it required little attention, for it was to remain relatively unknown for centuries. At one time, near the end of the eighteenth century, the buildings around it burned, but they were replaced, and the garden survived them unharmed.

The rock garden at Ryoan-ji entered the twentieth century still ignored by most of the world, omitted from guide and history books, bypassed in favor of more prominent and traditional relics of Kyoto's past. Ryoan-ji existed as a modest Zen temple until suddenly, around the year 1930, the garden was "discovered" and the world was confronted with the enigma and essence of all Zen wisdom compounded at once in the small rock garden at Ryoan-ji. Photographers converged on the garden, a natural subject for black-and-white photography, and spread photographs of it around the world. It was not long before the rock garden was better known than the temple.

"Ryoan-ji? No. . ."

"The rock garden. . ."

"Oh, the *rock* garden, of course!" And this stranger to Kyoto now knew exactly what was being discussed, despite the city's large population of rock gardens. None has been so exhaustively photographed, so often recorded on film, as the one at Ryoan-ji.

Unfortunately, the publicity that sought out Ryoan-ji's garden also served to distort and confuse the outside world. Like the face of the abbot of Koto-in, the face of this garden transmitted only a hollow outline to photographic paper, and photographers who felt it necessary to "shoot" the place from new angles produced distortions that had little to do with the original intent of the garden's fifteenth-century designer. Nor were photographers alone in their assault on the place. They were joined by the literalists, who were anxious to pin down the garden's meaning.

These people called the rocks of the garden islands, mountains, tigers, dragons, temples, and symbols of all other kinds. Similarly they called its raked gravel bed such things as clouds, rivers, and the sea.

All this has overinflated the little garden and ably confused those who have never seen it. The photographers seemingly prove that this is but a random collection of rocks that one can as well see in a book at home as by taking the trouble to go there. Their wild angles, and the varied "solutions" offered to the garden's "enigma," are enough to convince one that perhaps there are two, three, or even four of these gardens, all similar, all different. Above all, the barrage of publicity is enough to persuade any sane man to avoid seeing this place at all costs.

It was in such a mood of suspicion and reluctance that I first visited Ryoan-ji, more in hope of getting it over with than in the expectation of pleasure. But it was not anything like what I expected. The photographs I had seen were dreary and stark next to this gentle, delicate arrangement of rocks that had such subtle character and texture. As to the various explanations of the garden's "meaning," I considered each one in turn and quickly forgot them. They meant nothing next to the pleasure of sitting there on the sun-filled verandah, watching the rocks in their court of white gravel.

There were little patches of moss growing about the bottom of the rocks, and some of them had microscopic lavender flowers that one could easily mistake for sunlight or miss altogether. Here and there lay a fallen pine needle, or a stone of the garden border that had drifted out of place. Beyond the wall, tall trees rose up and beckoned from the world outside, and birds flew about in them and sounded their calls. The sun poured down on the raked white gravel and then up into one's face—softly, making it warm. The boards of the dark corridor which led to this sunny place squeaked when an occasional visitor came, and once in a while there were the rustling noises of someone getting up, or sitting down, or silently walking about, the way it is in an empty cathedral.

One's concentration was great but effortless. It consisted simply of random thoughts, but they seemed to flow more easily here, and occasionally they were weighted down by some vaguely noticed facet of the pattern of rocks that momentarily halted the mind and then eased it gently back onto its own deep paths. Nothing moved in the garden, but there was a great feeling of life and motion there. It was rewarding to be here watching it. It was important to be here. The important thing about this place was just to be able to come to it. This was something that all the photographs and interpretations were unable to replace: the thrill of watching the garden.

After that first visit I no longer avoided Ryoan-ji but went back often. The garden changed with different weathers and different times of day; perhaps it was best under the fresh dew of breaking morning, when the corridor boards seemed to creak more sharply and the whole temple slowly to arise and shake off its sleep. But even in the pouring rain this garden is beautiful.

The attraction of Ryoan-ji's garden is so great, and the focus upon it so sharp, that few people who come to it see the temple which surrounds it, although Ryoan-ji has considerable interest and charm. In the dark shadows of the altar room there is a fine life-sized statue of Hosokawa Katsumoto, sitting there looking skeptical and comfortable not thirty feet from the thousands of people who pour through his former home. His tomb and those of his relatives are arrayed across the hill behind the temple, and the same hill shelters the tombs of several emperors, spread about a beautiful glen that is close to the temple but hidden from it. A path winds out of this glen to other imperial tombs, and elsewhere paths roam over a precinct that is surprisingly large and pleasantly remote from the crowded city. Ryoan-ji is all paths and trees, opening up below on the spacious Heian pond with its tiny islands and shrine. Here is none of the barren yard so often found at Buddhist temples, but a pleasant, roaming park that preserves the mood of the long-lost Heian era.

Every year thousands of people come here. They swarm up the narrow lane from the electric car platform and arrive at the gate in buses and taxis. They pour by the pond and head straight for the garden. Except for the uncaring herds of school children who are brought here every spring, virtually all those who come are fulfilling a wish to see this garden, no matter how many times they may have seen it before. They see nothing else here: the garden is enough; it alone is worth the trip.

Once they arrive, Ryoan-ji's visitors sit on the wide wooden steps in the sun and look out at the garden, and then the question begins: here is a group of stones set into a bed of raked white gravel, surrounded by a slanting mud wall beyond which are trees of various sizes, all of which somehow materialized after the Onin War. What does it all mean? What questions can it answer?

The answers can only be found by going there.

# 11 The Rise and Fall of the Toyotomi: Daigo-ji and Sambo-in

"I mean to do glorious deeds and I am ready for a long siege, with provisions and gold and silver in plenty, so as to return in triumph and leave a great name behind me. I desire you to understand this and to tell it to everybody."                                   TOYOTOMI HIDEYOSHI[1]

TOYOTOMI HIDEYOSHI (1536–98), Oda Nobunaga's successor.

THERE is a famous old pagoda at Daigo. Looking across the fields of that quiet little village, one can see its upper stories and eloquent spire poking out of the trees at the foot of a thickly wooded ridge. It seems to be standing alone on the far side of the ancient highroad. The near side is lined with farmhouses, their fields strung out behind them, but across the road one sees only green trees and the pagoda. This pagoda did stand alone for the entire sixteenth century, and even then it was old: it has stood at Daigo now for more than a thousand years.

For most of its life it has been surrounded by the halls of Daigo-ji, a large temple of the Shingon sect. Daigo-ji was nearly seven hundred years old at the time of the Onin War, but in that war the temple was largely destroyed: in its lower precinct, nothing survived except the pagoda. For a century thereafter, while Japan was bathed from head to toe in civil war, the Daigo pagoda stood by itself between the hills and the highroad.

Meanwhile the powerless Ashikaga hung on as shoguns, potentially at the mercy of the first man who could gain control of the state. Finally, it was Oda Nobunaga who answered an imperial plea and took the necessary steps to bring a century of anarchic civil war to its end.

Nobunaga's approach was one of brute force: it was he who razed Mt. Hiei in 1571. By 1582 he had nearly completed his task of crushing rebellious factions when he was attacked and killed,

---

1. From a letter to his wife written during his siege of Odawara, May 17, 1590, and translated in G. B. Sansom, *Japan, A Short Cultural History*, New York, 1943, page 410.

33. "The Momoyama garden ... shows a flamboyancy, color, and vigor that distinguishes it from all others." Sambo-in's garden and its famous weeping cherry tree. Courtesy of Asano Kiichi.

34. "Daigo-ji, supplied with halls from other temples and new ones of its own, became an important temple again." Daigo-ji's cherry-tree avenue at festival time. Hideyoshi's paulownia crest decorates the curtains. Courtesy of Asano Kiichi.

35. "Its center was a garden, a garden whose richness was—and perhaps still is—unequaled." Sambo-in's garden as seen from the teahouse Chinryu-tei. Courtesy of Asano Kiichi.

36. "... the most famous stone in the garden is named Fujito-no-ishi...." Section of Sambo-in's garden showing Fujito. Courtesy of Asano Kiichi.

37. "A small *karesansui* garden ... containing three stones which were selected to express different moods of river water." Section of Sambo-in's garden showing the Three Stones of the Kamo River. Courtesy of Asano Kiichi.

at the Honno-ji in Kyoto, by one of his own generals. He had ordered this man to make a troop movement in relief of a second general, one Hashiba Hideyoshi, who was caught in an unsuccessful siege. Instead, the man turned on Kyoto and murdered his lord.

Now Nobunaga was dead, killed by his own man, and for a moment the nation wavered, unpropped and ready to keel back into the chaos it had come so close to escaping.

## HIDEYOSHI

It was Hashiba Hideyoshi who rescued the state. He squeezed a peace from his enemies, marched back to Kyoto, and within two weeks defeated the mutinous army and killed the assassin. Hideyoshi did not stop there: finding Nobunaga's sons in his way, he pitted them against each other, made peace with the weakened survivors, and continued his conquest of the country until by 1585 it lay at his feet, and a relieved people accepted his rule and the peace which it brought.

Briefly, this was the rise of a family which had yet to be named, the Toyotomi. And what of their leader?

"He was the son of a certain Nakamura Yanosuke, and was born in the village of Nakamura in Owari. His father dying soon after, his mother married into the Chikuami family, by whom he was educated. In his childhood, he was called Hiyoshi. His parents destined him to become a bonze, so they placed him on [sic] the Komyo-ji, a neighboring temple, but at the age of 15, he made his escape and went to Totomi, where he entered the service of Matsushita Yukitsuna, castellan of Kuno. The latter, having learned one day that [he] was from Owari, gave him 6 *ryo* to purchase a coat of mail for his master, like the one Nobunaga wore. The young man took the money, used it to procure clothes and weapons, but instead of returning to his master, he changed his name to that of Kinoshita Tokichi, and went to Nobunaga. The latter admitted him into his service, and soon noticed his brilliant intellect. . . . "[2]

The castellan of Kuno was not the last man to feel the sting of

2. E. Papinot, *Historical and Geographical Dictionary of Japan,* Tokyo, 1909, page 693. Oda Nobunaga came from Owari too—hence the mission to purchase armor.

this fellow "Hiyoshi," for the latter was a man who changed his name as he rose through the ranks, and rose through the ranks as he changed his name. By 1562 the first name Hideyoshi had attached itself to him, and in 1582, when he began his campaign to succeed Nobunaga, it was Hashiba Hideyoshi who swept the country.

In a country where the names of towns, areas, provinces—and even men—are changed often, that Hideyoshi was rarely seen twice under the same name might not seem unusual; but it was unusual, for Hideyoshi changed names because he had none of his own which commanded respect. This set him apart from the group of men he joined and eventually mastered—the barons and warlords of Japan, whose surnames receded into the past beyond memory or record. "Nakamura Hiyoshi" (中村日吉) inspired no awe, but "Hashiba Hideyoshi" (羽柴秀吉) most certainly might.[3]

In Hashiba Hideyoshi we have the only man in Japanese history who governed the country after being born a farmer's son. He was small and ugly, and was called Saru-san (Mr. Monkey) behind his back, but this did not prevent him from engineering a straight-line rise by his own extraordinary abilities. When he reached the top, there were only two positions which his birth prevented him from holding: those of emperor and shogun. Hideyoshi had himself appointed *kampaku*,[4] the highest position outside those two, and saw to it that there was no shogun. At the same time he took the surname Toyotomi, a name which, having scaled the wall to his objective, he kept, and by which he is known to history.

Under Toyotomi Hideyoshi Japan entered the most colorful and short-lived great period in her history.

The two driving spirits of this period were the wealth concentrated in a few hands and the hefty materialism that was Hideyoshi's answer to everything. His poor background made him insensitive to the tastes of a previous age that had focused on the mysteries of Zen and the philosophy of restraint. He and his comrades, as one writer says, "wanted and got an art which was grand

3. "Hashiba" he made up from parts of the names of two friends.

4. *Kampaku*: the minister who acted as intermediary between the emperor and other officials. By reducing the "other officials" to empty title-holders, Hideyoshi took all their power for himself. In this appointment too he broke a traditional restriction to certain families.

in scale, manly in design, and ostentatious in technique to give substance to their own desires."[5] They wanted, and they got. They got it because they had tremendous wealth at their disposal and because sudden power belonged to one man as it had belonged to none for centuries.

Politically, Hideyoshi's materialism stretched his ambition beyond the shores of Japan: he threw the country into an extraordinary invasion of Korea in the hope of adding that country and China to his own. At home, he had a national land survey made, and he built a great walled moat around Kyoto, parts of which exist today. He rebuilt the ravaged capital with narrow, "riot-proof" streets, so that within his new rampart he had absolute control. By his quick, decisive, and unprecedented political actions Hideyoshi made Japan his private fief; then he turned to the arts, which bowed on every level before his exuberant gale.

In military architecture, the old ways of half-serious wooden fortifications, hidden mountain camps, and fast, tricky warfare were extinguished by great strongholds that mushroomed up out of the plains, the greatest of them all Hideyoshi's castle at Osaka. Warfare now meant open siege, and the slotted keeps and massive stone walls of these castles were built to withstand it.

Ordinary architecture, too, moved towards grandeur. Hideyoshi led the way with his fabulous Kyoto palace, Juraku-dai, where he received the emperor and held parties for giving away mountains of gold coins. Although Juraku-dai's splendor was unequaled, Hideyoshi only used it for eight years; then he tore it down and built another palace, this time at Fushimi outside the city. This one was so grand that its individual gates and buildings, which still stand here and there about Kyoto, are to this day the most prized possessions of the temples and other places that own them.

In the field of painting, wall murals became fashionable, depicting such manly subjects as jungle beasts, birds of prey, and giant, twisted trees—invariably against backgrounds of gold leaf.[6] Artists had to paint on a huge scale to match the vast di-

5. R. T. Paine and A. Soper, *The Art and Architecture of Japan*, Penguin Books, 1960, page 92.

6. The gold backgrounds not only exhibited one's wealth but also helped illuminate the enormous dark halls and rooms.

mensions of Hideyoshi's halls, and they had to use the strongest colors they could find to overcome the glare of the gold. Refinement in painting was forgotten in the face of styles that would show off one's wealth and power.

The art of ornamental carving gained acceptance and greatness under Hideyoshi. It became an integral part of architectural design; ornate transoms and friezes covered buildings both inside and out, their intricacy vying with their realism to astound the onlooker. Birds, animals, and flowers were carved with amazing accuracy: as I heard an old man say one time when he saw the Fushimi gate at the Hokoku Shrine, "If those cranes only had eyes, they would fly away."

Another art to which Hideyoshi gave life was that of sculpture. It had lain dormant for centuries, but he revived it by setting out to equal the huge Daibutsu of Nara, the eighth-century creation of the Emperor Shomu. He would build one for Kyoto, Hideyoshi boasted. Not only that, but what had taken Shomu twenty years would take him five. He did it in three, and when it was destroyed in an earthquake seven years later, only death prevented him from building it again.

He pushed his way into the refined pockets of gardening and tea ceremony, too. He turned his back on the quiet, black-and-white gardens of the Zen sect and promoted opulent displays that had ponds, islands, massive and numerous stones, and trees of all kinds—even palms. Display was the thing—bold display that emphasized nothing more than sheer wealth. The garden at Ryoan-ji has fifteen rocks; Hideyoshi's at Sambo-in has 800.

His answer to the tea ceremony, that refined art which inhabited the $4\frac{1}{2}$-mat room, was to hold a ceremony of his own to which he invited the entire population. He did it at the Kitano Shrine in November 1587. It was as if, by massive mockery, he meant to drive this art of intimate gatherings right out of Japan.

There were few areas of life that escaped Hideyoshi's gigantism, and fewer still that were the same after it hit them.[7] Fur-

---

7. The tea ceremony did survive this period in a form close to that of pre-Hideyoshi days. Perhaps this was due to Kobori Enshu, who at Hideyoshi's request built the Katsura Rikyu, uninfluenced by his patron because he had exacted the three famous conditions that Hideyoshi should spare no expense, set no time limit, and never visit the place until it was done. Hideyoshi never

thermore, there was little reason for resistance, because the out-size projects of Hideyoshi bestowed wealth upon everyone connected with them. Far from resisting him, men sought out his patronage.

A typical project resulted from his visit to Daigo-ji to view flowers in 1598. The temple and its sub-temples had now lain in ruins for more than a century. There was nothing to recommend the place except its old pagoda—itself battered by an earthquake two years before—and a famous collection of cherry trees. It was to see the latter that Hideyoshi came. While he was there, Daigo-ji's abbot, aware of the possibilities, approached him and persuaded him to restore not only Daigo-ji but also one of its sub-temples, Sambo-in.

Such a job was the work of a day for Hideyoshi. Although he died the same year, the work was put through as he planned it. Daigo-ji, supplied with halls from other temples and new ones of its own, became an important temple again. Sambo-in, on the other hand, had its religious aspects virtually stamped out: Hideyoshi saw it as a headquarters for future flower parties and conceived there a network of pleasure pavilions around an unrivaled garden. Sambo-in as Hideyoshi restored it not only pushed the other sub-temples of Daigo back into obscurity but challenged Daigo-ji itself. Hideyoshi eliminated Sambo-in's past and replaced it with a monument to his own Momoyama period.

This was a man who not only unified his country beneath him but set out at once to conquer another, who not only built Japan's greatest palaces but tore them down at will. In a country with the highest respect for lines of class, Hideyoshi started at the bottom and emerged at the top. He used gold for everything—for power, to paint on, to eat from, to swing doors on—"the very privies are decorated with gold and silver, and paintings in fine colors. All these precious things are used as if they were dirt. Ah! Ah!" one man said.[8]

Nothing held Hideyoshi back but his own mortality; he had

saw it, for he died before it was finished, but Katsura Rikyu was Enshu's answer to the Kitano Tea Party, and it carried the refined arts through this ebullient period into the following century, when places like it sprang up again, among them Shugaku-in Rikyu.

8. Sansom, *op. cit.,* page 438.

the answer for everything but death. And if, in imitating him, his successors failed to capture his boldness and could not manage his scope, the pedestrian quality of their imitations only testifies the more eloquently to the rarity and freshness of this man who charged the arts of Japan with a pungency, daring, and strength which have yet to be matched.

## DAIGO-JI AND SAMBO-IN

To keep the power and the state for his son, Hideyoshi set up a complicated guardianship that involved all the most powerful lords in the country, arranged in such a way that they were played off against each other and their energies channeled to the well-being of his child heir. Like all such arrangements, this one worked well in the beginning, when rebellion was still dangerous and the relationships between these men remained as Hideyoshi had understood them. But only two years after his death, one of the five principal guardians, Tokugawa Ieyasu, successfully usurped the positions of his fellows, and after a short war emerged as the sole power in the country. He was named shogun and catered to Hideyoshi's son while his own power was still unsettled, but in 1614 he found an excuse for further war, besieged the Toyotomi in their castle at Osaka, and finally destroyed this short-lived family altogether, replacing their line with his own.

Under the Tokugawa, all the buildings of the Toyotomi in Kyoto were dispersed as part of the effort to spread that family's influence to the winds. It is perhaps a tribute to Hideyoshi's extravagant artistry that these buildings were not simply destroyed. Nevertheless none of his creations in Kyoto were left intact; only Sambo-in at Daigo seems to have been far enough removed from the city to escape the program of dispersal.

At Sambo-in, Hideyoshi's spirit lives on. Rarely has a temple in restoration changed its character so fully as this one did. When he rebuilt Sambo-in, Hideyoshi, a man whose religion was himself, thrust aside its old gods and boldly took their place.

As the new god was mortal, he surrounded his temple with a high wall and secreted and narrowed the single way in to protect himself from unwelcome visitors. Inside this sanctum he created a miniature world more glorious than anything outside.

Its center was its garden, a garden whose richness was—and perhaps still is—unequaled. It has ponds, islands, bridges, waterfalls, streams, trees, shrubs, and—above all—rocks: in about an acre, hundreds of the finest rocks in the land, carefully arranged so the qualities of each are displayed without diminishing the total effect of splendor.

The rocks form a dense and complex network. It is so dense that, when one watches it a while, it begins to generate tension. Nowhere are the eyes allowed to rest: the rocks lead them on, pull them from one to the next, vie with each other to attract attention. The competition between these rocks begins to annoy one. Why did Hideyoshi allow this tension to enter his sanctum?

The rocks are a microcosm of Hideyoshi's world—a true microcosm, because most of them were given him by men—liege lords who had to express their homage in every possible way. Hideyoshi was supreme among these men because he maintained them in tense equilibrium, under pressure he never relaxed and from which he himself was not free. It could not be relaxed, for that would bring anarchy, and anarchy would dissolve the kingdom of the mortal god. The tension followed him everywhere, even into the garden of his flower-viewing pavilion. To Hideyoshi, this was probably a small price to pay for the godly position to which he had risen.

Hideyoshi was clever: he got used to the tensions of state and he controlled them easily. But he could not maintain them after he died, and his son was too young to man the controls. Hideyoshi's network of power survived him but briefly, and then it was torn apart and replaced, to live on only in the little world of Sambo-in's stones.

It must irritate his spirit when travelers come to Daigo and pass by his rich creation—unseen behind its high protective wall—and walk on to Daigo-ji to see the famous pagoda, the only structure that was there before he came.

It is peaceful around the pagoda. Uphill from it there is a little park of plain pools, next to the Benten Shrine. The pools flow silently into each other, and the landscape around them is plain. This is the sort of place where one feels at peace, where the tensions of the world flow out of a man. Here is the still, glassy water; there, the pagoda stretches toward the open sky.

When Hideyoshi first came here, he must have been impressed by the pagoda's venerability. He wanted something similar for the line of his descendants. When he died, he may have thought he had started a ruling family that would last. As a practical man, he probably realized that his descendants could not rule forever, but even so he must have expected them to hang on longer than the two years it took Ieyasu to make himself shogun!

# 12 The Tokugawa: Nijo Castle

TOKUGAWA IEYASU (1542–1616), founder of the Tokugawa line of shoguns.

TOKUGAWA IEMITSU (1603–51), third and most powerful in the line.

TOKUGAWA IEMOCHI (1846–66), the fourteenth Tokugawa shogun.

TOKUGAWA KEIKI (1837–1913), the fifteenth and last shogun, also known as Yoshinobu.

THE TOKUGAWA were more successful than Toyotomi Hideyoshi at keeping the national power in the family. They held it for two and a half centuries, and when one considers their unimaginative methods, this was an accomplishment.

The first Tokugawa appeared in the thirteenth century, in what is now Gumma Prefecture, in the mountain country of central Japan. A member of the prolific Minamoto family—one Yoshisue, a second cousin of Minamoto Yoritomo's father—settled in a town there called Tokugawa and took its name.

By the fifteenth century Yoshisue's descendants had moved south and were established in the town of Okazaki, which stands today about twenty miles southeast of Nagoya. Here the family remained for several generations, gradually enlarging and strengthening its holdings. During this period there were several occasions when the Tokugawa were attacked and threatened with destruction, but the military acumen of the family leaders always managed to see them through.

It was in Okazaki that Tokugawa Ieyasu was born in 1542. He entered a world that was torn by civil war, and even before he was old enough to fight he helped his family's cause as a hostage. In that time of shifting loyalties it was common to bind an alliance with hostages; Ieyasu served his father as one when he was five, was captured by the enemy, and later rescued.

In the meantime his father had died, and the leaderless family domains had begun to disintegrate. The young son set out to regain them. He found himself at war with Oda Nobunaga, but

38. "It is said that Nijo's garden was originally laid out without trees so that the shogun would not be saddened by the sight of the passing seasons." Nijo-jo's garden in winter. Courtesy of Nozaki Shigyo.

they came to terms, and Ieyasu returned to personal conquest. Several years later, after Ieyasu had expanded his territories considerably, he came to Nobunaga's aid in various campaigns. On one occasion Ieyasu's eldest son was considered to have betrayed his father and Nobunaga by his relations with one of their enemies, and Ieyasu had him commit suicide. It was a time when one's military situation ruled everything else—even the life or death of one's son.

When Nobunaga was assassinated in 1582 Ieyasu withdrew from the continuing wars, but later he re-entered them to fight Hideyoshi. Once again he made peace with his opponent and became his ally. Then, while Hideyoshi ruled the country, Ieyasu busied himself with his own interests again: he continued to extend his control eastward and eventually built himself a castle at the then small town of Edo. By the time Hideyoshi died, Ieyasu held most of the country between Nagoya and Edo.

Ieyasu was one of the five guardians Hideyoshi appointed for his son, and as soon as Hideyoshi died, Ieyasu moved into Kyoto and set about consolidating the power for himself. He paid lip service to Hideyoshi's son but was in reality working to squeeze everyone out of the picture, the boy included. Before long he was accused by the other guardians of usurping their positions; opinions led to alliances; and the alliances led to war. In 1600, at Sekigahara, Ieyasu defeated his opponents in battle. From that time on, the Tokugawa family were the uncontested masters of Japan.

Like most people in Japan, Tokugawa Ieyasu and his relatives had had no experience in governing the whole country. It was only recently that the country had been pulled together, and there was no tradition of meaningful national politics. The Tokugawa, like other barons, had only governed feudalities.

Their sole aim was to preserve control of the country for themselves. Unlike Hideyoshi, they had no ambitions to conquer neighboring nations, nor did they have the aesthetic streak that had run through the Ashikaga shoguns. The Tokugawa were simply powerful barons who had a talent for war and provincial politics. They imagined the country as little more than an overgrown barony and set out to rule it that way. In their own fiefs society had been divided into classes and groups whose only

common tie was the baron; so across Japan the Tokugawa shoguns divided the people into rigidly defined groups that they
were determined to keep separate from one another. With bar-
riers and checkpoints they compartmentalized the nation geo-
graphically too, so there would be no great movement from
place to place. With a baron's understandable respect for allies
and enemies, they awarded domains in such a way that their
former enemies were surrounded by Tokugawa allies and cut
off from each other.

Various means were used to weaken the nation's barons.
Their families were kept as hostages in Edo, where the Tokugawa established a governmental seat. Their armies, their castles—almost every detail of their lives was prescribed by the
shogun, who took pains that there should be no deviation.

In short, the Tokugawa plan was to use what methods they
knew to keep Japan exactly as it was when Ieyasu became shogun. They reasoned that if nothing were allowed to change, the
pre-eminent position of their family would not change either.
Anything new—for example, the presence of foreigners or
Christianity—was suppressed. The country was closed to outsiders and locked in position within. It is to the credit of the
Tokugawa power that this rigid, unyielding approach kept
them at the top as long as it did. Inevitably, no matter how oppressive their controls, changes would come to Japan as the years
and decades passed by; yet for 268 years they ruled as if nothing
were changing at all. Perhaps it was their apparent success at suppressing change that made them blind to the changes that eventually undermined them, releasing the nation from their grip.

THE TOKUGAWA AND KYOTO

One problem for which Ieyasu had no precedent when he became shogun was the city of Kyoto. Throughout history Kyoto
had proved troublesome to those who conquered it, especially
those who did not know its ways. Ieyasu, like Nobunaga and
Hideyoshi before him, was an outsider to the city—he was a
general and a politician, while Kyoto men were civilians,
priests, artists, scholars, or members of the court. In few respects
did Ieyasu have anything in common with this capital city he
conquered, and his answer to its challenge was to withdraw to

a capital of his own, leaving behind a massive fortress to deter unrest. He would keep his distance and deal with the city on the coldest, most warlike possible terms. War he understood; Kyoto he did not.

Very shortly after Ieyasu became shogun, he began building Nijo Castle on a broad site near the center of the city. The castle's growth went on for many years under different shoguns: huge stone walls rose around the property, and inside them were placed halls and keeps, many the former possessions of Hideyoshi. This castle was intended to be the cornerstone of Tokugawa policy not only in Kyoto but in all of western Japan—this is how Ieyasu defined its role in his famous legacy: "The protection of the Castle of Nijo shall be entrusted to some reliable and trustworthy Fudai [allied lord] of good lineage, instead of to that of the Commander-in-Chief; he shall be called 'The Kyoto Representative,' and on all occasions of disturbance the Thirty Western States shall take their orders from him."[1]

In the early years of their regime the Tokugawa used Nijo for shows of strength, which they apparently felt were necessary to remind Kyoto and the west that the power at Edo was not a myth. Now and again the early shoguns marched on Kyoto at the head of representative armies and took up residence in their castle. One of these visits became the occasion for marrying a Tokugawa girl to the emperor, a noteworthy achievement considering the Tokugawa lineage.[2] A later appearance culminated in a visit by the emperor and his Tokugawa consort to Nijo Castle. This was in 1626, and apparently the shoguns were satisfied that their message was sufficiently clear, for after that occasion some of the castle buildings were removed, and eight years later there occurred the last trip to Kyoto that a shogun would make for 230 years. From 1634 on, the Tokugawa were content to let the bastions of their castle speak for themselves. The castle lay dormant, a fitting symbol of the general inactivity in Kyoto during the two centuries between 1650 and 1850. For after 1650 Kyoto itself saw little change: there were no important temples

1. J. Murdoch, *A History of Japan*, London, 1925, page 805.
2. The only recorded precedent of imperial marriage to a member of a baronial family was the marriage of the Emperor Takakura to Taira Toku-ko, but in that case her lineal background was improved by the method described in chapter 5, note 2.

built, no struggles for power—there was no power there. The population, with the active government gone to Edo, remained constant at about half a million people. The city, with this castle settled into its heart, entered two centuries of relative lethargy.

## THE CASTLE AND ITS OWNERS

It always seems ironic to see a picture book of Japan in which the city of Kyoto is represented by a view of Nijo Castle. This is often the case, yet nothing could have less to do with Kyoto than Nijo Castle. The castle is a symbol of Kyoto's occupation by a group of outsiders, and there was never a chance that anything native to Kyoto would influence its design. If outside influence affected the Tokugawa builders, it was the influence of those other Nagoya men, Nobunaga and Hideyoshi. The castle was a fortress in the tradition of the fortress architecture that they introduced: specific influence can probably be traced to Hideyoshi's short-lived downtown palace, Juraku-dai.

If it does not represent Kyoto, Nijo certainly does represent the men who built it. Although it is modest in size compared to many other castles, and although its interior emphasizes ceremonial halls rather than battlements, Nijo Castle shows us what great power the early Tokugawa shoguns had. The castle's location, in the heart of the capital city, gave it an importance that could not be surpassed by greater castles in more distant places. The very fact that the Tokugawa did not hesitate to fit it out inside for ceremonies rather than siege is a clear indication of their surpassing power—this was their western stronghold, yet they made little effort to fortify it seriously! Inside the buildings too, the formidable array of decorative art work speaks of power. None but a great national ruler could have commanded such a broad range of talent to decorate his castle.

But if these interiors show the Tokugawa power, they also show that it was new. The display is overwhelming. Nothing is left to the imagination; no wall space is left bare. Everything in sight is decorated in the costliest and most obvious possible way: a nail cover, in most buildings a simple medallion large enough to cover the nail, becomes here an eighteen-inch gilt frieze, replete with intaglio animals, birds, flowers, and—in the center—the Tokugawa family crest. A long-acknowledged ruler like the emperor would have no need for such display, but the Tokugawa shoguns used every possible means to make their changed circumstances obvious. Nijo Castle contains some of the largest and most intricate wall carvings ever made, as well as what must be Japan's largest paintings and the ubiquitous nail covers. Medallions and giltwork are everywhere. It is hardly an example of the tasteful restraint that one usually finds in Kyoto.

In the plan of the buildings and rooms one finds a miniature plan of the entire Tokugawa political system. As one walks through the buildings, he works past anterooms until he reaches a large reception hall, and then, after a narrow hallway, he finds himself working past anterooms again. They are bigger this time, and *their* reception hall is grander. The pattern continues; one wonders where the repetition will end.

This is just one example of how fully the Tokugawa compartmentalized society. So rigid was their separation of groups that they built a separate complex of anterooms and reception halls for each rank of people which the shogun expected to receive. The lower, less welcome ranks were kept to the outer halls, where bold, rich paintings would speak to them bluntly. More trusted lords were allowed deeper into the buildings and greeted in more refined surroundings designed to flatter and impress them. To insure that groups did not mix, various means were used to make access from one building to the next difficult or impossible.

The final building contained the shogun's personal apartments where, with no one to intimidate, he could afford to make use of the most delicate styles of painting. Thus, because it happened to suit their political purposes, the Tokugawa employed an unusually large number of painters to decorate their castle, ranging in style from the massive pines of Kano Tanyu in the outer halls to the fragile landscapes of Kano Koi in the shogun's own rooms. Similar remarks could be made about the artisans they employed in other fields—carving, metalwork, cloisonné. The great diversity of art which one sees in Nijo Castle is a happy result of the Tokugawa political system. We may be sure that a taste for artistic variety had nothing to do with it: if it had seemed politically preferable, they would no doubt have had one man do everything.

For the great power and great wealth that enabled them to create such things as Nijo Castle, the Tokugawa had to pay the price of great suspicion. Treachery was always a possibility. Knowing how they had gained their position—both the major battles that brought it to them had been won by what we would call treachery—the Tokugawa knew well how it might be lost. They were uneasy and suspected everyone. At Nijo Castle the separated halls and buildings, together with great corridor doors that could seal off whole areas, were one form of protection. Another was the bodyguard rooms that were installed adjacent to every room that the shogun might use. The shogun wanted the presence of these rooms to be obvious and had them fitted with ornate, tasseled doors. Even in his own quarters, open to no one except his female attendants, one wall is adorned with an ornate door to the bodyguard room. For similar reasons the castle had two kitchens, one of which was to serve the shogun alone.

This, then, is the picture Nijo Castle gives us of the Tokugawa shoguns—immensely powerful politicians who were determined to keep their freshly won position at all costs. But there is one more, less significant, aspect of the castle that may provide a final insight into the personality of these men.

It is said that Nijo's garden was originally laid out without trees so that the shogun would not be saddened by the sight of the passing seasons. In other respects, apparently, the garden was like other natural gardens. Consider for a moment a garden that has ponds, rocks, bridges, waterfalls—but no trees. How barren must it have been, how out of place in a country famous for man's attempts to unite with his natural surroundings! In the shogun's attempt to ignore the seasons, one is tempted to see the hope that he could also ignore his own mortality, now that he was ruler of all Japan. Wasn't the other ruler, the emperor, divine? Did the shogun hope that divinity would somehow rub off on him too? His buildings are perhaps the most ornate, materialistic structures that a Japanese man ever raised for himself. His garden was huge too, but he did not allow the cycles of nature to take place there. Nevertheless the absence of falling leaves in the shogun's garden did not stop the seasons from changing, any more than the weighty, grotesquely ornate family mausoleums at Nikko and Edo brought closer to life the dead shoguns under them. It must have been discouraging to learn that the man at the top of society was no more impervious than the man at its bottom.

The Tokugawa shoguns were worldly, practical men, with few religious inclinations and no desire to wait until life ended to seek the treasures of the world. No Tokugawa shogun retired to the priesthood, the way some previous shoguns had done. Buddhism declined in their era, and more worldly philosophies took the helm. Theirs was a period of repressive, unimaginative politics and competitive materialism. The requirements of politics determined everything else. Even the period's finest products—such as the Kano paintings at Nijo—were only a coincidental by-product of political considerations.

### DEFEAT BY SURPRISING ENEMIES

Nijo Castle was never besieged, but some of its buildings fell, and the Tokugawa shogunate collapsed there. The fine condition of the parts of the castle which stand today attests to the lack of assault by the "Thirty Western States" during the long centuries of Tokugawa rule. The castle found a worthier foe in lightning and fire, which over the years took away its innermost buildings and principal keep, leaving behind the Ni-no-maru (i.e., the "second ring" in the castle's concentric design) and the moats and stone walls.

Like their castle, the Tokugawa shoguns were not destroyed by defeat in the field. If rebellion had been their only problem, they might be ruling today, for long experience had taught them how to suppress human enemies. As national rulers, however, they faced problems other than direct rebellion for which their background had not prepared them. One was the direction of a national economy; another was relations with foreign countries.

In the economic field, the shogun's "corrections" to the financial landslides which overwhelmed Japan often only made the situation worse. By the 1860's deteriorating economic conditions had so weakened the country that the shogun was unable to resist a second unexpected force, the pressure from foreign governments to end Japan's isolation. He found it necessary to gradually submit to the requests of these foreigners, despite heavy popular opinion against such concessions. As the pressure mounted on both sides, the shogun sought relief by asking the practical advice of the emperor, something the Tokugawa had never done, but the emperor insisted upon the expulsion of the foreigners. When the shogun did not do this, the emperor demanded that he come to Kyoto to explain his failure to act; so in 1863 Tokugawa Iemochi, with but three thousand retainers, became the first shogun to visit Nijo Castle since Iemitsu had come and gone at the head of three hundred thousand troops in 1634.

These visits became frequent as the situation grew worse. The emperor presented Iemochi with a sword symbolic of his command to expel the foreigners, but neither the sword nor the command increased the latter's power to do so. During the next few years confusion dominated Japan's public affairs as popular feeling both for and against contact with the outside world increased and the shogun's power to take reasonable steps in either direction diminished. Western Japan was in open rebellion when Iemochi died in 1866. He was succeeded by the reluctant fifteenth shogun, Keiki, at about the same time that the emperor died and was succeeded by a fifteen-year-old boy.

This was the Emperor Meiji, who would lead Japan into her greatest revolution. At this time, however, he was too young to have influence, and the vacuum created by the unwilling shogun and the child emperor was filled by the powerful lords of western Japan. In 1867 they addressed the shogun and requested that he resign. Keiki, who had lived most of his short term at Nijo Castle, there acceded to their request in the fall of the same year. Finally, early in 1868, the emperor accepted this resignation and abolished the office of shogun, bringing to an end the system that had ruled Japan for most of the time since the end of the twelfth century.

The emperor did this in the Grand Audience Hall of Nijo Castle. Nijo fell, and the shoguns were turned out of it without a siege. The age had finally arrived when castles were not enough to keep a man in power.

# 13  Emperor under Edo: Shugaku-in Rikyu

GO-MIZU-NO-O (1596–1680), 108th emperor (1611–1629), designer and founder of Shugaku-in Rikyu.

THE EMPEROR Go-Mizu-no-o ruled during the final downfall of the Toyotomi and in the following years when the Tokugawa tightened and consolidated their strength. After his father died in 1617, Go-Mizu-no-o was persuaded to take the shogun's daughter as his consort, and on a later occasion it was he and his consort who were the guests of the shogun at Nijo Castle. This man was in the unenviable position of being emperor during the time when the Tokugawa were doing their best to establish themselves, at the expense of him and others.

Go-Mizu-no-o never was on warm terms with the shoguns, and when he had fathered an heir by his Tokugawa consort, they mounted pressure for his abdication. He resisted all harassments, and then his son died. The shogun continued to treat him badly, however, and in 1629 the emperor, without the slightest warning, suddenly abdicated and made his daughter Japan's first empress since Kyoto had become the capital.

Strangely, after Go-Mizu-no-o's abdication, the shogun's attitude changed to one of kindness and patronage. He was encouraged to build a retirement villa, and he spent many years debating various sites. It was not until the 1650's that he settled on the village of Shugaku-in, in the foothills northeast of Kyoto. Go-Mizu-no-o had a long life ahead of him, however, and after the villa was built he visited it regularly for about twenty-five years, right up to the time of his death.

In the meantime four of his children succeeded one another to the throne, with Go-Mizu-no-o the force behind them all. He was certainly the main imperial figure of his century.

As had always been the case in the past, the shoguns preserved a powerless imperial house as a symbol of their own legitimacy, but the Tokugawa policy of reasonable financial support was

39. "Buildings at Shugaku-in emerge as part of the garden in which they reside." Rinun-tei and its great hedge in Shugaku-in's upper garden. Courtesy of Sato Tatsuzo.

173

40. "Another act of Go-Mizu-no-o was to paint a name tablet for each of the buildings which he had designed." Kyusui-tei's plaque, Shugaku-in. Courtesy of Sato Tatsuzo.

41. "... Kyusui-tei, where the symbolic devices of different mat levels, different floor materials, and a plain hanging cornice combine to create in a single space an unmistakable separation." Shugaku-in's Kyusui-tei. Courtesy of Sato Tatsuzo.

something new. Past regimes had stripped the emperor of power by keeping him poor, so that his funds would do little more than meet the bare necessities of continued existence. The Tokugawa shoguns, however, took a different approach to this problem. They were well aware that Kyoto traditionally softened those who became enmeshed in its various cults, and they set out to preserve the emperor's weakness by keeping him busy with trivia. They revived and supported all manner of old imperial ceremonies that had not been performed for centuries, and they encouraged such harmless projects as the erection of Shugaku-in Rikyu. If the emperor was occupied with meaningless rites and powerless arts, they reasoned, he would remain weak while retaining a desirable dignity.

Thanks to this policy, the emperors and ex-emperors found themselves the possessors of moderate wealth, while the Tokugawa enhanced their own reputation as legitimate advocates and patrons of the imperial family.[1]

The position of Go-Mizu-no-o must have been surprisingly similar to that of the present emperor. Like today's emperor, Go-Mizu-no-o had sufficient means to retain his dignity but was totally lacking in political power. It had been so long since an emperor had actually ruled his country that he was probably regarded more as a kind of holy man than as any sort of a political figure. His sanctity protected him, and his political sterility made him of no use to the ambitious, so that he had little need for physical defenses.[2] Go-Mizu-no-o and his kin lived unthreatened and in relative peace.

THE BAMBOO GATE

There are no stone walls around Shugaku-in Rikyu, nor is there a ticket booth in front of the gate. One cannot pay to get in, and no one ever tried to invade the place. The bamboo gate

1. Despite their generosity, however, the shoguns watched the imperial house and those around it closely and kept a close accounting of the uses made of imperial funds. Their wariness of the emperor's associations is exemplified by the "Bridge of Eternity" at Shugaku-in, a handsome structure donated to the villa by a provincial governor. The gesture was not appreciated by the shogun, who had the man commit suicide.
2. The two recorded assassinations of emperors were engineered by imperial relatives, in both cases prior to the seventh century.

is closed to intruders, and for those who have permission to come it is fitted with a small door, to enable them to enter without infringing on the imperial prerogative of "using" the gate. They may see the villa, but they may not use it, and whether by coincidence or design, he who steps through that door must bow down low.

Formerly only distinguished national guests were brought here, and they wore morning coats and long dresses for the occasion. Gradually these restrictions relaxed, until now those with permission may come, and there is no apparent requirement for dress. The villa is shown at appointed times, and the visitors are punctual. Further, despite the lack of regulation, they are noticeably well dressed for the occasion, and their manner as they await the imperial tour is quiet, respectful, and subdued. These traits are not limited to the more reverent older people, but appear in youthful visitors as well. They contrast markedly with the appearance and manner of these same people in a public place, and they show that, among certain groups at least, a very definite residue of respect for the emperor has survived to this day.

BIWA AND BODYGUARDS

As the paths of Shugaku-in Rikyu lead one from garden to garden, detailed evidence unfolds that the emperor's life was the very antithesis of the shogun's, so much so that they must have seemed like rank foreigners to each other. Nijo Castle is a product of physical strength that contains the imprint of force. Shugaku-in, on the other hand, presents a study in restrained artistic taste. The most refined essence of a culture is carefully set forth here, its fragile delicacy something that could never survive downtown.

The most obvious example of the contrast lies in the buildings themselves. Buildings at Shugaku-in emerge as a part of the garden in which they reside, like delicate plants or trees carefully shaped for human habitation. They have a surprising interior flexibility as well as a carefully planned union with their surroundings.

Most of them are frail things that would not withstand the onslaught of a man's shoulder. One pavilion of the upper garden, called Rinun-tei, has two rooms with no permanent walls at all, but just sliding screens on all four sides that make them totally accessible to the garden and to each other. When a cool breeze is needed during Kyoto's hot summer, the screens are simply removed.[3]

In every detail the buildings of Shugaku-in reflect the pure aesthetics underlying the imperial taste. The architecture is simple and conservative, as thoroughly refined as the emperor himself. Decoration is kept to a minimum, and of paintings, some pavilions have none. The most "ambitious" paintings are those of the Okesho-den,[4] in the central room of which are pasted up small, hazy representations of the "eight views of Shugaku-in." Other paintings are small and unimportant, and in most cases the reason is obvious: these buildings were constructed for viewing nature, and the scenes they look out upon are the true paintings of Shugaku-in. The artistic energies of the creator went into the garden outside, and no attempt was made to rival it, or even to distract from it, by artificial depictions inside the buildings.[5] Shugaku-in's sole purpose seems to be to bring its inhabitant closer to nature. What room would there have been in such a scheme for the shogun's garden of bare, unchanging rocks, or his wall paintings of cherry limbs whose blossoms never fell?

Here and there small details illuminate the artistic character of the strong-willed retired emperor who created this place. In a room of one pavilion there is an extra alcove, about the right size to hold a man, set between the tokonoma and the shelf alcove. The canons of Japanese room design are so strict that one notices this variation immediately. Go-Mizu-no-o had it added to provide him a place to store the imperial lute, or *biwa*.

Another act of Go-Mizu-no-o was to paint a name tablet for each of the buildings which he had designed. The calligraphy on these tablets is the sole exterior decoration for those buildings. In

3. Such openness would have been too risky for the shogun, who kept his castle cool by sealing out the sun and breeze completely.

4. The Okesho-den is relatively ornate and seemingly out of place at Shugaku-in, but it was not originally part of the villa. It was the dressing room of Go-Mizu-no-o's consort, which was removed to Shugaku-in after her death in 1678. The ornate character of the building is perhaps best explained by her Tokugawa lineage.

5. An acknowledged exception: the fish paintings of Okesho-den, such fine rivals of reality that a net was painted over them, as some say "to hold them in." But see the note above.

one case, where the name characters are enclosed in knotted, delicately entwined octagons, we are permitted to imagine the old man poring over a revolutionary and intricate tablet design, a pleasant task to break the monotony of his everyday life. Other name tablets are simpler, but their simplicity does not lessen the fascination of the bold, ragged brush strokes firmly executed across the silky, naked wood.

The simplest element of design was carefully studied and re-fined before being incorporated into these buildings. A wooden box for storing storm screens—a necessary wart on nearly every Japanese building—was built on hinges so that it could be folded back out of sight. Sliding paper screens were hinged from the top instead of being confined to their usual lateral grooves in rooms where the view and the sunlight made this desirable, thus creat-ing a form of awning that was undoubtedly pleasant in summer. Rooms varied in size from fifteen mats down to one and a half, and in one small pavilion Go-Mizu-no-o created three "rooms" without a single partition between them.

This was Kyusui-tei, where the symbolic devices of different mat levels, different floor materials, and a plain hanging cornice combined to create in a single space an unmistakable separation —three rooms, yet from each of them one could see out on all four sides of the building. . . .

GO–MIZU–NO–O

It is a cool, gray fall morning. Not an ideal day, yet Shugaku-in's natural splendor seems to illuminate any weather: even today the kaleidoscopic hedges glow in spectrums and rainbows like great polished, pearly shells from the South Seas. In the upper garden, walking along the east bank of the pond, one passes the Bridge of Eternity and crosses the narrow gorge spanned by the curving Maple Bridge and climbs up the small island there to Kyusui-tei, the solitary pavilion at the northern end of the pond.

One stops momentarily and looks in at the pavilion's carefully divided space. In the far corner, hanging out over the garden, are the six small raised mats, enclosed by a neat lacquer sill, reserved for the emperor. It is not difficult to see the old man sitting there in his Buddhist robes, his garden behind him, his piercing eyes, ignoring the puffy aging flesh around them, scanning the room. His religious attire puffs up around him as if he were permanently planted there. Despite a pursed, toothless mouth, Go-Mizu-no-o's bald fortress of a head and those high-set, narrow eyes make it plain to see why he has been the power behind his reigning children.

His eyes dart to the opposite side of the building, to the board-floored pantry where two attendants huddle together preparing tea. For a split second he glances at his companion in the ante-room, but only long enough to assure himself that the man has not moved—he is still sitting there, blandly unaware that his boredom is so obvious.

What is on the retired emperor's mind? There is the name tablet which he wrote out for Kyusui, which was hung up recently, and which this fellow did not even notice. The retired emperor has become used to the dull people with which he is surrounded. He looks out to his left, thinking of the valley of maples out there across the pond, its leaves even on this cool gray morning gradually drying and stiffening towards that approaching fall day when they will parch and rattle under the autumn sun and force one to shield his eyes as he looks at them. It is a great event, that annual show of color.

It is a little chilly. Go-Mizu-no-o's eyes widen again as he looks about his pavilion. The tea is coming now, but perhaps after the tea he will start back and proceed to a warmer place more suited to the day. Predictably, his companion pronounces that an excellent idea. But secretly Go-Mizu-no-o likes this weather—one must understand a day like this one before he can truly enjoy the red maples when they come; on the other hand, there is no point in lengthening the morning in the hope that this fellow will eventually understand. On their way back, Go-Mizu-no-o thinks, they can stop at his "pavilion in the clouds," Rinun-tei, and look out over the distant reaches to his capital city, Kyoto. From that uppermost of upper vantages the old man can almost see the people down in the capital of this island country that he rules.

And can there be any question that he rules? If he did not, then why would he be here among his maples while the citizenry attended to less exalted tasks in the distant city below? About others admittedly he knows little, but Go-Mizu-no-o once saw the vast, dark, soulless halls of his minister the shogun, and he has never envied him.

The seated form of the old ex-emperor slips back into the past, and the modern visitor turns away from an empty Kyusui-tei, his mind filled with thoughts of this sage old man and the sequestered life he led. Somewhat later on that cloudy morning, having seen each of Shugaku-in's three delicate essays on the combined arts of gardening, architecture, and calligraphy, the visitor bows low to stoop through the door in the bamboo gate, stepping through to the world outside, to the village of Shugaku-in. He wonders to himself: how much longer will the emperor rule?

# 14 Baron under Edo: Nijo Jinya

OGAWA HIRAEMON, seventeenth-century rice dealer, builder of Nijo
Jinya.

NEITHER the emperor's Shugaku-in villa nor the shogun's
castle at Nijo was what one would call a typical home, for the
Edo or any other period. Each in its way showed that its owner
was a man who played a special role in his society. For the common citizen—the farmer, merchant, artisan, or soldier—there
was no possibility of attaining either the sudden opulence of the
Tokugawa or the inherited remoteness and elevation of the emperor. The requirements of survival—including tribute to both
rulers—kept such visions in the realm of the impossible.

The large mass of common people provided a neutral and
firm base to society which did not change very much from century to century. They were the constant in each regime's formula
of power, upon which the latter depended—probably more than
it realized—to remain unchanged. They did remain unchanged,
and even today in many sections of Japan the basic elements
which have traditionally constituted the poor man's life are easy
to find. The ox and hand plow, the fish and rice diet, the paper
and wood house—these and many other aspects of the lives of
the poor exist today as they have existed for centuries.

In other areas of everyday life there has also been a noticeable
lack of change: inns, for instance, remain the same drafty,
crowded, thin-walled, noisy, and sometimes charming places
they have been ever since the peaceful Edo period introduced the
civilian traveler to Japan. Today we live in a time when the centuries seem to have caught up with Japan, when these traditional
elements seem about to be tossed aside. Nevertheless, at least
until this postwar period, it is noteworthy how little conditions
were altered for the great mass of the people by the steady stream
of political upheavals at the top.

As in any country, the people in Japan's history whose lives were subject to the most fluctuation were those whose careers were actually tied to the political events of the day. Among those who rode up and down with the machinations of the powerful were the priests of the various Buddhist sects and the shifting class of feudal barons.

The baron was a man whose independence and power varied inversely with the centralization of the national government. In time of chaos, when no single force could hold Japan together— as, for instance, during the century of war that preceded Oda Nobunaga—the baron was the most powerful man in the land. People within his domain depended on him for protection and paid for this local stability with heavy tributes and fierce loyalty. On the other hand, the power of the individual baron did not necessarily increase when the total number of barons decreased, because the average baron was not capable of regional or national leadership, being unable to command undivided loyalty outside his own fief.

When Tokugawa Ieyasu became shogun, he set out at once to sap the power of the barons to choke off the threat of a rival. By a series of careful checks he drained the strength of each one to the exact point where there was just enough to support his present status without any left over for personal ambition. As they did with the emperor, the Tokugawa shoguns attempted to give the barons an appearance of power while actually withholding it from them. They wanted their barons to appear strong enough to maintain local order and obedience—but to be no stronger.

The effect of this on the baron was to place him in a delicate balance: on the one hand, he had to act strong locally; on the other, he knew that too much display of force would offend and anger the shogun. Thus the shogun could march into Kyoto at the head of a giant army, but the baron's very presence there placed him under suspicion of conniving with the emperor, and everywhere he went he had to beware lest his own comparatively small display of strength accuse him of excessive ambition. The size and force of his encampment, the number of his bodyguards —the slightest detail which bore on the baron's potential political power was carefully observed by the shogun's spies.

As one method of controlling the individual barons, the Tokugawa allowed only a limited number of them to have castles

42. "Although this *jinya* was built as much for fighting as for everyday living, the devices which make it an ambush . . . are so well-concealed that all but the most acutely trained observers would never know they were there." Nijo Jinya. Courtesy of the Asahi Shimbunsha.

43, 44. "...a hallway where a shifted hook lowers a secret staircase." Nijo Jinya. Courtesy of Nijo Jinya.

(*shiro*), forcing those outside that number to do what they could within the walls of a private home. The result of this restriction was a sort of armed house called a *jinya*, or encampment house, that lay somewhere between an ordinary house and a genuine castle. Since the *jinya* was usually imposed on a man who would have preferred to build a *shiro*, it was characterized by great surreptitiousness and concealment, for the baron would make it into as great a stronghold as possible without seeming to have built an unauthorized *shiro*.

To further prevent barons from consolidating their strength in the distant provinces the shogun established a requirement that all barons travel, at regular intervals, between Edo and their own domains, dividing their time between the two places. By keeping their families hostage in Edo, the shogun exerted his will on the barons even when they were at home.

One of the effects of this regulation was to fill the main highroads of Japan with a continuous flow of barons and their retinues going back and forth between the provinces and Edo. Barons traveled as they never had before, and since they required adequate accommodations and self-protection en route, there grew up a second class of *jinya*—commercial *jinya*—which might best be described as fortified inns. These buildings were unique to the Edo period, before and after which there was no need for them. They grew out of the requirements of the times and, like their private counterparts, incorporated covert devices and hidden fortifications to make themselves inwardly strong while outwardly adhering to their limitations as inns. A subtle fortress-inn which enabled the traveling baron to combine his own security and dignity with a humility imposed from above, the commercial *jinya* was a fixture in the highway cities and towns of Tokugawa Japan.

### THE OGAWA HOUSE

Ogawa had been a baron in his own right. As a follower of Nobunaga and then of Hideyoshi, he had held a castle in Shikoku that had given him a sizable income. That all vanished into the air, however, when Ieyasu dispossessed him in 1600.

Now, after a span of poverty, he was making a comeback of sorts in Kyoto. He had bought some land there and had entered the rice trade. His business prospered, and soon he was able to secure the account of the imperial household, which not only brought financial success but gave to Ogawa certain special privileges, such as riding in and out of the imperial precincts instead of going on foot. About this time, too, he branched out, spreading his operation into pharmaceuticals.

It was undoubtedly his connections with the imperial household, coupled with his own truncated career as a feudal lord, that brought this man in contact with the upper echelons of Kyoto society, including the various barons that came and went from time to time. Ogawa was on good terms with many of them, and he got in the habit of providing them with lodging when they came to Kyoto. Before long he realized that he had unwittingly branched out again: this time he had become an innkeeper, and whether because there was no politic way to escape it or because he simply saw it as a good financial possibility, he decided to build himself a real baron's inn.

Ogawa was a man of taste who could be expected to do such a job with care and craftsmanship. When he had been in the service of Hideyoshi it was he who was selected to build a $4\frac{1}{2}$-mat teahouse in preparation for his lord's flower-viewing party, with results that apparently pleased Hideyoshi greatly. Now when he set about building his manor house—his *jinya*—Ogawa made use of the best builders and materials he could find, and apparently did not rush the job, for it is said that he spent thirty years at it.

The result of this labor of love was a spectacular example of a *jinya*, the like of which does not stand today and indeed may not have stood in the era of its building. Nijo Jinya—so named because of its location—not only had the attributes of an inn and the built-in armor of a baron's camp, but it was supplied with revolutionary components, both decorative and practical, that were in some cases centuries ahead of their time. Chief among them was a system of protective devices—many of which were pure inventions—designed to hold off that primary destroyer of Japanese buildings, fire. Undoubtedly the *jinya* would not be standing today if they had not done their job, for it was located in a crowded neighborhood and on at least one occasion survived a fire which leveled the entire area around it, the Great Fire of Temmei.

The Temmei fire has been called "one of the biggest fires in the history of the world."[1] It occurred in March 1788, when with the help of an untimely gale a small blaze exploded and raced across Kyoto from east to west for more than three days. When it had finished its work, the entire heart of the city was a charred ruin.

Nijo Jinya lacked ramparts or even distance to separate it from neighboring buildings, all of which burned—but it survived. Its fireproofing system was undoubtedly what saved it. The Temmei fire was the most severe test ever placed on Ogawa's network of clay doors and slides, sheathed roofing and removable shingles, and his complex water system. That the *jinya* passed this test may well be its most notable achievement.

In the unusual, however, Ogawa did not limit himself to preservation devices. Throughout the *jinya* one sees decorative elements that stand out as unique—china nail covers, a bath using early examples of tile, or a painting done about sections of inlaid glass, which in those days was a rare commodity.

This is an exciting building. Its basic forte is the skill with which its fireproofing devices and hidden armament were installed, in both cases without disturbing the structure's aesthetic appeal. Although this *jinya* was built as much for fighting as for everyday living, the devices which make it an ambush are not only put back out of sight, but they are so well concealed that all but the most acutely trained observers would never know they were there. It is only when their hidden nature is revealed to the visitor that he can gain a true appreciation of the imagination and foresight that were possessed by the rice dealer Ogawa Hiraemon.

## "BARON NAGATSUKA"

When one sees Nijo Jinya, he finds it difficult not to daydream, to imagine the place under siege, to insert himself into the in-

1. Ponsonby-Fane, *op. cit.,* page 406. I have taken much information on the Temmei fire from this source. A contemporary map shown opposite page 407 marks the extent of the fire, with the area of Nijo Jinya completely blacked out.

trigue which could have happened there. This was not the type of building that would attract the usual warfare—massive assaults, front-line combat. Its hidden fortifications made Nijo Jinya a place for cunning and trickery. The attacker would have to assault this place—and its inhabitants—with his mind as well as his arms.

Even today an imaginary baron slips noiselessly through the halls, combating with the wiles of the *jinya* the evil intentions of an imaginary assassin in priest's clothing. They sit in the main parlor, Baron Nagatsuka granting an interview to this priest whom he has reason to trust as an informer. The priest hesitates —he pulls a knife—he lunges at the baron. What does Nagatsuka do? There is little he can do, except to call out for help. Does help arrive in time? Perhaps not, if it has to come from the hallways, but the assassin has overlooked the parlor's singular clerestory window, an innocent-seeming access for light connected to a hidden room, through which a bodyguard can drop at once— perhaps even before his lord calls out, for the acoustic chamber has provided him with every word.

Nagatsuka is saved, but it is not long before he seems to be cornered again. His back to the angle of a dark hallway, he finds himself cut off from his men while enemies close in on both sides. It is a blind corner; how can he escape? If he is agile enough he will make it, for there is a miniature garden set into the wall be- hind him, and while its artistic rocks are cutting into the faces of the enemy, Nagatsuka will be scaling the carefully spaced half- timbers to the ceiling. When the attackers rush to the corner to drag him down, they will find that he is gone, and if they look closely at the dark space up by the ceiling, they may see a small triangular opening, hardly noticeable there.

This takes the baron to a story concealed between stories, all of which would be a revelation to his attackers, because they still believe, from their earlier appraisal of the heavy roof outside, that this is a one-story building. In reality there are three, in addi- tion to the hidden 'tween-story where Nagatsuka now hides.

As the visitor continues through the building, the imaginary battle follows him. Nagatsuka may be upstairs, but downstairs one of his men is sure to get trapped in the corner tearoom, with the enemy having cut off all exits. There is no escape but to leap into a nearby closet, and even that seems a poor opportunity, for no sooner is he in than they storm the room from both sides, and in moments the closet's paper door has been slashed to ribbons, pierced by a dozen swords. Is the man killed? Hardly, because this closet has a back door. The door leads to a hallway, where a shifted hook lowers a secret staircase, and thus he escapes and his pursuers learn for the first time that the building continues overhead.

Upstairs, an assassin charges down the dark hallway after his prey and reaches out to grab him when—he drops into a blind staircase and—whether or not his neck is broken—is sealed into place by a heavy flooring that is quickly slid over him. In the dark he had missed the subtle dogleg of the hall which a single side step had enabled the fleeing man to pass. His companion may not fall into the now-filled staircase, but farther on he will undoubtedly stride into one of the gopher holes in the floor, and while his ankle is being broken, the rest of him will be pitched headlong into the stone courtyard below, for the hallway ends without warning here.

So it goes at Nijo Jinya. Does Baron Nagatsuka escape his would-be assassins? One would surmise that he usually did, and further that very few of his confused enemies would leave this curious building alive to warn the next party that tried to take it. From whatever side they came, the outsiders would need the sensitivity of bats to escape the surprises that awaited them.

Yet the visitor finds, as these successive subtleties are revealed, that one additional question occurs to him: did these events ever actually happen? A suspicion lingers that the imagined battle is the only one Nijo Jinya ever saw.

Did people while fighting actually have time to scale walls, to raise and lower secret staircases, and to draw back trap doors; and did the opponent actually fall down the staircase and, once down, stay there long enough so the lid could be lifted over him? Did bodyguards actually leap from the secret-silent compartment next to the clerestory window—or did they leap only to find that their lord had already been killed? These devices are just cunning enough so that one wonders if they were actually useful. Was anyone ever killed at Nijo Jinya? Perhaps not, but perhaps, on the other hand, the knowledge that in such a place there might be a surprise at every corner was the final persuader to stay an assassin's hand.

## THE JINYA'S SIGNIFICANCE

Nijo Jinya makes it obvious how little the baron had in common with the emperor, that lonely man who lived in an imperial vacuum. Its overwhelming practicality establishes it as something the emperor would have been unable to understand. He was completely removed from the practical problems that were the everyday life of the baron, and the idea of a building being useful as a defense against fire or enemy would probably have struck him as strange.

The shogun, on the other hand, would have understood this building's uses, but he would have prided himself that his own halls were richer and more refined. His castle, of course, was a much greater structure than the unpretentious *jinya,* but despite this the houses of shogun and baron had much in common. Both were noteworthy for the obvious suspicion with which those inside regarded all outsiders. The shogun and the baron faced the same problems; the difference lay in the ways they attacked them. The cramped nature of the *jinya,* its cautious richness, and its conventional appearance all reflect the deep abyss that separated the baron from his former peer.

Yet despite the fact that the *jinya* has but faint and timid traces of the magnificence of the shogun's castle, and virtually none of the beauty of the imperial villa, it holds great interest because it reveals how the ordinary baron lived. In Japanese history it was the rule for the buildings of rulers to survive, while those of lesser citizens did not. Nijo Jinya would not be an exception to that rule had it not been for the inventive genius of its merchant-baron-builder.

# 15 The All-Time Temple: Kiyomizu

IF THERE is one Buddhist temple that spans Kyoto's history, has been important and well known in all periods, and yet is not overassociated with any one of them, it is Kiyomizu-dera, known to all simply as Kiyomizu. This temple is a unique and inseparable part of Kyoto. It would be difficult to imagine a Kyoto that lacked Kiyomizu, yet strangely the temple has little connection with the Buddhism of that city.

The beginnings of Kiyomizu antedate even the conception of the city which became Kyoto. It is older than Enryaku-ji and preceded the Tendai sect in Japan. The temple was born when a priest from Nara came to its site in answer to a vision, and the sect he brought with him was a Nara sect—the Hosso. Kiyomizu was founded as a temple of the Hosso sect.

Like the other Nara sects, the Hosso fell into decline as Kyoto and its own forms of Buddhism ascended. The Nara sects were left behind and gradually lost their power. Today only a few great temples of the Hosso sect survive, and all of them, except Kiyomizu, are in Nara. As for Kiyomizu, it stands alone in Kyoto as a major temple which does not belong to one of the local sects.

One might expect that this would have singled out Kiyomizu for extinction long before now, but quite the reverse seems to be true. One can only speculate at the reasons this "alien" temple survived so handsomely in Kyoto. It may be that, belonging to no local sect, Kiyomizu was able to stay friendly with all of them —at least after the early period of wars between the Kyoto and Nara temples. By not being tied to a Kyoto sect, Kiyomizu was not pulled into the fierce religious wars by which they decimated one another, nor was it subject to the cycles of success and failure, hope and despair, which followed the newer sects in Kyoto, wound up as they were in the politics of city and nation.

When one considers how the Zen sect rose with the warrior

class and the Jodo among the poor, and how the Tendai monks excluded those of the Shin for centuries, and later expelled the Nichiren, only to be destroyed themselves by Oda Nobunaga—when one considers in addition how Buddhism itself was persecuted in the Shinto revival of the nineteenth century, as the individual sects had always been persecuted whenever their political supporters fell—when one considers all these things, it would seem that belonging to an old, dormant sect was to Kiyomizu's distinct advantage.

To look at the temple today, one would be encouraged to such a conclusion. It probably attracts more visitors than any other place in Kyoto. Why? One reason is undoubtedly its magnificent view. But beyond that, this temple attracts the members of all Buddhist sects. Jodo believers do not visit Shin temples, Shin believers do not visit Zen temples, Zen believers do not visit Tendai temples. But Jodo, Shin, Zen, and Tendai believers all visit Kiyomizu. It has attained neutrality with old age; its uniqueness attracts all.

Nevertheless one wonders to whom Kiyomizu turned for active support during its long history. Who wanted to keep it alive? Why, whenever it burned, was it always swiftly rebuilt, whatever the political mood of the day?

To answer these questions one must turn to the temple's popularity and to its location. Apparently Kiyomizu has always been a popular place for all kinds of worship. As a temple devoted to Kannon, it was one of thirty-three such temples that comprised a standard route of pilgrimage for those who sought the mercy of that popular deity. Kiyomizu's eleven-faced, thousand-armed Kannon also had a widespread fame for effecting easy childbirth, in the hope of which large numbers of expectant mothers and their families would come here. In addition, its religious "neutrality" apparently enabled Kiyomizu to house the services of other sects on occasion, as it did those of the young Jodo in its Amida hall in 1188.

These and other facets of the temple's versatile religious personality gave it a widespread popular backing of which there is still hefty material evidence right at the temple itself. The numerous stone lanterns and *koma-inu* (mythical guardian dogs) about the grounds, and the unequaled horde of giant paintings

45. "This gigantic, homely, and unforgettable structure dominates the temple completely." Kiyomizu's Hon-do. Courtesy of Kiyomizu-dera.

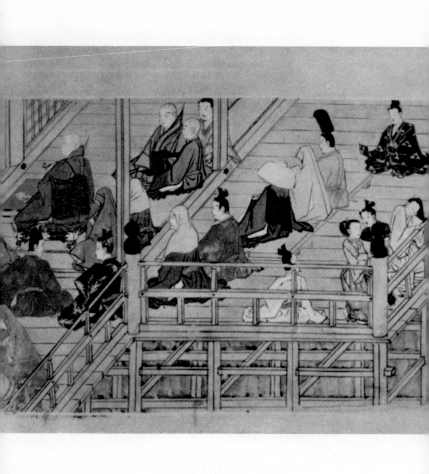

46. "If there is one Buddhist temple that spans Kyoto's history...
it is Kiyomizu-dera. . . ." Honen preaches the Nembutsu at Kiyomizu. From the scroll *Honen Shonin Eden* (Biography of St. Honen).
Courtesy of Chion-in, Kyoto.

47. "It is principally because of its location, on the edge of a high hill overlooking the city, that Kiyomizu has always been a national landmark." Kiyomizu-dera as seen from the Hokoku-byo. Courtesy of Asano Kiichi.

48. "... another large hall with its own large platform. ..." Kiyomizu's Oku-no-in. Courtesy of Asano Kiichi.

hanging up under the eaves of the buildings—especially of the main hall—all were the gifts of parishioners. So too were the famous iron *geta* and staffs near the main hall, the dragon fountain nearby, the Asakura Hall, and numerous other valuable items that need not be listed. As evidence of heavy popular support in past years, the temple abounds in donations and thank offerings, and even they only represent gifts since the last great fire in 1629.

Undoubtedly this great and real popularity of Kiyomizu was what made it expedient for governments of all complexions to support the place and to rebuild it promptly after each of its numerous fires. This was an easy way for a government to win the support of the people. Conversely, lack of interest in the fate of Kiyomizu was a reasonable guarantee of popular opposition. These considerations undoubtedly influenced such powerful men as Toyotomi Hideyoshi and Tokugawa Iemitsu, both of whom patronized the temple heavily.

To Kiyomizu's widespread religious appeal one must add its unique and beautiful location as a second factor which contributed to the spread of its fame. It is principally because of its location, on the edge of a high hill overlooking the city, that Kiyomizu has always been a national landmark, known even to those who never saw it as a place to be confused with no other. The beauty of this site made the temple a natural literary setting that was rarely neglected in works involving Kyoto. In real life too, Kiyomizu saw more than its share of trysts, and its combination of isolation from and nearness to the city, together with its useful view, made it a natural rendezvous for such secretive types as spies, scouts, and rebels. The truly national knowledge of Kiyomizu's location and the military advantage of its high ground made it a rallying point for whole armies mobilized for war. In these respects its site contributed to Kiyomizu's fame. "Meet me at Kiyomizu," one could say, and there was no mistaking what he meant.

Its use as a camp site was not always to the temple's advantage: military engagement and the carelessness of soldiers accounted for some of the temple's fires. Earthquakes, accidents, and the relatively poor supply of water on the hill also contributed to the temple's destruction from time to time.

But Kiyomizu never lay in ruins long. From the time of its first building, when around the year 800 Japan's first great shogun gave it his own home, to the time of its last, a great restoration in 1633 patronized by the most powerful shogun of them all, Kiyomizu has never needed to look far to find a powerful backer who would keep it alive.

## KIYOMIZU'S BIZARRE CHARACTER

Perhaps because Kiyomizu has attracted such widespread support its character is eclectic and bizarre. It is limited to no era and represents none. Even though most of its earlier relics were destroyed in the temple's many fires, it is still composed of elements from every possible source, and somehow each one seems to take on a uniqueness which could only happen here. In time these elements range from a statue of Kannon worshiped by the pregnant wife of the Emperor Shomu—he built the great Buddha in Nara in the 740's—to the excellent stones in the garden of the priests' quarters, donated by Toyotomi Hideyoshi, to an endless procession of objects that have been given the temple right down to the present day. In spirit, too, they contain a wide variety of associations: there are many facets of Kiyomizu that seem more closely attached to legend and myth than to the intellectual order of imported Buddhism. The temple has somehow entered the roots of the country, where Shinto dwells. For example, its waterfall, far from being the solely decorative stream one sees at most temples, is sacred, and its waters have a purifying religious value that seems closer to Shinto's pantheism than it does to Buddhist doctrine. A hill in the back of the grounds, covered with ranks of worn images of Jizo and various other Buddhas, also has a surprising aura of the primitive about it. It is not of course a direct connection with Shinto, but these and other parts of Kiyomizu have an elemental nature which is unmistakable yet which does not seem misplaced.

In its way Kiyomizu might be likened to St. Mark's in Venice. Like the latter, it seems to have been caught between two cultures—in this case the intellectual Buddhism of the mainland and the local persuasions of tradition, superstition, and Shinto worship—and to have solved its dilemma by accepting elements

from them both. Nothing displays the strange character that results from this mixture better than the main hall (Hon-do) itself.

This gigantic, homely, and unforgettable structure dominates
the temple completely. Its dancing stage and orchestra wings—
themselves reminders of Japan's ancient court dances—hang out
in the air on great scaffoldings that disappear down into the tops
of trees rising beneath them. Its huge, humpbacked shingle roof
—and how many Buddhist roofs are shingled?[1]—seems to grow
right out of the nearby slope of Higashiyama; it is a monster
whose vast extremities can hardly be encompassed in a single
view. Its heavy bow, its strange scalloped corners, its unmatch-
ing elements—every homely detail belongs to this roof alone.

In underneath it, among the giant pillars that hold it up in the
air, one looks up to see great paintings of horses, strident black
on gold, loaded up under the eaves together with paintings of
numerous other subjects. These famous horses—it is tempting to
relate them to the horses of St. Mark's—are everywhere, hung
haphazardly and without pattern in the dark as if the sole motive
were to get them up out of the way. But if they seem strange,
what can one say for the elephantine painting on the back wall
of the Hon-do, hanging unnoticed out under the eaves? This is
a case of size determining location, for clearly this battered work
could fit nowhere else. There it hangs, naked to storm and rain,
gradually fading away under the huge roof which does not project far enough to protect it. Few who come here see it, for few
walk behind the Hon-do, and as each year passes there is less of
it to see. Above it on the roof, large plants lie hidden among the
shingles, waiting only for a good strong rain to stand them up.
Surely no temple is quite like this one!

Wherever one turns, the rich character of Kiyomizu strikes
him in the eye. Its famous view of Kyoto is a fine one, but finer
still are the varied and unusual perspectives of the temple itself,
unique sights that present themselves as one walks about the
grounds. The glory of Kiyomizu is its visual richness, as photographs are constantly reminding us. Rare is the person who visits

1. Generally speaking, few, for Buddhism brought tile roofs with it from
China and only where local style was overpowering lapsed back into shingle.
On the other hand, Shinto roofs are usually shingle—where they are tile it is
often a sign of Buddhist influence.

this place without first having seen photograph after photograph of it hanging out over its cliff, but equally rare is the person whose first sight of the temple is that majestic sweep of halls that he has seen in so many photographs. It is unfortunate that this place where one's sense of sight has such great potential rewards await-ing it is usually approached by a narrow, shop-lined lane which sneaks up on the cliff from the side, thus depositing the visitor right in the midst of Kiyomizu's halls before he has had a chance to appreciate their location.

Because I feel that strong visual impressions are Kiyomizu's great reward to the visitor, I set out to create a situation in which one's first sight of the temple would reveal something of its un-usual character, instead of offering only the quasi-flatland same-ness that is seen in so many less interesting places. The result of this effort is set forth on map 21, which offers not only what might be called the "right" approach to Kiyomizu, but also a picturesque walk of less than a mile. This walk passes through an area that is surprisingly rural and quiet when one considers its nearness to the city. It takes one through a small village, a quiet wood, a peaceful, isolated graveyard, and as it gets higher the path begins offering fine views of Kyoto, framed in the distance by nearer slopes and tall, bare, leaning "umbrella" trees. Then it reaches a bridle path that soon leads one to a small pagoda.

It is a pleasant surprise to come upon such a delicacy in the middle of a wood. The pagoda is aged and weatherworn, but it is also diminutive, fragile, and feminine. Appearing in such a quiet, wooded place it commands one's attention as he draws near and begins circling around it, but not for long, for as he gets to the other side he is suddenly aware of something else in the background, as if a giant had just materialized to protect this delicate thing. It is the cliff, and Kiyomizu.

It is like being in a small boat on a calm sea and suddenly en-countering a battleship under full steam. The buildings of the temple are fanned out across the far side of the intervening val-ley. One's eye snags on the silhouetted pagoda, then swings back to the giant Hon-do, then travels down the line again to the pagoda and past it, to roofs which sink down the slope and trail off in a distant view of the city. From this vantage Kiyomizu seems to surge straight out of the mountain on a glacier-like march right down to the city streets. The buildings seem quite near, and the Hon-do does not appear large, until—as might happen with the lone battleship—one sees his first people there. Perhaps he is looking for reasonably sized people to be walking about the grounds. Failing to see any, looking more closely, he suddenly notices movement everywhere, like insects crawling on a mound. These tiny figures are the people, and with that realization the halls behind them seem to mushroom up into the sky.

This is seeing Kiyomizu at its best. It is difficult to abandon this view, and when one finally does, the path leads back into the woods again and the sight of that great temple is cut off completely—it disappears, as if it had been an unreal vision. Just now it had dominated everything, yet here, moments later, it is completely gone.

The path through the woods is short. As one goes on, the Hon-do begins to appear again. Small sections of it show through the trees, and the people standing about on its platform are larger, and occasionally their noises can be heard. Now the Oku-no-in, another hall with its own large platform, lies directly ahead; it is crowded with people who are peering over the edge and gazing out across the distant city quite unaware that someone approaches from the woods so close by. The path leads around behind this hall, and then right onto the platform, and standing among these same people one sees the Hon-do huge and close, separated from the Oku-no-in by but a few yards of deep empty space. Looking beyond that great hall, one sees the flat city of Kyoto spreading out in the distance.

A SPRING EVENING

One day I came to Kiyomizu at dusk. It was June, and there was still a definite chill in the air. The crowds were gone, and the temple was empty, as it is only near the end of the day. The sun had been down for some time, and behind Kyoto a dull red sky was flickering out and taking with it all detail in the shadowy city below. Soon Kyoto, and a little later Kiyomizu, would be shrouded in darkness. But at this moment Kiyomizu was silhouetted sharply in the afterglow, waiting patiently for the city to take the first taste of night.

I walked up to the Hon-do to look from the dancing platform. I stepped out into the false light of the white sky from among the heavy, close-standing pillars and looked out over a black and white world. A sound attracted my gaze to the sacred waterfall below, and I looked down through the cool evening air.

There was a man standing in the waterfall. The water fell on the back of his neck. He wore, for all I could see, a shapeless white garment which could have been the cotton kimono of a pilgrim or even underwear. The cold water poured steadily on the back of his neck, and with head bowed he danced about under it—not moving away, just slowly dancing where he stood, right in the center of the fall.

There was no one else about. I stood on the dancing platform looking down, and the dancing pilgrim moved yet stood still in the cold falling water below me. He made strange howling noises, and they floated up into the empty, cool night air. They were not loud noises, but they spread easily through the emptiness surrounding us both.

Somehow that pilgrim, and his howling noises floating up around him, and the night closing down on the city and slowly working up to the temple on the hill, all managed in a moment to come together and express my deepest feelings about Kiyomizu-dera.

# PART TWO
## Guide

# 神泉苑 Shinsen-en Sacred Spring Garden

1. HISTORY. Kyoto was founded in 794, and Shinsen-en was apparently completed by the end of the century, for there is record of a visit by the Emperor Kammu in the summer of 800. The garden covered about 33 acres, shaped in a narrow rectangle running north and south. The section which remains today was in the approximate center of the original garden.

The garden was used for all forms of imperial entertainment and also for certain religious services. Its numerous buildings were built and arranged in imitation of Chinese styles.

"Detailed particulars of the buildings in the gardens are unfortunately not available, but from old books and traditions it appears that the Kanrin-kaku was the principal. . . . Its exact site and dimensions cannot now be ascertained, but it contained the imperial throne and seats for the crown prince, princes of the blood, ministers, etc., and must have been of considerable size. The roof had dolphin finials, and a red-lacquered balustrade surrounded the building. Right and left were separate pavilions, probably connected to the main building by corridors. Mention is also made of the eastern and western fishing pavilions, doubtless on the edge of the lake, and of the eastern and western waterfall pavilions. The gardens were enclosed by a fence, and there were gates on all sides, the principal one being on the east."[1]

Shinsen-en fell into decay during the 12th and early 13th centuries as the old Imperial Palace burned several times. In 1227 the last attempt to rebuild the old palace ended in fire. Meanwhile, however, there had occurred a civil war in 1221, and one of the victors, Hojo Yasutoki (1183–1242), had Shinsen-en restored. In succeeding centuries the garden again fell to ruin. Early in the 17th century its remains were given to To-ji, a metropolitan temple of the Shingon sect, and it was restored again by its new patrons, who also built a Buddhist temple on

1. Ponsonby-Fane, *op. cit.*, page 98.

the grounds. There is evidence that, at that time, Shinsen-en was still considerably larger than it is today, for the back of Nijo Jinya (q.v.) apparently looked out over its pond, where there is now a school playground. If this is so, it would indicate that the pond in the 17th century extended south of its present location and was at least twice its present size.

2. SHINSEN-EN TODAY. The present garden is about a tenth the size of the original one. Its grounds contain a pond (Hojoju-ike), an island, a bridge called Hojo-bashi, three Shinto shrines, and one Buddhist temple. The pond and island may reflect a configuration of the old garden. The Shinto shrine on the island is dedicated to Zen-nyo-ryu-o (lit., "pious woman dragon king"). It is apparently the modern successor to the shrine of the same name, whose annual ceremonies the public was permitted to attend as early as the 9th century. Along the east bank of the pond stand a Benten shrine and an Inari shrine, the latter with its customary superfluity of *torii* (Shinto gates). Both are small.

The Buddhist temple is on the west side of the grounds. Its main hall, Shinsei-den, contains an image of Kobo Daishi (or Kukai, 774–835), founder of the Shingon sect. Other halls, and a belfry in the northeast corner of the grounds, are part of this temple. A group of stone images of Jizo, guardian of children and wayfarers, which stand in the southeast sector, belong to it too.

In a major renovation begun in 1963, a new gate and wall were added on the north side of the grounds, and a sizable building (Hojo) was brought from To-ji and re-erected next to the Shinsei-den.

Shinsen-en is the only part of the original palace grounds that has survived in any semblance of its former state. Of the rest of the great palace enclosures, no trace remains—it was all built over centuries ago.

Festival Noh plays are given here in the early part of May.

# 延暦寺 Enryaku-ji

1. GENERAL HISTORY. Enryaku-ji was founded in 788, six years before the capital was moved to Kyoto, by the priest Saicho (767–822, posth. Dengyo Daishi). Its location atop Mt. Hiei to the northeast of the city was selected so it could protect the future capital from the evil spirits said to come from that direction. Originally called Ichijo-Shikan-in, it was formally named Enryaku-ji, after Enryaku, the year name of its founding, by the Emperor Saga in 823.

The monastery grew quickly in importance and from the 11th century onward, aided by its own army, it maintained the primacy of the Tendai sect and the lesser positions of all others by brute force. At the height of its power Enryaku-ji is said to have had 3,000 temples on Mt. Hiei. These were divided into three precincts and sixteen quarters: the Eastern and Western Precincts (five quarters each) and Yokawa (six quarters). (See map 14.)

In 1571 the general Oda Nobunaga invaded the mountain, razed the temples, and slaughtered the priests. No building now on the mountain was there before Nobunaga.

The monastery was re-established during the period 1585–1650 under the patronage of Toyotomi Hideyoshi and the Tokugawa shoguns. At present it comprises about 130 temples, the main cluster of which stands at an altitude of about 680 meters on Mt. Hiei (850 m.). Enryaku-ji is headquarters for the largest of the three branches of the Tendai sect in Japan. Although it has never regained its former size and power, it is nevertheless formidable among the temples of modern Japan in the number of its buildings, the size of its grounds, and the magnificence of its location on Mt. Hiei.

2. MUDO-JI-DANI (無動寺谷 the valley of the motionless temple). A complex of five or six buildings about one mile south of and below the top cable-car station on the Sakamoto side of Mt.

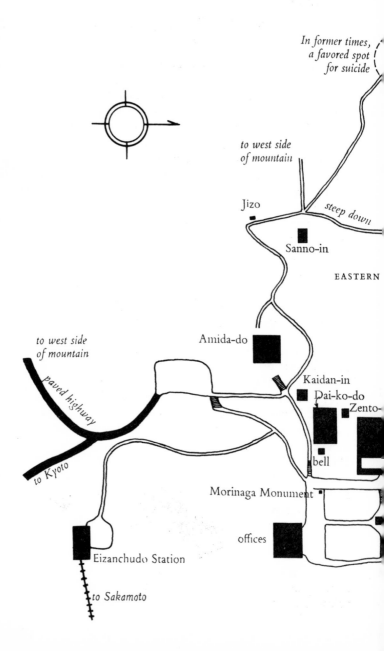

abandoned ropeway ho

*In former times,*
*a favored spot*
*for suicide*

*to west side*
*of mountain*

Jizo

*steep down*

Sanno-in

EASTERN

Amida-do

*to west side*
*of mountain*

Kaidan-in

Dai-ko-do

Zento-

*paved highway*

bell

*to Kyoto*

Morinaga Monument

offices

Eizanchudo Station

*to Sakamoto*

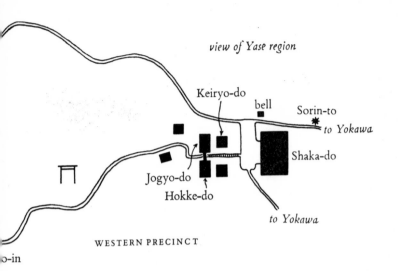

view of Yase region

Keiryo-do

bell

Sorin-to
to Yokawa

Shaka-do

Jogyo-do

Hokke-do

to Yokawa

WESTERN PRECINCT

o-in

n-chu-do

MAP ONE
Enryaku-ji

延暦寺

SHOWING THE PRINCIPAL BUILDINGS OF
THE EASTERN AND WESTERN PRECINCTS

Hiei. Its main hall is the Myo-o-do. This building receives its name from Fudo Myo-o, who is worshiped here. Fudo ("immovable") subjugates evil and evildoers by the sheer force of his wrath. He is one of the five ferocious "light kings" (Myo-o). The life-sized image of Fudo is said to be over a thousand years old, the work of So-o (831–918), one of the many distinguished early priests of Enryaku-ji.

In this temple the priests of the Tendai undergo one of their three "difficult practices," in this case that of rising daily at about two o'clock a.m. and spending the entire day walking the mountain and praying at each of its temples. A "unit" of this practice is a hundred days; the whole term is a thousand.

Mudo-ji-dani was first settled about the year 865. Other halls at this place include Benten-do, Homan-in, Daijo-in, and Gyokusho-in. Myo-o-do and Daijo-in can be seen from the top cable car station on the Sakamoto side of Mt. Hiei.

3. SANNO-IN (山王院 Mountain King Temple). When he returned from studying in China in 858, the priest Enchin (814–91, posth. Chisho Daishi) founded a temple on the mountain called Senju-in. It was located next to the Sanno Myojin shrine, a shrine to one of the Shinto gods of the mountain, and soon it came to be called Sanno-in. In 873 Enchin became head of Onjo-ji, a Tendai temple in Otsu, and about a century later doctrinal differences between the "main line" of thought and that of Enchin's followers came to a head, the latter were forced to leave the mountain and go to Onjo-ji, and the sect was split into two branches. Aside from its connection with Enchin, Sanno-in is of minor importance. Its present small building, which houses an image of Senju Kannon (thousand-armed Kannon), probably dates from the 17th century.

4. JODO-IN (浄土院 Pure Land Temple). The temple was originally erected by Saicho, the founder of Enryaku-ji, to house a statue of Amida which he himself had carved. Amida is the Buddha who rules the Western Paradise, or Pure Land—hence this temple's name. In 854 Ennin, one of Saicho's disciples, made a tomb for his deceased master here.

The present Jodo-in consists of three buildings which date

from the early Edo period. The main hall houses an image of the founder to which is made a daily offering of food. To the west is the Amida-do, which houses Saicho's image of Amida. The image is not displayed but is kept in a box shrine in front of which stands a copy of it.

Behind the main hall to the north stands the third building, Saicho's tomb. It is surrounded by a stone fence in front of which an incense pattern is kept burning. The numerous stone lanterns and miniature pagodas here are offerings to Saicho. To the left and right of the tomb stand a linden tree and a *sarasoju* tree, respectively.

They represent the linden tree under which Gautama Buddha disseminated his teachings, and the *sarasoju* under which he passed from this life into Nirvana.

Jodo-in is the scene of another of the three "difficult practices." It is called "sweeping hell," and consists of early rising, prayer, and sweeping, the latter usually lasting about six hours. Anything and everything is swept, and the visitor will notice the broom scratches on the ground and the spotlessness of the area, extending even to the walls around the temple. Any priest staying at Jodo-in must perform this practice daily as long as he is there, the minimum period being three months.

Some priests, performing a different kind of practice, stay on the mountain without leaving it for periods of twelve years; in 1961 I met one, Mr. Nakano, who had chosen to spend his twelve years sweeping at Jodo-in. It was his third year, and although he could not eat meat, fish, or eggs, and his complexion was quite green, he looked strong and healthy, and when we interrupted his isolation he became quite talkative. In 1963 his health was good, and he had begun to have a certain fame around Kyoto. He hopes to make a world trip after coming down the mountain in 1970.

5. JOGYO-DO (常行堂 Endless Walking Hall). This is the western of the twin temples near the Shaka-do in the Western Precinct. Its history gives some idea of the vicissitudes undergone by both of them. The first Jogyo-do of Enryaku-ji was built in the Eastern Precinct in 848. The Western Precinct received its own Jogyo-do on the present site in 893. The latter burned in 1154, was rebuilt in 1155, burned again in 1271, was rebuilt in 1285, and burned a third time with the rest of Enryaku-ji in 1571. The present build-

ing dates from about 1595. The one in the Eastern Precinct, and another erected in Yokawa in 968, were not rebuilt after 1571.

The second of the four "religious practices" (not to be confused with the three "difficult practices") of the Tendai sect takes place at Jogyo-do. It consists of constant walking accompanied by the chanting of the Nembutsu ("Namu Amida Butsu," or "Save me, Amida Buddha").

The interior of the building is bare save for a small image of Amida, facing south, seated before a gold halo *(kohai)* covered with Bodhisattvas.

6. HOKKE-DO (法華堂 named after the Hokke, or Lotus, Sutra). Hokke-do is the eastern of the twin temples. First built in 825, it, too, now dates from about 1595. It houses an image of Fugen Bosatsu seated on an elephant. Except for this image the interior of Hokke-do is bare.

Fugen is one of Shaka's attendants (cf. Shaka-do below) and in a trinity sits on Shaka's right. The elephant is symbolic of Fugen's self-possession and occult powers attained by the practice of nearly all the possible religious disciplines.

The third of the four "religious practices" is performed here. It is based on the Lotus (Hokke) Sutra and consists of walking and sitting—reading the sutra while walking, and meditating upon it while sitting.

The two buildings, surrounded by ambulatories and devoid of furnishings, are obviously designed for walking; they are connected to each other by a covered corridor. Together they are called Ninai-do, or Benkei-no-ninai-do ("Benkei's burden halls"), referring to the legendary 12th-century priest-strongman Benkei, who is purported to have raised both buildings by shouldering the corridor between them.

7. SHAKA-DO (釈迦堂 Shaka Hall), receives its name from its principal image, Shaka Nyorai, the historical Buddha also known as Gautama. It is the oldest building of those presently at Enryaku-ji and has an interesting history, because it was originally a hall of the rival temple Onjo-ji.

The year of its original construction is unknown, but this hall dates from the early part of the Kamakura period (1185–1392), when its building style was developed.

The necessity of accommodating increasingly large congregations as well as priests—the latter often performing secret rituals—in a single building led to the construction of a "fore-hall" across the front of the basic temple. At first these fore-halls had their own roofs; by the 13th century, methods had been devised to enclose the temple proper and its fore-hall under a single roof. In later centuries the single roof increased in size and massiveness. The present heavy roof on Shaka-do is a mutation that may have been made as late as the 17th century.

Until the late 16th century this building was the main hall (Kon-do) of Onjo-ji in the plain south of Mt. Hiei. Thus in 1571 it was spared Nobunaga's fire, since Onjo-ji had sided with him, and later when Toyotomi Hideyoshi seized control of the country and destroyed in its turn Onjo-ji, he did an incomplete job and this building survived. Hideyoshi, in granting permission for the rebuilding of Enryaku-ji, awarded the remains of Onjo-ji to the project, and this building was flaked, carried up the mountain, and rebuilt as the Shaka-do of Enryaku-ji. Only very recently it was repaired extensively and it is now in outstanding condition.

As the main hall of the Western Precinct, Shaka-do was once the scene of many of the important ceremonies of Enryaku-ji. Since the monastery was reduced from its former size, however, the three precincts have been smaller and less independent, and Shaka-do no longer shares the importance of the Kompon-chu-do of the Eastern Precinct (para. 13 below).

The image of Shaka was carved by Saicho, but again it is not revealed, a copy being displayed in front of the box that houses the original. At the four corners of the altar are Shi-tenno (four heavenly kings), traditional guardians of Buddha who stand watch on the four main points of the compass.

The Shi-tenno are associated with various colors and attributes. Briefly, these are as follows:

N.  Tamonten ("who hears all"); blue; spear, cudgel, miniature pagoda
E.  Jikokuten ("upholder of the state"); green; sword, spear

S.  Zochoten ("mighty"); white; sword, spear
W. Komokuten ("who sees all"); red; spear, rope, brush-pen, scroll[1]

The interior of Shaka-do is divided into three sections: (1) the wide raised floor across the front of the temple, for the worshipers; (2) a "well" or sunken stone floor in the temple proper, for the priests; and (3) a raised altar in the middle of the "well" on which are placed the religious images and attendant ornaments. This configuration is a characteristic of Enryaku-ji halls that is duplicated in the Kompon-chu-do.

During services the well is dark, while the two raised floor spaces are lit. The altar is on the same level as the floor for the worshipers. The significance of this arrangement is simply stated: there is equality between god and man, but they are separated by a distance unbridgeable by man. The darkness in the well is the darkness of society which keeps man from god. The priests work where society is darkest, and by their work and prayer bridge the gap between man and god.

The significance of the three lanterns in front of the altar and the three gold chrysanthemum crests on the ridgepole outside is discussed below under the Kompon-chu-do (para. 13).

8. SORIN-TO (相輪橖 a storyless pagoda). This pagoda consists only of the nine-ringed spire *(sorin)* usually found at the top of a pagoda building. It is supported by crossed metal arms and rests on a vault which contains 23 Buddhist sutra manuscripts. The original Sorin-to, 45 feet high, was built by Saicho in 820; it reached its present state in a major restoration in 1895. The Sorin-to at Rinno-ji, Nikko, was built in imitation of this one.

9. YOKAWA (横川). This is the name of the third or northern precinct of Enryaku-ji. It contains several buildings, the most important of which are the Chu-do (中堂 Central Hall) and the Shiki-ko-do (四季講堂 Four Seasons Lecture Hall).

Ennin (794–864, posth. Jikaku Daishi), the third head priest of Enryaku-ji and historically one of its most important figures, studied at Yokawa, copied sutras, and built two temples (which no longer exist) to house them there. The famous priest Eshin (942–

1. As listed in William Watson, *Sculpture of Japan,* Viking, 1959, page 215.

1017) also studied scriptures there, at the Eshin-in, and many others famous in Tendai history are connected with the history of Yokawa. Eshin's tomb is close to Eshin-in.

The Chu-do was first built by Ennin in 848 to house an image of Kannon, the goddess of mercy, but the hall, which was rebuilt in 1694, burned in 1901. It has only recently been rebuilt again. The Four Seasons Lecture Hall was first constructed in 967, and the present building dates from 1653. It houses an image of Ryogen (912–85, posth. Ganzan or Jie Daishi), its founder, and gets its name from the lectures on the five Mahayana sutras which are given there during each of the four seasons.

Yokawa is where the third of the three "difficult practices" takes place. It consists of a term of remaining indoors and praying for at least six hours every day.

Yokawa is a few miles north of Shaka-do; from it paths lead down the mountain to Sakamoto.

10. AMIDA-DO (阿弥陀堂 Amida Hall), is the uppermost of the important buildings of the Eastern Precinct, and it is the newest temple of Enryaku-ji. It was built in 1937 and houses a large image of Amida.

Amida, the ruler of the Western Paradise, is the Buddha who receives the souls of the dead and allows them to enter his kingdom. His name means "infinite life" or "boundless light"; the transition from these intangible concepts to the form of a Buddha is apparently the result of attempts to bring them into the realm of easy human understanding.

In the Amida-do are said prayers for the welfare of the dead. The spirit of a dead person is believed to reside in his mortuary tablet (ihai), and here such tablets cover the walls to left and right behind the image of Amida.

11. KAIDAN-IN (戒壇院 precepts-platform temple). The central image of Kaidan-in is that of Shaka. The present building dates from 1604, the heart of the Momoyama period. Elements representative of this period are the curved gable built into the upper roof and the cusped-arch windows at the corners of the hall. The latter were introduced in the architecture imported from China

by the Zen sect and later spread into the buildings of other Buddhist sects.

A temple named *kaidan* is a place where Buddhist priests receive moral precepts *(kai)* and are ordained. Before Kyoto became the capital, there were only three ordination halls in Japan, all in Nara, and the Nara temples guarded their monopoly jealously. When Saicho came to Mt. Hiei, one of his ambitions was to receive imperial sanction for his temple to have its own ordination hall. The power of the Nara temples was such, however, that he did not achieve this in his lifetime. After Saicho's death, permission was finally granted, and in 827 the first Kaidan-in at Enryaku-ji, and the fourth in Japan, was built. Since that time the Kaidan-in has been the scene of Tendai sect ordinations, and many famous priests, including the eventual founders of other sects, have entered their priesthood here.

12. DAI-KO-DO (大講堂 Great Lecture Hall). The former Dai-ko-do burned to the ground on October 11, 1956. It was an impressive, double-roofed structure of the early Edo period. To replace it, a large hall was brought up the mountain from Sakamoto and rebuilt on the Dai-ko-do foundation. This hall (in Sakamoto it was the Sambutsu-do and housed an image of Amida) was first built in 1634 and formerly stood just south of the Sakamoto cable-car station.

The new Dai-ko-do was dedicated in 1963. Its image of Dai-nichi Nyorai, the Buddha patronizing learning, was brought from Mudo-ji-dani to replace the one lost in the fire.

Mudo-ji-dani had two images of Dainichi: the one of the Taizo-kai and the one of the Kongo-kai, the two heavenly worlds depicted in *mandala* paintings. The former is the one which has been transferred. Both are of the early Edo period.

Behind Dai-ko-do a small building called Zento-in marks the spot where Ennin once lived. The present structure was built after the fire. It is not much used today.

Enryaku-ji's belfry stands off the southeast corner of the Dai-ko-do. It was not burned in the fire.

13. KOMPON-CHU-DO (根本中堂 Fundamental Central Hall). This building is the heart of the whole monastery. The first Kompon-chu-do was built by Saicho himself to house an image of Yakushi

Nyorai which he had carved. It was completed in 794; at that time it *was* the monastery. Since then the fortunes of the building have waxed and waned with those of Enryaku-ji and the whole Tendai sect.

"The history of this structure illustrates both the simplicity of early Tendai and the subsequent rapid advance towards size and magnificence. At the outset it was a shingled chapel to Yakushi, only 30 by 15½ feet in plan and 12 feet to the eaves. In the 880s it was rebuilt on a much more impressive scale, eleven bays across, with a full ambulatory. It was burned down in 935 and rebuilt—apparently in the same form—by 940. Even at that size it could not accommodate the demands made on the national headquarters of the sect. The single aisle across the front was hopelessly inadequate. Out of the inconvenience suffered by clergy and laity alike came a remodelling in 980, in which a magobisashi [an additional width across the front made by extending the overhang of the roof] was added. Thereafter, as the dedication record put it metaphorically, 'the dove-coloured throng might soar and move about without hindrance; the flocking pigeons had a place to rest.' The present Komponchūdō shows the results of a still later alteration, using the mature raidō [fore-hall] formula."[2]

It was, of course, burned with the other buildings in 1571. The present hall dates from 1642 and measures 123 by 78 feet in plan and 32 feet to the eaves.

Kompon-chu-do lies in style between the unrestrained boldness of the Momoyama period and the material extravagance and overdecoration that followed in the Edo period. Here the two have begun to mix, but the presence of Edo elements is not strong enough to weaken the magnificence of this building in its setting on the mountain among towering trees. Ornate carvings hang in the outside corridors, but they are unpainted and unobtrusive. The black-and-gold ornament under the eaves is difficult to see, although it can be viewed closely from behind the Dai-ko-do. The copper roof on the outer corridors and the curved gable over the entrance are further evidence of the period in which the present Kompon-chu-do was built, although these corridors existed in a simpler form prior to 1571.

2. Paine and Soper, *op. cit.,* page 217, note 5 (page 280).

Inside, the giant pillars are made of *keyaki* (zelkova) wood. The coffered ceiling is decorated in typical Tokugawa fashion: each square contains a flower painting provided, at the shogun's command, by each of the different feudal lords of Japan, painted in his province and brought to Enryaku-ji as a kind of offering to the shogun.

The floor is arranged in different levels, as it is in the Shaka-do, although here the scale is more impressive: the altar truly seems to "float in blackness."

The altar is a building in itself, complete with bracketed eaves. It is crowded with images and religious objects, the accoutrements of a "high church," which the Tendai sect most certainly is. Saicho's Yakushi is hidden within the altar, and the copy displayed in front of it is guarded by a Shi-tenno. Figures of Nikko and Gekko complete the Yakushi trinity.

Yakushi Nyorai is usually regarded as a god of healing, or more widely as a god who cures all pain and suffering, whether mental or physical. His twelve vows, which include the elimination of famine and the propagation of right understanding, are directed against very real human problems. This strong materialistic appeal probably helps explain his popularity. Nikko and Gekko are deities of the sun and moon, respectively.

In front of the altar are three large lanterns with the imperial crest—the sixteen-petaled chrysanthemum—on their windows. This crest also appears three times on the outside ridgepole of the hall, as it does at Shaka-do. The lanterns are said to have been lit by Saicho and never extinguished during the succeeding centuries. The crest, it is said, was originally that of the monastery, which gave it to the Emperor Kammu, founder of Kyoto, after which time it was used by the imperial house. Finally, the number three (three lanterns, three crests) is probably connected to Mt. T'ien-t'ai in China, the Chinese headquarters of the Tendai sect, over which three stars are said perpetually to shine. The symbol of the Tendai sect, which appears on the neckbands worn by some of its priests, is these three stars of Mt. T'ien-t'ai.

There is a monument near Kompon-chu-do in the shape of a small obelisk supported by a tortoise. It was made in 1921 and is dedicated to Morinaga Shinno (1308–35). This prince, the son of the Emperor Go-Daigo, became a priest and, in 1327, head abbot of the Tendai sect. He later re-entered the political scene to lead revolts against the Kamakura shogunate, but his enemies calumniated him. His father, who believed them, had him imprisoned. Subsequently his jailors, themselves about to be defeated in a battle, murdered him before fleeing. As a priest Morinaga took the name Sonun; he was also called Daito-no-miya.

14. MONJU-RO (文殊楼 Monju's Belvedere). The present Monju-ro is said to be the same age as the Kompon-chu-do—that is, rebuilt in 1642. It resembles the earlier Monju-ro in shape, although the latter was larger and apparently had fine detail work similar to that on the former Dai-ko-do. Once again cusped-arch windows are used. Monju-ro's 17th-century design is called *wayo-toyo-kongo-zukuri*: a mixture of native and Chinese styles.

Stairwells on either side of the building lead to the upper—and only—floor, where the image of Monju, surrounded by his Shitenno, sits facing east. All were carved about 1700 by an unknown sculptor.

The deity Monju is a counterpart of Fugen Bosatsu, whom we encountered in the Hokke-do. Where Fugen usually sits on Shaka's right on an elephant, Monju is found on Shaka's left, astride a lion and carrying a sword. His Sanskrit name, Manjusri, means "wonderful virtue" or "wonderful lucky omen," and he is worshiped as the god of wisdom.

On the back wall hang wooden tablets written by the parishioners and offered to the god. The ceiling, lacking exposed beams or other interruptions, is called a *kagami tenjo* or mirror ceiling. A low balcony runs around the upper story, from which there is a fine view of Lake Biwa.

In the Monju-ro takes place the first of the four "religious practices" which have been mentioned above. In this practice the devotee sits facing west in meditation lasting ninety days, at the end of which time evil is broken and the truth realized.

Before Enryaku-ji was burned, the Monju-ro of the Eastern Precinct was one of a cluster of four buildings, the others being Zuijii-do, Jogyo-do, and Hokke-do, or one for each of the four Tendai "religious practices." Of these, however, only Monju-ro was rebuilt after 1571. At present Enryaku-ji has no Zuijii-do.

Down the stone steps to the east of Monju-ro one comes to Sanjo-shuku-in ("lodging house atop the mountain"), and the road there leads down the mountain to Sakamoto, two kilometers away.

15. HIE JINJA (日吉神社), a Shinto shrine. While the proper name of this shrine is Hie, the more popular reading of the same characters is Hiyoshi. This shrine is inextricably entwined in the history of Enryaku-ji.

When Saicho began establishing his temple on the top of the mountain, he worshiped the Shinto deity Oyamagui-no-Mikoto, which he claimed to have found there, renamed the deity Sanno, or Mountain King, and eventually re-established it in a shrine at the foot of the mountain. His worship of a Shinto deity did not involve religious conflict but was considered more as an act of loyalty to the emperor, for Shinto gods were the imperial ancestors. Shintoists claim that Saicho, by doing this, was merely subverting the national religion and bringing it under the wing of Buddhism. There is no doubt that this recognition of Shinto deities by Buddhism was the beginning of a long period of Buddhist growth and supremacy which kept Shinto effectively subdued until the Meiji Restoration of 1868. Even during Saicho's time the various Shinto gods (the final number enshrined was seven, known as the "seven mountain gods of Hiei") which his temple recognized were being compared to Buddhas, and eventually they were identified with various Buddhas. This practice spread throughout Shinto in later years, even to the extent that Buddhist images were set up in Shinto shrines.

During the centuries when the priests of Mt. Hiei made their raids on Kyoto, they always carried a sacred miniature shrine (*mikoshi*) from Hie Jinja with them at their head, for it was sacrilege to obstruct or harm the *mikoshi*. This religious ruse worked effectively for centuries, until eventually someone dared to smash the *mikoshi* and was—as he had suspected—not disintegrated on the spot.

Although there have been at various times shrines to these mountain gods named Sanno both atop the mountain and at its foot, their worship is now centered in Sakamoto, where Saicho first brought the presence of Oyamagui-no-Mikoto. The Hie

Shrine there has many unique aspects, some of which are the following:

a. To approach it one crosses a large stream called Omiya-gawa by one of three large, heavy stone bridges. Their curved design is considered unique, and they were built in 1586.

b. The *torii,* or gate to the shrine, is also unique, in being surmounted by a pointed gable which resembles a mountain—or even the Japanese character for mountain (山). This shape derives from the "mountain gods" enshrined there, and the style is called Sanno *torii.*

c. The roofs of the shrine buildings proper are an unusual shape, being cleverly curved, overhanging far in front but cut off short in back so that they resemble a woman holding her skirts up.

These bridge, *torii,* and roof styles are all particularly associated with Hie Jinja.

The shrine is divided into west and east sections, the latter being the newer. The western shrine is approached by the upper of the stone bridges. One passes through a Sanno *torii* and continues to the Ro-mon, or high gate, which is Buddhist in style and marks the entrance to the shrine.

It is not uncommon for Shinto shrines to claim certain animals as their "messenger animals," and in the case of Hie this honor goes to the monkey. Caged monkeys are therefore seen on the premises, and up under the eaves of the Ro-mon, at each of the four corners, perches a small, carefully carved monkey.

The present buildings of the western shrine date from the Momoyama period, the late 16th century. The eastern shrine is smaller and its buildings more orthodox in construction and slightly newer.

16. SAKAMOTO (坂本, Foot of Slope). This town at the east foot of the mountain is on one of the two routes from Enryaku-ji to Kyoto and is also enroute to the rival temple, Onjo-ji; so it naturally grew up as the lowland headquarters of Enryaku-ji. Warlike expeditions from the temple passed through here, emperors came here—both to worship at the Hie Shrine and to beg help of Enryaku-ji in war—and priests of Enryaku-ji built their temples here. Even today there are more than fifty Tendai temples clustered in the center of Sakamoto, most of them still active, and

there are many more in the suburbs of the town. The main streets are lined solid with temples and here also one finds the religious boys' schools of Enryaku-ji—lower, middle, and upper.

The Sambutsu-do, mentioned above as replacement for the burned Dai-ko-do, was just south of and across the stream from the cable-car station. Nearby is a Shinto shrine, Tosho-gu. Both were built in 1634 in imitation of their more famous counterparts at Nikko. The original bridge leading to them was also built in 1634 but fell in a washout in 1935.

The other temples in Sakamoto are too numerous to mention individually, but it is sufficient to say that the town remains today as a peaceful stronghold of the Tendai sect.

# 三千院 Sanzen-in

*Sanzen* (三千 3000) is an abbreviated form of *sanzen-daisen-sekai* (三千大千世界 3000 great thousand world), or the greater part of the Buddhist universe times a thousand cubed, which was the vast system to which Shaka Nyorai (Gautama Buddha) directed his ministry. The universe was divided into three worlds, six paths, and myriad subdivisions that formed a system no less complex than that of Dante. Only its four highest heavens were not in the *sanzen-daisen-sekai* ministered to by Shaka.

1. GENERAL HISTORY. In 788 Saicho founded a small temple on Mt. Hiei to serve as a temporary shelter for his image of Yakushi while he was building the Kompon-chu-do. In the 9th century this hall was rebuilt and enlarged, and a detached temple was added to its domain in Sakamoto, at a place called Kajii (梶井 Paper-Mulberry Well). In 1118 a prince of the blood, Saiun (1104–62), the second son of the Emperor Horikawa, became abbot of the temple at Sakamoto, and it thus became a *monzeki*—a temple with a royal abbot, or one in which royalty resides.

In the meantime the famous priest Eshin (942–1017) had built his Ojo-gokuraku-in on Uo-yama (Fish Mountain) in Ohara in 985 (see map 18). This was the future main hall of Sanzen-in, and its first connection with the *monzeki* in Sakamoto came when Saiun was asked to take charge of it in 1155. From that time the Ohara temple was a detached branch of the Kajii *monzeki* of Sakamoto. Saiun became head abbot of the Tendai sect in 1156, and many of his successors at Sakamoto also attained this position.

The headquarters of Kajii *monzeki* continued in Sakamoto until 1698, when the Tokugawa shogun offered its 43rd abbot a large site in downtown Kyoto, and the *monzeki* was moved there.[1] The move to Kyoto increased the importance of the

1. This site was on the east side of Kawara-machi where the Prefectural Hospital now stands, and was retained by the family line until 1908.

branch temple at Ohara, which now became the temple residence of the abbot. Still, he went there only for important ceremonies, remaining the rest of the time at his Kajii-no-miya (Kajii Palace) in Kyoto.

In 1868, during the suppression of Buddhism that followed the Meiji Restoration, all *monzeki* were disestablished. The royal line of Kajii abbots was secularized and became nobles named Nashimoto. They continued to live at the former Kajii-no-miya in Kyoto, but the Buddhist articles and relics of the *monzeki* were transferred to the temple in Ohara. The period of suppression was short-lived, however, for in 1871 *monzeki* were allowed to re-establish themselves. Ohara now became headquarters of the Kajii, or Nashimoto, *monzeki,* and the temple there was named Sanzen-in for the first time. This new importance enabled Sanzen-in to restore buildings and improve their appearance. Although its history is long, it is only in the last century that Sanzen-in has assumed the independence and stature it now has as the Kajii *monzeki*.

The temple's historic value, however, derives from the 10th century, when Eshin built its first hall. Eshin was a pioneer of the Amidist movement in Japanese Buddhism, and this hall and its image of Amida are his best-preserved creations. Few images this old are preserved in such fine condition.

2. SHIN-DEN (宸殿). Sanzen-in is fronted by a tunnel of cherry trees and cut off from the outside world by a stone wall done in the 16th-century castle style. There is a large *katsura* (cercidiphyllum japonicum) tree opposite the Goten-mon (Palace Gate). The Shin-den is the northernmost of the three buildings and is usually the first to be shown to visitors.

The Shin-den and Kyaku-den (see below) were originally built here in the 16th century out of materials from the Imperial Palace, Kyoto. The original Shin-den was completely destroyed —with cause and date unknown—and the present structure is a reconstruction done in 1926. The building has four rooms.

a. THE WEST ROOM contains two venerable pieces of sculpture. The seated Kuze Kannon was done in the middle of the 13th century by an unknown sculptor. It is made of camphorwood and has a metal crown. The image is said to be copied from a

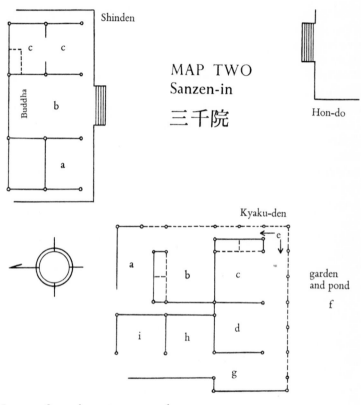

MAP TWO
Sanzen-in

三千院

Shinden

Buddha

Hon-do

Kyaku-den

garden
and pond

Letters refer to the text, para. 2 and 4

similar image belonging to the Shi-tenno-ji in Osaka. An un-usual feature of Kuze Kannon is that she comes apart at the neck. When this was first discovered a letter was found in the interior cavity, which had been written by one Nakatomi Gyohen in 1246 and which helped to date the statue.

Kannon, technically of neither sex but popularly conceived of as female, is one of Amida's two assistants, but has emerged as a kind of "goddess of mercy." Kannon's Sanskrit name, Avalokitesvara, comes from a passage of the Lotus Sutra that says, "if one should happen to hear the name of Kannon and call upon his name with all his heart, he [Kannon] would *at once be conscious of the calling* (avalo-

**225**

kitesvara) and bring him perfect deliverance."[2] Extremely popular in Japan, Kannon appears in many forms—with a thousand hands, eleven heads, horse heads, or, as here, in the more usual human form.

The second image is of Fudo Myo-o. Said to be over a thousand years old, it is attributed to Ennin (794–864). The flames which envelop Fudo's body culminate in the bodies and heads of five mythical birds who will purify our crimes. With threatening sword and awesome grimace Fudo terrifies us to repentance.

Drums sometimes displayed in this room were actually used by the emperor when the building was dedicated in 1926.

b. THE CENTRAL ROOM is the altar room of this hall and contains an image of Yakushi Nyorai said to have been carved by Saicho. The plaque above the entrance to this room says "Sanzen-in" and is the calligraphy of the Emperor Reigen (1654–1732). This room is designed in miniature imitation of the Shishin-den of the Imperial Palace, Kyoto, from which also comes the name of the building.

c. On THE EAST SIDE of the Shin-den there are two rooms. The outer one has *fusuma* (sliding screens) depicting the edges of a pond and a rainbow. They were done at the time of the building's reconstruction by Shimomura Kanzan, who was commissioned to do them by Sir C. N. E. Eliot, author of many books on Buddhism and at that time British Ambassador to Japan.

The inner room contains a raised *tatami* (mat), the elevated floor traditionally provided for imperial use, which was used by the emperor at the dedication ceremonies.

Hanging on the wall is a rubbing of a complex Chinese calligraphy said to have been executed in a single stroke. The small box in the alcove is decorated with a mulberry leaf and a cross-hatch design: it is a sort of caricature of *kajii* (cf. para. 1 above). The mulberry leaf also appears on the main doors of the Shin-den, and serves as a crest for the Kajii *monzeki*.

3. OJO-GOKURAKU-IN (往生極楽院 Temple of Rebirth in Paradise) or HON-DO (本堂 Main Hall). On the cedar-moss lawn to the east of the path between the Shin-den and the Hon-do stands a statue

2. Coates and Ishizuka, *op. cit.,* page 100.

of Jizo, the guardian deity of children and wayfarers. The nearby garden was originally made in the 12th century by Shiba Hosshi. It is called Ukiyo-en (有清園 Pure Presence Garden), and its pond is Kudoku-ike, Charity Pond. A maple tree to the left of the path is said to be three hundred years old; beyond it is another Jizo. Sanzen-in is famous for the color of its maples in the fall.

The Hon-do was constructed by Eshin in 985 and rebuilt once, in 1143.

Originally this building was profusely decorated inside; every exposed surface was painted, whether with pictures of deities or pure decoration. The concave ceiling—called *funazoko* because its shape resembles that of the inside of a boat—was covered with pictures of Buddha's 25 Bosatsu; the walls depicted the Diamond and Womb worlds of Shingon philosophy—complicated, highly formal paintings in which hundreds of Buddhas are depicted in precise positions (it is said over 3000 such figures once covered the walls); the rough-hewn pillars, and the beams and walls, were decorated with ornate, colorful designs.

The paintings on the "boat ceiling" have disappeared, leaving it bare and dark. The wall paintings—which may have been done by Eshin, or by someone else as late as the 12th century—survive only in framed fragments hanging about the hall. Traces of the wall and beam decoration can be made out here and there, particularly on the partition behind the central image. This partition was once decorated on both sides, but the original surface of its back is gone.

The principal image, of Amida, was sculptured by Eshin in 985. Among its distinguishing characteristics is the method of construction, for it is hollow and made from many carefully fitted pieces of cypress wood. Earlier sculptures were invariably of a single piece, and hence tended to be tall (often standing) and narrow. Amida's relatively human countenance is indicative of the more benevolent concepts of Buddhism after the Nara period. The halo *(kohai)* behind Amida, also Eshin's work, deserves close examination. Besides its profuse ornamentation, it contains the detailed images of 13 different minor Buddhas.

The method used in the construction of hollow images, called *yosegi-zukuri* (寄木作 assorted-wood construction), should be commented upon. The image is built up of thin wood sections, or blocks, but before the finish is applied it is covered with linen or other fine cloth glued on in layers until the joints of the wood are effectively covered and the surface is smooth. Black lacquer is then applied in coats of increasing fineness that eliminate all trace of the cloth, and finally the image is gilded. Where old images are worn or damaged one can often make out the layers of construction by looking closely.

Amida's two attendants, Seishi and Kannon, are also of hollow joined cypress, but they date from a century to 150 years later than Amida. The only date related to either of them is found on the platform under Seishi—1148. The images could be of that date or earlier. Certainly the Heian "benevolence" mentioned above is more pronounced in these figures than it is in Amida. Their kneeling position is unusual, as the attendants in a Buddhist trinity generally stand.

Seishi and Kannon always accompany Amida when he comes to receive the soul of a dying man. Kannon bears a lotus blossom on which to deposit the soul and Seishi prays for it. Kannon's name is discussed above; Seishi Bosatsu receives his Sanskrit name, Mahasthamaprapta, from the following passage of the Meditation Sutra: "With the light of wisdom the Bodhisattva Seishi shines over all sentient beings, and as he has *the highest authority* (mahasthamaprapta) easily brings them deliverance from the bondage of the three evil states."[3] As Kannon represents mercy, so Seishi generally represents wisdom.

The black lacquer platform around the three images is old but of uncertain date. It is inlaid with designs in mother-of-pearl.

At Sanzen-in the Amida trinity faces south. From the introduction of Buddhism to Japan until the 11th century this was the customary direction for all temples to face. However, the introduction of mountain monasteries such as Enryaku-ji had forced exceptions to this rule where the terrain made adherence impossible. Then later sects which emphasized the arrival of Amida from the Western Paradise adopted a new uniformity in which their temples always faced east. This trend began within a century of the building of Ojo-gokuraku-in.

There is a fine camellia tree southwest of the hall.

4. KYAKU-DEN (客殿 Guest Palace). The Kyaku-den was built in 1587. After the *monzeki* moved to Kyoto in 1698, it became the

---

3. Coates and Ishizuka, *op. cit.,* page 100.

temple residence of the abbot-prince, although apparently he used it rarely. Kyaku-den received the relics of the *monzeki* when they were sent from Kyoto in 1868. Since 1871 it has been a true *monzeki* residence, and to reflect its increased stature Kyaku-den was totally refurbished early in this century. All the *fusuma* date from this restoration. The building is usually shown to visitors last; so the rooms are discussed clockwise from the northeast corner of the building (see map 2).

a. HALLWAY EAST-WEST. At the east end of this hallway there hangs a painting of Eshin by an unknown painter, done after his death. In a small altar at the same place is the image of Ganzan Daishi.[4] The curtain of this altar is decorated with the sixteen-petaled chrysanthemum crest, associated both with the Tendai sect and with the imperial family.

b. LIVING ROOM, 8 mats. On the north wall is a portrait of Ennin, third head priest of Enryaku-ji. The *fusuma* were painted in 1909 by Takeuchi Seiho. The scene is near modern Hakone in eastern Japan, seen at dawn. The painting is in black and white, but the addition of an olive sky casts an impressive gloom over the scene. It covers the south and west walls and on the north wall extends to the small cupboard panels over the tokonoma (alcove). On the left panel of the cupboard is painted a small cuckoo in flight, the only moving object in a vast expanse of stillness.

c. AUDIENCE ROOM, 8 mats. The tokonoma here contains a painting of Gundari Yasha Myo-o, another of the five wrathful light kings (Myo-o), who is believed to be Kannon in another form. The anger in his face reflects his reaction to the crimes of mortals. He has eight arms, and green snakes around his legs.

The *fusuma* in this room were painted by Kikuchi Hobun in 1909–10. The scene is evening on the coast of the Inland Sea near Suma-Mikage, and the birds depicted are coastal plover.

d. WAITING ROOM, 8 mats. This room is a waiting room for servants or visitors; therefore it has no alcove. Lacking permanent walls, it can be opened into the adjoining rooms in order to enlarge them.

Its twelve interior *fusuma* were painted by Suzuki Shonen in

4. See under Enryaku-ji, para. 9.

1905. The painting, which has the mood of an El Greco, shows Shaka Nyorai on a mountain among pines, practicing acts and sayings which will give him wisdom. The peasant praying on his knees next to him bears a striking and presumably intentional resemblance to Seishi Bosatsu of the Hon-do in both his posture and his position. Another interesting aspect of this painting is that the pine tree branches form the portrait of a dragon. The head is on the extreme left, while other branches form the claws and tail.

e. The HALLWAY along the exterior of these rooms is for armed guards of the prince and under normal living conditions would be screened off from the rooms inside.

f. Kyaku-den faces south on a SMALL POND AND GARDEN, Juheki-en. This arrangement of building and garden is called *shinden-zukuri,* a court style introduced in the Heian period and often found at *monzeki* temples. The pond is meant to resemble the shape of the character *shin* (心 heart, mind) and is therefore called *shinji-gata* (*shin*-character pond). This shape is very popular around Ohara.

g. HALLWAY in the southwest corner of the building. The glass case on the west wall holds many of the *monzeki* articles which were brought to Sanzen-in when the Kyoto *monzeki* was disestablished. The top shelf contains, among other things, wooden and paper letters and messages from various emperors.

The screens here were painted by Imao Keinen, a disciple of Suzuki Shonen (see para. d above). The painting is an interesting treatment of the subject of old age. Turtles are shown in a pond. Usually they are a symbol of longevity, but here they appear tired, and they are surrounded by lotus plants—some of them broken—which recall both the lotus pond in the Western Paradise and approaching death. There is a sadness about this pond which we whom it surrounds must share. The painter was sixty-five years old when he did these screens.

h. SIX-MAT ROOM. The only light for this small room comes from a peculiar tall skylight which reaches up through the ceiling to the roof far overhead. The *fusuma* on its south side, covered with the *kajii* crest, correspond to the north *fusuma* of the room described in d above. The *fusuma* on the north wall actually belong to the peripheral hallway (as a and e above), which is why they do not fit exactly here. They portray ducks on both sides, painted by Michizuki Ryokusen.

This room contains a screen on wheels which dates from the late 16th century. The cart of the latter is lacquered, and the painting of a huge flower on the upright panel is in the Momoyama style, although it was painted by Kamizaka Seka in the Meiji period. This screen is called *gosho-guruma* (御所車 palace cart).

i. Another six-mat room, north of the above, in which are displayed royal washing basins and water pitchers, huge and finely lacquered in black with the imperial crest in gold.

It is possible, of course, that the portable items in these rooms will not always be in the locations listed above.

# 平等院 Byodo-in
# Temple of Equality

1. UJI (宇治). A summer resort noted for its cormorant fishing and firefly hunting, Uji is most famous for its green tea, which was formerly raised for emperor and shogun alone. Since its cultivation began here more than seven centuries ago, Uji tea has been considered the finest in the land. At the north entrance to Byodo-in there is a large upright stone which is a monument to Uji tea. It was erected in 1887.

The Uji Bridge was first constructed about 647 by the priest Dosho (629–700), Japanese founder of the Hosso sect, and is renowned both for its longevity and for the colorful events connected with it. It was the scene of great battles in 1180 between Minamoto Yorimasa and the Taira and in 1184 between Minamoto Yoshinaka and his cousin Minamoto Yoshitsune. Lying on the road between Kyoto and Nara, it was the scene of numerous other encounters, and it figures prominently in many novels, including the famous *Genji Monogatari*. The small parapet near its west end is reputed to mark the spot where the war lord and connoisseur of tea Toyotomi Hideyoshi once dipped water for his brew. A dipping ceremony is held here annually on October first.

There is a stone pagoda on an island south of the bridge. It is a restoration of one erected by Dosho to commemorate the completion of Uji Bridge.

2. BYODO-IN: GENERAL HISTORY. The greatest of the Fujiwara ministers, Michinaga (966–1027), had a villa on this site which his son Yorimichi (992–1074) enlarged and converted into a temple in 1052. The Phoenix Hall was completed in 1053, and the Emperor Go-Reizei, Yorimichi's son-in-law, visited the place in 1067. The following year Yorimichi retired to Uji, where he lived out the remainder of his life. At this time the Byodo-in had 33 buildings, seven of them pagodas, but of them all only the Phoenix Hall has survived.

Byodo-in suffered long periods of neglect after the Fujiwara family lost its power in the 12th century. A great fire in 1483 apparently carried away all the buildings except the Phoenix Hall and the newer Tsuri-dono, including a last five-storied pagoda. Since that time the Phoenix Hall has had some periods of restoration—between much longer periods of neglect. Major work was done on it about 1680, and more recently between 1950–57, the latter at a cost of more than seventy million yen (about $195,000).

The present Byodo-in consists of only three structures: the Phoenix Hall, the Tsuri-dono, and the bell tower. The temple is maintained by the government, assisted by two neighboring temples, Jodo-in and Saisho-in.

Byodo-in was originally a temple of the Tendai sect, but its emphasis upon the worship of Amida caused it to be used in later centuries by the Jodo sect.

3. HO-O-DO (鳳凰堂 Phoenix Hall), called Amida-do until the Edo period.

a. THE GROUNDS are dominated by the large pond in front of the hall, which at one time apparently surrounded it completely. This must have protected the building from nearby fires. The present configuration of the pond dates from the late 16th century, when Toyotomi Hideyoshi built the dike which now separates it from the river and cut it down to a small stream behind the Phoenix Hall. The setting of the hall on the pond is a direct imitation of Chinese styles which had been introduced to Japan in painting and were popular during the Heian period. The pond can also be said to represent the lotus pond of Amida's Paradise.

The single stone lantern in front of the Phoenix Hall is probably as old as the building itself. In later centuries the single lantern gave way to twin lanterns, and the large openings in this one—which make it purely decorative, unable to shield a candle—are an element of the older lantern styles.

b. THE BUILDING. In shape it resembles a phoenix landing with wings outspread. The "wings" of the building are held off the ground by columns to heighten the effect of weightlessness. They are useless ornamentation: there is no access to them and

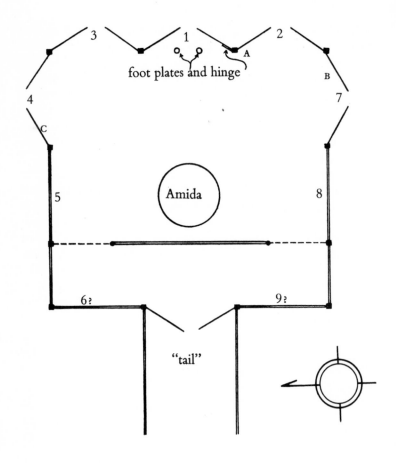

foot plates and hinge

Amida

"tail"

MAP THREE
Byodo-in Phoenix Hall

鳳凰堂

1–9  Levels of Paradise
A     Location of replacement statue
B     Painting of Amida's descent still visible
C     Painting depicting horses

their flattened interiors are too small for a man to stand in. The "tail" of the bird—the plain west wing of the building—is a controversial part that may have been added in a later century. In any case it contains nothing that is particularly noteworthy.

It is thus the "body" of the Phoenix—the temple proper—upon which interest centers. Its roof and foundation have recently been renewed, but the original wooden structure remains. Outside, the chamfered square columns are one indication of the building's age, for in later periods the chamfer grew smaller and eventually square columns were abandoned altogether. The faces of rafter ends extending out under the roof are decorated with ornate metal arabesques. The lower front roof itself is constructed in split levels characteristic of certain other Heian-period buildings, including the Hokai-ji, a temple near Uji. The small turrets at each end of the building—like most of its features purely ornamental—are reminiscent of similar structures which adorned the old Imperial Palace and which may today be seen on its modern replica, the Heian Shrine in Kyoto. Not surprisingly, the main roof of the Phoenix Hall is topped by twin phoenixes.

Inside, the visitor is presented with a tangible vision of Amida in his Paradise, slightly worn after 900 years here on earth. The doors in the front and side walls, and the walls in the back of the hall, still contain remnants of giant paintings that show dying souls being received into each of the nine levels of Paradise. All the interior beams and columns were once decorated with intricate colored designs which can still be picked out with a flashlight or spotlight, especially on the two columns of the partition behind Amida. Some sections of the ceiling and beam designs in the back of the hall have been restored to give an idea of their original appearance.

The ceiling is minutely coffered and was once covered with round bronze mirrors which, although blackened by age, can still be seen on the beams. Over the image of Amida there is a double canopy of cypress wood, ornately carved. The inner canopy is called *hanagai* (flower canopy) after its shape. The poles hanging from the ceiling once supported curtains.

In the midst of this ornamentation is the image of Amida, surrounded by the images of 52 followers which are fixed to the upper walls. It is not difficult to believe that these surroundings, seen through incense in the mirrored candlelight, must have convinced Yorimichi that he was indeed close to Amida and the Western Paradise.

There are two footplates with rings set in the sill of the front center entrance. These, and the lower hinge of the door on one's left as he approaches this entrance, are surviving metalwork of the original building (see map 3). The footplates are inlaid with gold. The other footplates and hinges are later—and relatively inferior— substitutes for lost originals.

c. THE SCULPTURE. The figures of Amida and his 52 attendants are the work of the sculptor Jocho (d. 1057) and his disciples. They are the only works in Japan today which are positively attributed to this famous sculptor, and coming as they did so close to the end of his life, they are considered to be his culminating accomplishment.

Jocho is not only admired as the sculptor who crystallized the new methods of the Heian period and bent them to style, but he was also the ancestor of several famous sculptors of later eras, most notable among them Unkei and his son Tankei of the Kamakura period.

Amida sheds serenity, calmness—the absence of desire. Seated with legs crossed, he appears balanced, settled, comfortable. His vacant stare seems to reflect nothing but inward thought. His high, smallish head and full chest are evidence of Jocho's loyalty to human proportions. His hands, folded in his lap in the "meditation position," denote the highest of his nine Paradises. His lips, neither open nor closed, make it seem that he is about to speak.

Amida's apparent serenity is broken if one kneels down before him, as Yorimichi must have done. It then transpires that Amida's eyes are directed straight down at the single worshiper, another strong indication of the personal use to which Yorimichi devoted this hall.

The figure is hollow, made of built-up sections of cypress like the Amida at Sanzen-in, but while the latter was a work executed in a revolutionary technique, this image shows the full potential of the established technique placed in the hands of a master. The figure is nine feet eight inches high. The *kohai* behind it, although it may resemble the original, dates from the later Kamakura period. It is also made of cypress, and has 13 minor Buddhas among its rising swirls.

Amida is seated on a stand of 64 lotus petals arranged in vertical columns of four—a departure which Jocho made from the more usual practice of staggering them.[1] The large platform under the stand was once inlaid with gold and pearl designs, now entirely picked out. The metal plates around the base of the platform, which depict animals and birds, were installed in the seventh month of the year Empo 8 (延寶八年 1680), as an inscription on one of them reveals. Most of the metalwork in the building dates from the great restoration of that time.

The 52 small figures about the upper walls are apparently replacements for Amida's more usual companions, Seishi and Kannon. The absence of the latter again emphasizes the personal nature of Yorimichi's communion with Amida. The small figures are made from single blocks of wood to which the projecting parts have been cleverly joined, and are about 20–25 inches in height. Their action postures and lively attitudes are unique among the sculpture of this period, and the musical instruments most of them hold are an interesting catalogue of the instruments used in that time.

Originally this heavenly host was painted and their backdrop was a mural depicting the 25 Bosatsu. During the Edo period it was decided that the mural could not be restored; so the wall was painted out, and the statues were mounted on boards painted with decorative cloud designs. These boards were in turn removed during the 1950's and the statues, which have become plain with age, are now handsomely mounted on the bare white wall. The original three-dimensional, many-colored frieze was an innovation not to be equaled until the gaudy days of the 16th century, but one cannot help feeling that the present arrangement is the finest one.

Only one of the figures is not original: the one closest to and south of the main entrance is a later copy (see map 3, "A").

d. THE PAINTINGS. The paintings around the inside of the hall, on the double doors and lower walls, are representations of souls

1. Prewar photos show these petals in a staggered arrangement, so their vertical arrangement must have been recreated during the restoration of the 1950's. This was, however, Jocho's custom. In arranging the petals of the lotus stand vertically he was virtually alone among sculptors.

being received into each of the nine levels of the Western Paradise by Amida and his heavenly retinue. They are attributed to an 11th-century painter named Tamenari, and show elements of the early Japanese national style. The partition behind Amida also contains an 11th-century painting, but it is not connected with the others, being of a Chinese pavilion with wings and towers not unlike those of the Phoenix Hall itself.

The Paradise scenes were placed about the hall in the order indicated on map 3.

The original locations of the sixth and ninth levels are not clear. The double door now at the back of the hall contains remnants of paintings which do not fit it, and since the side bays in back are now bare, it is thought that these paintings may originally have belonged to them. This has raised the further possibility that these two bays originally had doors, and that the center bay in back may or may not have had a door, thus adding to speculation that the back of the building was originally different than it is now, and that the "tail" was a later addition or mutation. The ill-fitting paintings were probably placed on the present back doors in the Edo period.

Unfortunately centuries of neglect and the autographs of those who visited the temple in its untended periods have badly disfigured all the paintings. As the damaged places reveal, these paintings were done on linen over wood.

The best preserved of them is that of the seventh level although it is covered with writing and dates, mostly from the Bunka and Bunsei eras (1804–1830). Nevertheless its left-hand door (map 3, "B") clearly shows Amida, Seishi, Kannon, and the attending host approaching the house of a dying man who is illuminated by their beam of light. The left-hand door of the fourth level (map 3, "C") also has a good section which shows horses and cherry blossoms. Here and there on the other panels interesting details can be made out.

e. THE "TAIL." This part of the building is simple in design compared to the rest, and besides the apparent changes in its doors, mentioned above, its cusped-arch windows indicate that it may have been a later addition, for such windows were introduced by the Zen sect in the 13th century. It is possible that the 16th century change in the configuration of the pond produced enough land for this addition.

The painted panels which were hung behind the small images in the Edo period now hang here in the "tail"; otherwise it is empty.

4. KANNON-DO (観音堂 Kannon Hall) or TSURI-DONO (釣殿). A "fishing hall" *(tsuri-dono)* was a building common to Heian period villas, and the position of this one north of the Phoenix Hall is probably an indication of the course of the Uji River before the dike was built in the 16th century. The present structure dates from the Kamakura period and houses an eleven-faced Kannon which was made in the late Heian period. Minor figures at the sides, Jizo and Fudo Myo-o (with two small guardians), are of the Kamakura period. The gold-leaf paintings of guardian deities on the box altar around Kannon date from the Edo period.

At the northwest corner of Kannon-do a small triangular plot set off by a fence marks the spot where, in 1180, Minamoto Yorimasa killed himself after the battle at Uji Bridge.

Yorimasa's tomb is at Saicho-in behind the Phoenix Hall, where many relics of him are preserved, including one of the earliest forebears of the present Japanese national flag.

Tsuri-dono served as a hiding place for the legitimate Emperor Go-Daigo in 1330, during the period of two emperors. It is said that he fished from the hall. He was captured there by the rival army and taken to Kyoto where, upon being required to turn over the imperial regalia—the symbol of imperial authority —he successfully palmed off a forged set.

5. BELL TOWER. The bell is said to be more than nine hundred years old and to have come from India. For a long time it was kept in the Tsuri-dono, but now it has its own belfry south of the Phoenix Hall. The little pamphlet given out by the temple says this of its bell:

"In Japan, there are three bells well known for their sonic beauty, lettering and shape. The bell of Miidera near Lake Biwa is the best for its sound, the one in Jingoji near Kyoto, for the beauty of its calligraphy, and the one here, for its shape."

# 寂光院 Jakko-in
## Solitary Light Temple

1. GENERAL HISTORY. A sign at the entrance to Jakko-in says:

*It is said that this nunnery was originally erected by Prince Shotoku around 600 A.D. . . . . According to the temple's history, the image of Jizo Bosatsu (Ksitigarbha–Bodhisattva), the guardian deity of children, in the main hall was carved by Prince Shotoku himself.*

This is unreliable history. Shotoku Taishi (572–621) was the first forceful proponent of Buddhism after it was introduced to Japan in 552. Although the capital was then near Nara, it is not impossible that he could have founded Jakko-in: Koryu-ji in western Kyoto, for example, was founded in his memory in 622. However, whether or not he originally founded it, Jakko-in as we know it today is a Tendai nunnery—the Tendai sect reached Japan two centuries after Shotoku's time—and everything in the nunnery with the possible exception of the image of Jizo centers on the 12th century or later, as does the role of Jakko-in in Japanese history.

When the Taira clan was annihilated by the Minamoto clan at Dan-no-ura in 1185, the only survivor of the slaughtered Taira was Kenrei-mon-in (1155–1213), daughter of the great Taira minister Kiyomori, widow of the 80th emperor, Takakura—who had died in 1181—and mother of the infant 81st emperor, Antoku, who had drowned with his grandmother at Dan-no-ura. She was brought back to Kyoto, where she became a nun at Choraku-ji. In the seventh month of that year her dwelling collapsed in an earthquake, and in the ninth month she went north to Jakko-in. She lived out the remainder of her life there.

In the late spring of 1186 the *ho-o* (retired emperor become priest) Go-Shirakawa, who had adopted her as his daughter when she was young, visited Kenrei-mon-in at her retreat.

All these events are minutely recorded in the *Heike Monogatari,* a historical novel of this period which is one of the most famous in Japan's history.

240

Kenrei-mon-in became head priestess of Jakko-in, and we are told that every one of her successors has been a princess from "a noted family." She died in 1213, and her imperial tomb is near the nunnery.

Although the buildings generally date from her time, a major restoration was performed on them in 1603 by Toyotomi Hide-yori, the son of Hideyoshi, at the instance of his mother.

## 2. THE BUILDINGS.

a. HON-DO (本堂 Main Hall). The outside, and the front half of the inside of this building are the work of Hideyori, who con-verted its original Chinese-style mud floor to the present Japanese floor. The rear half of the hall, however, is preserved from the 12th century.

The main image here is Jizo Bosatsu, holding his customary staff and jewel.

As the guardian of dead children and travelers, whether or not Jizo preceded her time, it was most fitting that Kenrei-mon-in, who lived out her life in prayer for her annihilated family, should pray to Jizo, both as the mother of the dead infant emperor (Antoku was born in 1178, ascended the throne in 1180, and died in 1185), and as the only member of the Taira clan who had returned from the long journey in retreat to the western end of Japan.

On the wall behind Jizo and above him on each side are shelves crammed with tiny Buddhist images, held onto them by wire netting. The number of images is variously given as 30,000 or 60,000; suffice to say there are many, far too many to count.

The back of the building—the older half—contains on the sides memorial tablets to the dead, and on the back wall two statues, set in glass cases. The one on the left is of Kenrei-mon-in, and the one on the right, of her faithful companion, Awa-no-Naishi. The statue of Kenrei-mon-in is said by the nunnery to date from the 13th century, but Ponsonby-Fane says it is a 17th-century work. She sits cross-legged, her hands raised in prayer.

The life-sized bust of Awa-no-Naishi is clothed in material said to have been used by Kenrei-mon-in herself, and the curtain that shields it inside the case is said to be material once owned by the infant Antoku. (*Heike Monogatari* says that Kenrei-mon-in gave the last remnant of Antoku's clothes to the temple in Kyoto where she became a nun.)

## MAP FOUR
Jakko-in (Sho-in)

寂光院

*Numbers refer to para.
2b. below*

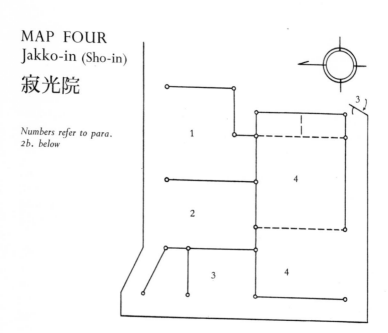

b. SHO-IN (書院 study or parlor). This is the building in which Kenrei-mon-in lived. It was restored in the 19th century, during the reign of the Emperor Meiji, at the wish of Komatsu-no-Miya, Akihito Shinno (1846–1903). The *fusuma* of the Sho-in were painted by artists of the Meiji period.

(1) The northeast room, seven mats. Its screens, painted by Hara Zaisen, show the peaceful bay at Dan-no-ura, where the Taira clan was slaughtered by the Minamoto.

(2) The northwest room, six mats. The *fusuma* painting of ivy arbors is by Tsuji Kako, who evidently took up the challenge from the following passage in the *Heike Monogatari's* description of Go-Shirakawa's visit:

"Pleasant was the sound of the water as it fell from the clefts of the time-worn rocks, and the ivied walls and beetling crags would have defied the brush of the painter. When His Majesty came to the cell of the former Empress, ivy was growing on the eaves and the morning-glory was climbing up them; the hare's-foot fern and the day-lily mingled together, and here and there was a useless gourd plant."[1]

(3) The west room, three mats, contains a monkey painted by Miyake Gogyo, who also painted the long-tailed cock on the door at the end of the south verandah.

(4) The south rooms, or *sho-in* proper, consist of an eight-mat chamber and its eight-mat anteroom; they can be converted to a single room by removing the screens between them. In the anteroom there are two boxes: one contains straw sandals said to have been worn by Go-Shirakawa when he made his visit; the other contains a piece of old wood said to be part of the ship from which Kenrei-mon-in's mother and son leaped to their deaths, and from which Kenrei-mon-in also leaped in her vain attempt to drown herself.

The inside room has portable screens painted by Tosa Mitsu-nobu (1434–1525). It has a framed needlework design of the characters for "Namu Amida Butsu" woven by Kenrei-mon-in from her own hair. Also, a box in the tokonoma contains a scroll of "Ohara Goko," the account of Go-Shirakawa's imperial trip *(goko)* and visit here in *Heike Monogatari*.

The partition between the two rooms has cutout designs of the chrysanthemum *(kiku)* and paulownia *(kiri)* crests, which are the ones used by the imperial house.

c. TEAHOUSE. Southeast of the Sho-in—below it on the hill and next to the pond there—is the teahouse built in 1929 by order of the present emperor.

3. THE GROUNDS AND GARDEN. Everything on the grounds, with the exception of the iron lanterns with the *kiri* crest from Toyo-tomi Hideyori's time, seems to be connected in some way with Go-Shirakawa's visit. The pond to the left of the entrance is in the popular *shin* shape.[2] The pine tree north of it, which was formerly covered with wisteria, they claim to be a thousand years old. The roots of a cherry tree, fenced off on the pond's south side, are said to be those of the tree to which Go-Shirakawa addressed his poem when he entered the nunnery grounds. Additional wood from this former tree lies under the bell.

1. Sadler, *op. cit.,* pages 246–47.
2. Cf. Sanzen-in, para. 4f, above.

This is how Jakko-in appeared to Go-Shirakawa when he arrived:

". . . the pond and trees of the ancient garden were dignified; the young grass had grown thick, and the slender shoots of the willow were all hanging in confusion, while the floating water-plants on the pond might be mistaken for spread-out brocade. On the island the purple hue of the flowering wisteria mingled with the green of the pine-tree, while the late blooming cherry among the green leaves was more rare than the early blossoms. From the eight-fold clouds of the kerria that was flowering in profusion on the bank came the call of the cuckoo, a note of welcome in honour of His Majesty's visit."[3]

The garden extends between the Hon-do and Sho-in; the waterfall which Go-Shirakawa noted [para. 2b(2) above] drops here in three stages to a small pond. Like the waterfalls of most "hill gardens," it is recessed and, dropping in stages that are hidden in the hill, it attempts to give the same impression that one would get from a much larger fall seen on a distant mountain. The mood of the whole garden, in keeping with the tale of Kenrei-mon-in, is a melancholy one.

The west gate leads to a path up the hill where there is a small, abandoned Shinto shrine.

4. KENREI-MON-IN'S TOMB. The tomb is on the same hill as Jakko-in, reached by a flight of stone steps east of the flight to the nunnery. It is not, in its present state, old, since all imperial tombs were restored after the Meiji Restoration, and this one was un-doubtedly put in its present form at the same time. Since the em-perors were powerless in her time, it is unlikely that Kenrei-mon-in originally had any tomb at all—at least no more than a simple marker. This would also have been in keeping with the strong Buddhist influence over imperial burials at that time.

5. OHARA (大原 Big Field). There are several small temples near Sanzen-in. Other points of interest include (see map 18):

a. OHARA MAUSOLEUM. An imperial tomb close to Sanzen-in that contains the remains of the Emperors Go-Toba (82nd, ruled

3. Sadler, *op. cit.*, page 246.

1184–98) and his son Juntoku (84th, ruled 1210–21). For more on Go-Toba, see chapter 7. Both died in exile—Go-Toba in 1239, Juntoku in 1242. The tombs were finally identified and restored about 1888.

b. OBORO-NO-SHIMIZU (朧の清水 clear water seen in the hazy moonlight). This is a tiny spring under a shrub on the right-hand side of the path of Jakko-in. *Oboro* (vague, hazy) implies hazy moonlight and its season, spring. The sign here says that on her way to Jakko-in Kenrei-mon-in saw her face reflected in this pool by the moonlight—hence the name. In *Heike Monogatari,* however, she comes to Jakko-in on a rainy fall day. Perhaps she made the moonlight trip some other time.

c. OHARA WOMEN. The women of Ohara are noted for their fine posture, which results from the unusual practice of carrying bundles—especially of twigs or bracken—on their heads. At the present time it seems fair to say that the decreased need for such a method of transporting bracken, and the increased number of visitors to Ohara, have changed this practice from one dictated by necessity to one dictated by tourism. It is successful, for a woman topped by a bundle of twigs is the nationally recognized symbol for Ohara.

Concerning the women of Ohara, Murray's *Handbook* (1894) says: "From time immemorial, nurses for infants of the Imperial house have been drawn from among these stalwart women."

The current *Official Guide to Japan* has this to say of them: ". . . the women carry heavy loads on their heads and thus they have a very fine bearing. Their dress is also peculiar, as they wear narrow *obi* (sashes), and cover their heads with kerchiefs while over their legs and arms they wear white cotton-cloth. Parties of these naive peasant-women may frequently be seen in the streets of Kyoto, selling flowers or carrying heavy merchandise." They are not so naive, nor so likely to be seen in Kyoto, today as they were back in the days when the *Official Guide* first printed that statement.

# Anraku-ji and Honen-in

*Anraku-ji, Honen-in, Ginkaku-ji, and Jodo-in all lie on the path that was used for his daily walk by the famous Japanese philosopher, Nishida Kitaro (1870–1945). Since the tomb of the Emperor Reizei and the nunnery Reikan-ji also lie on this path, brief notes on these two places have been added here for the reader who wishes to follow Nishida Kitaro's route, as well as a map (map 5) of the route.*

## 冷泉天皇 桜本陵 Reizei Tenno Sakura Hon-ryo Emperor Reizei's Cherry Tomb

REIZEI (lit., cold spring) was the 63rd emperor. Born in 950, he ruled from 967–69. He was sickly and was unable to go to the palace for his enthronement ceremony. Poor health induced him to abdicate two years after ascending, but curiously he lived on in retirement until 1011.

The imperial tombs of this period were very modest, in contrast to the great mounds raised over earlier emperors. New philosophies, the Buddhist practice of cremation, and imperial poverty all contributed to the small size of Heian tombs. This tomb was lost and forgotten for several centuries. When all the imperial tombs were restored after the Meiji Restoration, Reizei's was one of the last to be found. It was at that time—in 1888—that it was provided the standard stone and wood accoutrements which it has today.

The sanctity of the imperial tomb prevents its formal cultivation. Thus the tomb is little more than an overgrown plot of land. There is a moss path around it which makes a pleasant walk (one should explain his intentions to the guard—see appendix III), but the inner confine may not be entered.

A classic picture of life in Reizei's time is contained in the famous novel *Genji Monogatari* that was written about the year 1000. The names of Reizei and of his uncle the Emperor Suzaku are used in the book, but the emperors portrayed are fictional ones.

# 霊鑑寺 Reikan-ji
## Sacred Mirror Temple

1. GENERAL HISTORY. Reikan-ji is a nunnery of the Rinzai branch of the Zen sect. It was established in 1654 for the tenth daughter of the retired Emperor Go-Mizu-no-o, and she was named its founder. The temple received relics from the ruins of an ancient temple called Nyoi-ji which was farther up the side of the mountain (Nyoi-ga-take); among them was an image of Nyoirin Kannon and a sacred mirror *(reikan)*.

From the time of its founding until the Meiji Restoration Reikan-ji was a *monzeki* nunnery that always had a princess for its abbess. Since the Restoration its abbesses have been drawn from the nobility.

During the 18th century Reikan-ji ran somewhat to ruin, but it was restored by the Tokugawa shogunate early in the 19th century (1801–4).

2. BUILDINGS AND GARDENS. The principal buildings are the Sho-in (書院) and, east of it, the Hon-do (本堂). The former possesses paintings by Kano Motonobu (1477–1559) while the latter houses the image of Nyoirin Kannon mentioned above.

In this manifestation Kannon possesses a gem which enables the satisfaction of all worldly desires, and thus is worshiped as omnipotent.

The buildings are connected by a corridor and separated by a wall. Outside this wall there is a small sand garden which, when tended, is raked in symbolic patterns. Beyond the wall the inner garden has two levels: the lower level of moss and sand is a kind of link between the outside garden and the upper level, which is covered with flowering bushes and trees. A path leads under the corridor between the buildings to another section of the garden which is similar.

The flowering trees, which are particularly fine in the northeast part of the garden, include red and white camellias and plums

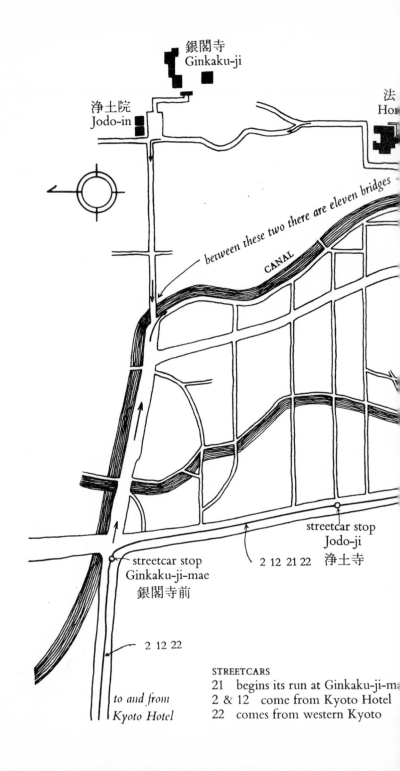

銀閣寺
Ginkaku-ji

浄土院
Jodo-in

法
Hon

*between these two there are eleven bridges*

CANAL

streetcar stop
Jodo-ji
浄土寺

2 12 21 22

streetcar stop
Ginkaku-ji-mae
銀閣寺前

2 12 22

*to and from*
*Kyoto Hotel*

STREETCARS
21    begins its run at Ginkaku-ji-ma
2 & 12   come from Kyoto Hotel
22    comes from western Kyoto

安楽寺
Anraku-ji

Two court ladies' tombs

■ Tombs of Anraku
& Juren

霊鑑寺
Reikan-ji

[Notre Dame
Convent]

冷泉天皇帝陵
Tomb of Reizei

示

Sakura-bashi*

streetcar stop
Kinrin-shako-mae
錦林車庫前

streetcar
barn

MAP FIVE
The Philosopher's Walk

*Sakura-bashi:
each corner of the
bridge has such a
stone post.

櫻
橋

NOTE: The route followed by Nishida Kitaro, the philosopher, is shown by **arrows**.

and cherries. There is also a white *ashibi* bush at the south end by the wall. It is a fine small garden.

The nunnery is not used to visitors, and although strangers are allowed on the grounds and readily admitted to the garden, it is difficult to gain access to the buildings without the help of an interpreter.

---

# 安楽寺 Anraku-ji
# Temple to Anraku

---

1. HISTORY. The events which led to the founding of this temple are fully recounted in chapter 7. Whether the temple was founded between Honen's return from exile in 1211 and his death in 1212 or at a slightly later date is uncertain. The tombs of the four principals in the scandal—Anraku, Juren, and the two court ladies—are all on the grounds of this temple.

Anraku was the son of the lay priest Morohide, a secretary of the Supreme Council of State, and he was noted for his ability at writing and speaking, so much so that in 1201, 1203, and 1204 he made trips to the seat of the shogunate, Kamakura, the last two times to fill speaking invitations. Juren, who was nearly forty when he was killed, was the son of Jippen, a samurai of the powerful Kofuku-ji in Nara.

Both tombs and buildings have undergone various restorations since the 13th century, but because of its small size Anraku-ji can be assumed to have changed little in most respects. It is, of course, a temple of Honen's Jodo sect.

2. THE GROUNDS. Like those of all temples in this area, the grounds of Anraku-ji are well planted and have fine camellia trees. They are divided by two paths which form a cross, intersecting in the middle of the temple yard. At the west end of this cross is the gate and entrance to the temple. At its north end stands the Hon-do, with two small thatched Shinto shrines nearby. At the east end, up some steps, are the tombs of the two court ladies, Matsu-

mushi and Suzumushi, surrounded by a low fence. These tombs were restored in 1897. The tombs of Anraku and Juren stand to the left at the end of the south path. They too have a low fence around them, and they were restored in 1904. There are many other tombs in the southern and eastern sections of the grounds and near the main gate, but these four are easy to find. A signpost where the paths cross points the way to them.

3. THE HON-DO (本堂 Main Hall). This is the chief building of the temple. East of it stand the apartments, and the small Shinto shrines previously mentioned are the only other structures on the grounds. Originally built in the 13th century, the Hon-do was later destroyed. The present building dates from around 1581. (To enter, see appendix III.)

The central trinity in this hall of Amida, Seishi, and Kannon is said to be the work of Eshin (942–1017). Near Seishi is a fourth image, of Jizo, which is said to be older than the trinity.

The left-hand altar also has a trinity of sorts. Here the central image is of Honen, enshrined in a miniature temple and covered with paper upon which is written countless times "Namu Amida Butsu" (南無阿弥陀仏). It is said Honen himself carved this image after returning from exile, but this is doubtful. At Honen's right hand on this altar is an image of Shinran Shonin (1173–1262), who founded the Shin sect based on the Jodo. The image is said to be about 600 years old, and to show Shinran at the time of his exile to Echigo. The third image is of Kannon, and is of uncertain date.

The right-hand altar contains images of Anraku, Juren, Matsu-mushi, and Suzumushi. The court ladies are depicted as nuns with Matsumushi on the beholder's left. Behind them are the two priests, Anraku being on the left.

The Hon-do deserves careful inspection. Neglected and rarely visited, it gives one a good picture of the fast-disappearing small country temple. In addition its images relate it to the three main figures in the history of Buddhist fundamentalism—Eshin, Honen, and Shinran.

# 法然院 Honen-in
# Temple to Honen

1. HISTORY. Honen-in was originally established about the beginning of the 13th century. It was uphill from its present site and possessed little more than an image of Amida and a roof to cover it. The latter was quickly destroyed in persecutions of the Jodo sect, and thereafter Amida sat bare on the hillside. Honen-in existed in this homeless Amida and its believers and had no structures of note until the middle of the 17th century. Then the present Hon-do was built, and buildings from the 16th-century Fushimi castle of Toyotomi Hideyoshi were brought here and attached to it. Since that time the temple has flourished.

2. GROUNDS AND MINOR BUILDINGS. There are two entrances to the precinct from the road. Their paths enclose a fine bamboo thicket which has occasional giant camellias. Cedars line the main walk, and the eastern and southern sections of the outer grounds are taken up by a peaceful cemetery.

There is a belfry to the right of the inner gate. The bell is rung only at 4 a.m. and 4 p.m.

Inside the gate one passes between two large oblong mounds of sand—a kind of *karesansui* garden. They have designs raked in them, which are redone by the priests in turns every three or four days. The mound on the right usually depicts water in some form —a whirlpool, a stream—while the one on the left usually shows a flower or leaf. The design depends on the season and upon the whim of the priest making it.

Past these mounds are two buildings—on the right a sutra storehouse, and ahead on the left the old bathhouse of the temple, which is no longer used. The small pond between them is about fifty years old.

The walk is paved in a rough and natural way reminiscent of tea-ceremony styles. It is forced to turn right and left by the main complex of buildings ahead. The right path leads around

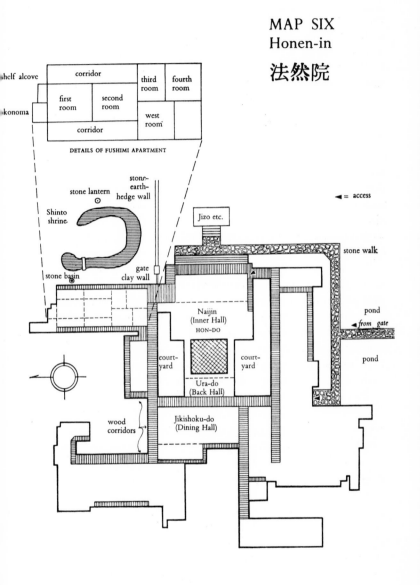

MAP SIX
Honen-in

法然院

DETAILS OF FUSHIMI APARTMENT

| shelf alcove | corridor | | third room | fourth room |
| | first room | second room | | |
| konoma | | | west room | |
| | corridor | | | |

stone lantern

Shinto shrine

stone-earth-hedge wall

Jizo etc.

◄ = access

stone walk

stone basin

gate
clay wall

Naijin
(Inner Hall)
HON-DO

pond

from gate

courtyard

courtyard

pond

Ura-do
(Back Hall)

wood corridors

Jikishoku-do
(Dining Hall)

to the east end of the Hon-do, across from which is a small shrine to Jizo set into the hill. There is also a large and symbolically marked replica of "Buddha's footprint" here. The left path leads to the entrance to the main complex of buildings, where the visitor is invited to knock on a board to gain free admission to the buildings and their garden.

### 3. THE MAIN BUILDINGS.

a. THE HON-DO. The Hon-do lies at the center of the main network of connected structures. The present hall dates from about 1640. It has a double roof and cusped-arch windows. Inside, its total area is about a hundred mats. The ceiling is bowed and ribbed in a style called *jabara-shiki*—"snake-body" or "bellows" —that is said to be duplicated only at Mampuku-ji in Obaku near Uji.

The image of Amida, like that at Anraku-ji, is said to be the work of Eshin. The position of its hands indicates the highest of Amida's nine Paradises. Before it, on the highly polished floor, lie 25 flowers that represent the 25 Bosatsu—a unique and beautiful display that is changed daily.

At the sides of the Hon-do are two courtyards, the northern of which contains three camellia trees—one red and white, one white, and one which blooms in seven colors. Nevertheless, the temple does not grow its "Bosatsu" flowers but finds it necessary to purchase them.

b. THE FUSHIMI APARTMENTS AND GARDEN. These rooms (two of 10, two of 8, one of 6, and two hallways of 10 mats each) were formerly an audience hall of Toyotomi Hideyoshi's Fushimi Castle. They were built in the late 16th century and transferred here in the 17th by the Tokugawa shogunate. The paintings are the work of Kano Mitsunobu (1561?–1608). The rooms have altogether only one tokonoma and shelf alcove; this indicates that they were originally used as a single unit. The host occupied the back room with the alcoves, and his visitor was shown to one of the other rooms, depending on his rank.

These apartments face onto the temple garden, which is set against a rising backdrop of deep woods. The garden is dominated by azaleas and contains a stone bridge, a stone tea basin (next to the building), and an old stone lantern. There is a crescent-shaped pond around an "island," from which steps lead up to a small Shinto shrine. The garden is separated from the rest of the grounds by a stone-earth-hedge wall.

c. OTHER DETAILS. Most of the other rooms in the main complex are apartments, studies, storehouses, and the like. The view to the west from the rooms on that side of the building is excellent. The priests' dining room, west of the Hon-do proper, contains an image of Monju.

*Ginkaku-ji and Jodo-in are discussed after Daitoku-ji, following the order of chapters in the first part of the book.*

# 大徳寺 Daitoku-ji
# Great Virtue Temple

1. GENERAL HISTORY. The priest Shuho Myocho (1282–1337, later Daito Kokushi) erected the first building of this temple in 1319, after he had studied the Zen sect at Kencho-ji in Kamakura and lived for twenty years among the beggars under Kyoto's Gojo Bridge to perfect his understanding. He converted the Emperors Hanazono and Go-Daigo to his sect, and with their backing his temple grew fast. It was officially sanctioned in 1324 and in 1333 was declared a place of worship for the imperial court.

The temple prospered until 1453, when it was damaged by a bad fire. Then in 1468 it was completely destroyed in the Onin War. In the 1470's the famous priest Ikkyu restored the temple with backing from the Emperor Go-Tsuchimikado.

During the 16th century Daitoku-ji was patronized by the prominent warriors of the time. It was in this period that most of its numerous sub-temples were founded. As one of the great Zen sect monasteries it prospered under the Tokugawa shoguns, but in the Buddhist persecutions that followed the Meiji Restoration it suffered considerable damage, especially to its sub-temples.

At present Daitoku-ji has more than twenty sub-temples on its grounds. Most of them are famous in their own right. The monastery possesses one of the finest collections of art treasures in Japan. Many of these are placed on display annually, in October.

2. THE BUILDINGS.

a. CHOKUSHI-MON (勅使門 Imperial Messenger Gate). This gate was constructed in 1590 and served as a gate of the Imperial Palace until 1640, when it was given to Daitoku-ji by the Empress Meisho. It is a fine example of the curved-gable style of the Momoyama period.

The tomb near the west side of the gate is that of Taira Yasuyori,

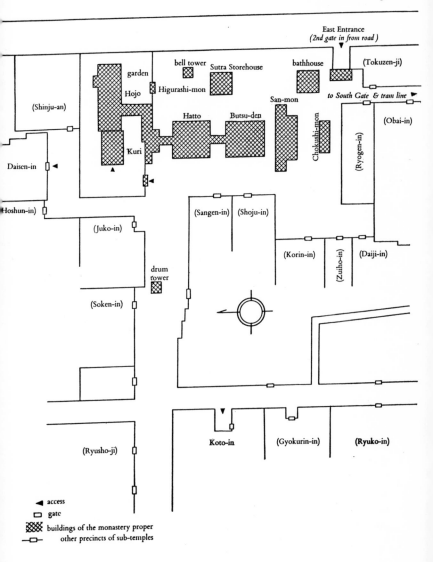

MAP SEVEN
Central Daitoku-ji

East Entrance
*(2nd gate in from road)*

(Shinju-an)

garden

bell tower

Sutra Storehouse

bathhouse

(Tokuzen-ji)

Hojo

Higurashi-mon

San-mon

*to South Gate & tram line* ▶

(Obai-in)

Hatto

Butsu-den

Chokushi-mon

(Ryogen-in)

Daisen-in

Kuri

Hoshun-in)

(Juko-in)

(Sangen-in)

(Shoju-in)

(Korin-in)

(Zuiho-in)

(Daiji-in)

drum tower

(Soken-in)

(Ryusho-ji)

Koto-in

(Gyokurin-in)

**(Ryuko-in)**

◀ access

gate

buildings of the monastery proper

other precincts of sub-temples

who was exiled after an unsuccessful plot to overthrow his family's ruling regime in 1177. He was later pardoned, but his dates are unknown.

b. SAN-MON (三門 Triple Gate). The lower half of this gate dates from a restoration of 1523–26, while the upper story was added about 1589 by the tea master Sen-no-Rikyu (1521–91). The latter section, profusely decorated inside by the painter Hasegawa Tohaku (1539–1610), contains several images, including a set of 16 Arhats originally brought from Korea.[1] There is also a statue of Rikyu himself, which when he first put it there so angered Toyotomi Hideyoshi that only the daring intercession of another priest prevented Hideyoshi from destroying the whole temple.

This gate has a plaque which says "Kimmo-kaku" (金毛閣 golden-hair pavilion), made by the 16th-century priest Sengaku Sodo, and the end-tiles of the roof are decorated with the character for gold (金).

The idea of a main gate with a usable second story was introduced in the Kamakura period by the larger Zen temples. In order to reach the upper story a stairway was needed, and since there was no place for one inside the structure, stairways were put up outside, at either end, and completed by a small entry house at the foot of the steps. In the Edo period these stairhouses grew until they became buildings of considerable size, such as those which can now be seen at the main gate to Zojo-ji, Shiba Park, Tokyo, or at the gate of Nanzen-ji, Kyoto.

c. BUTSU-DEN (仏殿 Buddha Hall). The present structure dates from 1665. Its principal image is Shaka, seated on a lotus blossom decorated with wheels, the symbol of Buddhist law. In two alcoves along the back wall are six other images, given in 1540; the three memorial tablets in front of Shaka are for the Emperor Go-Daigo, Daito Kokushi, and Tetto Giko (Daito's successor). The painting of two angels amid clouds and other now faded surroundings on the ceiling is by Kano Motonobu (1477–1559) and was originally in the Hatto (see below). The clouds and drag-

1. The Arhats often appear in the upper rooms of these gates. Usually associated with Hinayana Buddhism, they are beings who have attained Nirvana while still in this world.

on on the sliding screens behind the altar were painted by Kaiho Yusho (1533–1615).

Among the details of this building which make it characteristic of the architecture imported by the Zen sect are the cusped-arch windows, the tile floor, the suspended swinging wood doors, and the curved lateral interior beam—the last used in China to connect members on two levels but in Japan reduced to a purely decorative function.

The plaque hanging under the outside eaves of the hall says *kito* (祈禱 prayer) and symbolizes the use of the temple as a worshiping-place by Go-Daigo and other emperors. The large camphor tree in front of the building was given by Toyotomi Hideyoshi.

d. HATTO (法堂 Lecture Hall). Daitoku-ji's first building was a lecture hall, but it burned many times, and the present hall dates from 1636. It was presented by the Inaba family at ceremonies celebrating Daitoku-ji's 300th anniversary.

The sole furniture of the building is the abbot's throne near the back, with a canopy hanging over it. The dragon on the ceiling, a standard component of orthodox Zen sect lecture halls, was painted by the famous Kano Tanyu (1602–74). Architecturally the Hatto, like the Butsu-den, is characteristic of the imported Zen sect style, called *kara-yo*.

The Zen sect returned to the practice of pre-Heian Buddhism in which the worship hall was designed to hold the clerical congregation only. Thus the temple buildings, unlike those of the Tendai and Shingon sects, are symmetrical in plan without an extra space added for lay worshipers. In both the Butsu-den and the Hatto this symmetry is interrupted only by a raised platform in the back—in the Butsu-den it is the altar, and in the Hatto, the abbot's lecture throne.

Despite the dates of their building, halls like this Butsu-den and Hatto reflect the traditional style and alignment of Zen sect buildings. In rebuilding, original plans were followed, and the standard alignment of the halls was maintained. Japanese Zen sect monasteries owe to China not only many of their architectural standards but also the positions of their principal structures, which wherever possible were placed on a single axis, all facing south.

e. HOJO (方丈 Superior's Quarters). Although its origins go

back to the 14th century, the present Hojo dates from 1636, when it was rebuilt on its present site to make room for the new Hatto. It is a rectangular building opening on the wide side to the south, consisting of eight rooms:

(West)   A (12 mats)   C        E        G (12)   (East)
         B (24)                D (24)   F (24)   H (24)

The fusuma paintings of the Hojo are by Kano Tanyu. They are done in *sumi-e* (ink—i.e., black and white) and are of various scenes in China.

Room B has a plaque outside it listing the temples which belong to Daitoku-ji's wing of the Rinzai branch of the Zen sect. Inside rooms B and A are displayed portable screens of seasonal activities which are changed to correspond to the appropriate time of the year. These were painted by Kano Tansaku.

Room C is the altar room and contains the main image—Shaka—and memorial tablets.

Room D, the abbot's room, contains a hanging scroll of Yoryu Kannon by an unknown painter, which was presented by the imperial house during the Meiji period. It is noteworthy in that the painting is made up not of lines but of tiny written characters which taken together form a sutra text.

Room E, Ummon-an (雲門庵 Cloud-Gate Arbor), is dedicated to the founder of the temple, Daito Kokushi. His statue is installed in the back of the room, which extends out the back of the building. There are many memorial tablets along the walls of this room, and at its front is a small fire urn which is in the stylized shape of an octopus *(tako)*. This was brought from Korea by Kato Kiyomasa (1562–1611), a general of Toyotomi Hideyoshi's expedition there in the 1590's.

On the north wall of room F hang two tablets which record conversations between Daito Kokushi and the Emperor Go-Daigo. The plaques were carved in the Edo period. Between them hangs a third plaque that says *reiko* (霊光 spiritual light), written by the temple's 15th-century patron, the Emperor Go-Tsuchimikado.

Room G sometimes contains a portable screen of cranes by Kano Tansen (d. 1728).

f. HOJO GARDENS. There are two famous gardens next to the

Hojo. They are in the *karesansui,* or dry style, being made of white gravel, stones, and background shrubbery.

The larger one, south of the building, is typical of the Muromachi-period Zen gardens in style, although it has been attributed to the priest Tenyu Joka (1586–1666).

It is symbolic, two rocks in the northwest corner representing the stream or waterfall outlet of the conventional garden, and the bushes and rocks in the opposite corner symbolizing mountains and cascades. The flat gravel spaces in the center, raked with modest patterns, could be the sea. This garden is a good example of the type discussed in chapter 8. Although its interpretation can be generally outlined, the essence of its meaning undoubtedly goes much deeper than concrete representations.

The east garden, attributed to Kobori Enshu (1576–1647), is a small one of fifteen stones between the Hojo and a nearby wall. Its style is similar, but it uses the trick of "borrowed scenery" to extend itself to the distant horizon.

This garden is a famous example of the "borrowed scenery" type. The shrubs behind it are used to lead the viewer's eye smoothly from the rocks and sand into the background, which originally was an avenue of pines along the Kamo River and, beyond that, Mt. Hiei. Perhaps it was meant to remind one of Mt. Fuji, seen from the famous pine-clad sand bar of Miho. The general intent was to give the garden an added depth by linking it to the distant scenery. Unfortunately, the growth of nearby trees and the advent of telephone poles, electric wires, and houses between the garden and the distant pine avenue have considerably diluted the effect.

g. KARA-MON (唐門 Chinese gate[2]). This gate, across the larger garden from the Hojo, is a relic of Toyotomi Hideyoshi's Kyoto palace Juraku-dai and perhaps also of his later Fushimi Castle. It was moved to its present location in the Taisho era (1912–26), although Daitoku-ji has possessed it since the time Hideyoshi's mansions were broken up in the 17th century. Its ornate carvings, best seen from outside the garden, are attributed to the famous carver Hidari Jingoro (d. 1634). The gate has the alternate name Higurashi-mon (日暮門) which implies one could spend the day until sunset examining its ornateness without boredom. This is a name often given to gates of this type.

2. I.e., in the style *(kara-yo)* imported by the sect from China.

h. KURI (庫裡 Priests' Quarters). This building is connected to the Hojo on its east side. Destroyed many times by fire, the Kuri was last rebuilt in 1636 from the dismantled materials of the former Hojo. So it is a 17th-century building made from 15th-century materials, since that former Hojo had been restored by Ikkyu in the Bummei era (1469–86) and stood on the site of the present Hatto for almost 200 years, until it was replaced by the present Hatto, moved north and rebuilt as Kuri, and the new Hojo built next to it.

i. MINOR BUILDINGS. As is customary, the bathhouse, sutra storehouse, bell tower, and drum tower are arrayed to the sides of the main file of buildings. Bathhouses are a standard part of large Zen sect temples; this one dates from 1622. The sutra storehouse was built in 1636 and contains a revolving bookcase, together with a statue of the Chinese man who is reputed to have invented it in the 6th century.

*Of the numerous sub-temples I have selected Daisen-in and Koto-in to be included here, because they are representative and also readily accessible to outsiders.*

3. DAISEN-IN (大仙院 Great Hermit Temple). This temple was founded in 1509 by Kogaku Soko (1465–1548), a brother of Rokkaku Takayori (d. 1520), a well-known war lord of his time. It is a small temple, consisting of an outer belfry and three principal buildings, Kyaku-den, Kuri, and Hon-do or Hojo. The last, surrounded on three sides by dry gardens, is the most important of the three.

The Hon-do is designed in *hojo* style, facing south on its wide side and divided into the conventional three sections. It is, incidentally, an early example of this architectural style. Its two west rooms, of twelve and six mats, contain an image of Kannon. Their *fusuma*, depicting birds and flowers, were painted by Kano Motonobu (1477–1559). In the central room, the Hojo proper, the *fusuma* have landscape paintings by So-ami (1472–1523). There is a statue of the founder here. In the east rooms—again twelve and six mats—the screens depict agricultural scenes, and are by Kano Utanosuke (or Yukinobu, 1513–75).

Of the three gardens around the Hon-do, the small one on the north side (Middle Garden) is insignificant.

The garden on the east side of the building is one of the most famous in all Japan. It is attributed to Kogaku (some say So-ami) and dates from about the time of the temple's founding.

The garden's fame results in part from the fact that it is built around a single rock, which formerly belonged to the shogun Ashikaga Yoshimasa (1435–90). Taking this rock for a ship—which it does resemble—the designer surrounded it with many others, together with white gravel and some small trees and bushes, to create a detailed landscape fitted into a space only a few feet wide. In the northeast corner of the garden are distant mountains and cascades (shrubs and rocks). A river of gravel gushes under bridges, between islands, over a dam. The ship sails south in this river. Traditional "crane" and "tortoise" islands line the route, and in the distance lies a mountainous seacoast—really only a foot or two away.

The third garden, on the south side of the Hon-do, is plain white gravel with a single tree in the distant corner.

The tree is a *sarasoju*—the kind under which Buddha passed into Nirvana. The two gardens may be related, for as the ship—a treasure ship, the ship of life—passes under the final bridge it will emerge in the calm wide sea which leads to the *sarasoju* tree. The message of these gardens is beautiful, wistful, and deep.

4. KOTO-IN (高桐院 High Paulownia Temple, perhaps after the paulownia crest of the Hosokawa family). This small temple was established in 1601 by Hosokawa Tadaoki (1563–1645), a leading warrior of the Momoyama period. A relative, Hosokawa Gyokuho, was named the temple's founder. The temple's connection to the Hosokawa family has continued to the present.

Tadaoki was born in Kyoto, and became a follower of Oda Nobunaga. Although he married the daughter of Akechi Mitsuhide, another of Nobunaga's followers, when the latter assassinated their lord Tadaoki broke with him and supported Toyotomi Hideyoshi. He took part in Hideyoshi's Korean expedition, and when Hideyoshi died threw in with Tokugawa Ieyasu, figuring prominently in the battle of Sekigahara, which brought Japan under that man's sway. Tadaoki later distinguished himself in the Osaka campaign of 1614–15, and in 1619 retired to become a Buddhist priest, taking the name Sansai (三斎), by which he is often known. He was tutored in tea ceremony by Sen-no-Rikyu and became an expert at the practice, being credited with founding the Sansai school of ceremonial tea and originating the *nijiriguchi* (wriggling-in entrance) of teahouse design.

Tadaoki's wife Tama (1563–1600) was the third daughter of Mitsuhide. She was famed for her beauty. She married Tadaoki at sixteen, but when her father murdered Nobunaga in 1582, she was sent away. Later she was allowed to return. In the meantime she had been baptized and given the name Gracia (1587), and henceforth she was a devout Catholic. In 1600, when she and other women were threatened with becoming hostages of Ishida Mitsunari, a war lord opposed to Ieyasu, Gracia obeyed the orders of her husband and committed suicide or had herself killed rather than submit to the enemy.

As at Daisen-in, the principal building of Koto-in is the Hon-do, facing south and designed in *hojo* style. The original Hon-do was burned in the anti-Buddhist campaign that followed the Meiji Restoration; the present one was built about the beginning of this century.

The west rooms are of ten and eight mats. The eight-mat room is a tearoom with a *sho-in* bay[3] and large *nijiriguchi* set into its west wall. The name of the room, Horai, appears on a plaque hanging on the east wall. The plaque was written by Hosokawa Koshaku about fifty years ago. The north wall of the room is taken up by a tokonoma and a one-mat passage to the pantry behind it. The cutout pattern in the panel over the *sho-in* bay is *nejiri-zakura* (twisted cherry), one of the three crests of the Hosokawa family. This crest also appears on nail covers in this building.

The front center room is $12\frac{1}{2}$ mats. Behind it is the altar room.

The altar has three alcoves. The *left* one has memorial tablets of the Hosokawa family and a statue of Hosokawa Tadaoki. The *right* one has memorial tablets of temple abbots and others, and (back to front) images of Shaka (2) and Daruma. The larger Shaka image dates from the Kamakura period. Daruma or Dharma was the original founder of the Zen sect in China (ca. 520). The main figure of the *central alcove* is of the founder, Hosokawa Gyokuho, at its back. At the front are a memorial tablet to Nagoya Sanzaburo, a

3. This bay was the feature of a style of architecture named after it, in which more light was drawn into the study *(sho-in)* by building a bay out under the eaves of the roof.

Hosokawa
(kiri)

Hosokawa
(kuyoboshi)

Hosokawa
(nejiri-zakura)

founder of Kabuki who died in 1604, and an image of the eleven-faced Kannon housed in a miniature gold-leaf shrine. This image is said to date from the late Kamakura period, but its house, with detailed bracketing and ornamental elephant and lion heads, is an imitation of later Momoyama-period architecture. On the double doors of the house are painted in color the four Shi-tenno, guardian deities. The image and its decorated house are fine work that deserves close inspection.

The east rooms are, again, of twelve and eight mats. On the north wall of the former hangs a reproduction of a famous painting of peonies by Ch'ien Shun-chii, which the temple numbers among its art treasures.

The covered entrance on the east side of the Hon-do leads to the Kara-mon, the ceremonial gate of the temple.

The south garden of Koto-in is a plain carpet of moss broken by trees and a single stone lantern. The west garden is natural and unorganized. At its far side are Hosokawa tombs, with Tadaoki's set apart and marked by a lantern said to be of Korean stone. Tadaoki had this lantern, given him by Sen-no-Rikyu, replace the conventional marker over his tomb.

All three Hosokawa crests *(kiri,* or paulownia; *kuyoboshi,* or nine heavenly bodies; and the previously mentioned *nejiri-zakura)* are in evidence at this tomb. The *kuyoboshi* also appears on some of the larger roof tiles of the Hon-do.

The second building at Koto-in is Ihoku-ken (意北軒 north-intending eaves). It dates from the Momoyama period, before Koto-in was founded, and was once inhabited by the tea master Sen-no-Rikyu.

The first room shown here (at the building's southwest corner) is eight mats and has *fusuma* painted by Kano Yasunobu (1616–85). A gold screen displayed in this room was painted by Itto Tekizenshi. North of this room is one of six mats. The *fusuma* here are also by Kano Yasunobu. In both this room and the tearoom (see below) different scrolls are hung from time to

time; so it is impossible to identify them here. In my experience
the ones here were always by an old Zen master and those in the
tearoom by a member of the Hosokawa family.

Beyond the six-mat room is a tea pantry, west of which is a
4½-mat tearoom, Shoko-ken (松向軒 pine-facing eaves). The
mats in this room are of irregular sizes. The walls are reddish
purple, and many of the timbers are unfinished limbs of trees.
The plaque on the east wall says *shoko* (松向 pine-facing).

For those who have enjoyed the immortal Heian-period novel
*The Tale of Genji* a short pilgrimage to the tomb of Murasaki
Shikibu may be in order. It is close to the streetcar stop east of
Daitoku-ji-mae (see drawing). The present stones there are of
course modern and not from Murasaki's time.

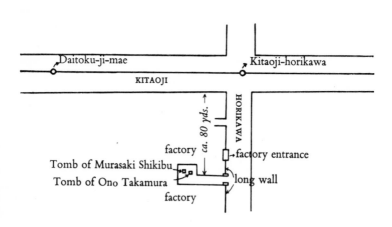

# 銀閣寺 Ginkaku-ji
## Silver Pavilion Temple

The proper name of this temple is Jisho-ji(慈照寺), after Ashikaga Yoshimasa's posthumous name, Jisho-in.

1. GENERAL HISTORY. Ashikaga Yoshimasa (1435–90), the eighth shogun of his line, began planning a retirement villa outside Kyoto as early as the 1460's. After he resigned in favor of his son (1474), he set about his project in earnest. His plans incorporated imitation of the Gold Pavilion of his grandfather Ashikaga Yoshimitsu. Yoshimasa was also influenced by the "moss temple," Saiho-ji, and apparently modeled his garden after the famous one there.

He selected a site outside the northeast corner of the city, up against the mountain Nyoi-ga-take, that was already occupied by part of the Tendai temple Jodo-ji.[1] Parts of Jodo-ji were removed to make way for the villa, and work began in 1480–81. The construction of the actual "silver" pavilion was completed in 1483, the same year Yoshimasa moved to his new home.

Building continued until the time of Yoshimasa's death in 1490. In all, a dozen or more structures were built, most of them designed to accommodate aesthetic pursuits: incense sniffing, tea tasting, moon gazing, poem composing, flower viewing, and so forth. Through his patronage Yoshimasa was instrumental in elevating many of these activities, particularly the tea ceremony, into the realm of fine arts.

After Yoshimasa's death, his villa was converted to a Zen sect temple in accordance with his wishes—again following the example of grandfather Yoshimitsu. It was named Jisho-ji, but its popular name became Ginkaku-ji, even though its pavilion was never actually coated with silver.

Ginkaku-ji suffered after the Ashikaga lost their real power. During the 16th century many of its buildings were destroyed,

1. This temple, said to have been built in the Heian period, had been through a fire in 1449.

and on at least two occasions armies camped nearby and burned much of the surroundings.

The temple was saved from oblivion by the attentions of the Miyagi family in the 17th century. For three generations they devoted themselves to its care and restoration. To the two original buildings still standing they added restorations of others. They rescued the garden by replacing the rotting pilings (which determined the shape of the pond). Thanks to the Miyagi work, Ginkaku-ji's garden is one of the most faithfully preserved from the Muromachi period.

After the Meiji Restoration, Ginkaku-ji went to ruin again, although fortunately no more buildings were destroyed. In this century, through the energies of its priests and public recognition of its historic value, the temple has been restored and maintained.

2. GROUNDS AND GARDEN. The restraint associated with the Zen sect and such arts as the tea ceremony is combined with a display of Yoshimasa's wealth at this temple. The path into Ginkaku-ji is bordered by a combination stone wall, bamboo fence, and hedge that is conservative yet at the same time is the product of wealth. The walks are paved with fine stones or slabs set in the simple "cleansing" patterns associated with the tea ceremony.

The garden is noted for its wealth of stones—both in groupings and in bridges—but despite their large numbers the stones are not so openly displayed here as they came to be in the gardens of later eras. Azaleas, varied trees, and fine moss tone them down and cause them to blend into the whole, producing a tasteful, rich effect. The garden is ambulatory *(kayushiki)* and is designed to open out now and then on carefully planned and controlled perspectives. It is believed that both the garden and the buildings of the original villa were the work of the versatile designer, artist, and connoisseur So-ami.

The tiny waterfall, called Sen-getsu-sen (洗月泉 Moon-Washing Fountain, because the ripples it produces wash away the moonlight), is a good example of the extreme degree of refinement to which the aesthetes of the Muromachi period aspired. The pond, Kinkyo-chi (錦鏡池 Brocade Mirror Pond), has its "white crane island" at the east end, upon which turtles sun themselves. "Crane" and "turtle" islands, intended to resemble their namesakes, were standard elements of these and later garden ponds, symbolizing longevity. Each rock that breaks the surface of the pond has a special name also—great inner rock, narrow river rock, floating rock, *zazen* (Zen meditation) rock, etc.

At the uphill end of the garden path there are a spring and some foundations that remain from buildings long ago destroyed. The spring is of special clarity and was used for tea water.

There is a second garden, of the *karesansui* or dry type, next to the main complex of buildings. It consists of two large white sand shapes, one a large plateau of rippled sand, the other a truncated cone of smooth sand. There has been much discussion about their age, for apparently they are not mentioned in writings before the Edo period.

They are called *Gin-shadan* (Silver Sand Beach) and *Kogetsu-dai*. They are sea and mountain, the former known to be shaped after the historic and beautiful West Lake (Jap. *Sei-ko* 西湖) near Hangchow in China. These sand shapes were meant primarily to assist one's imaginings under the moon.

There are two Shinto shrines on the grounds. One is in the northeast corner of the precinct, while a larger one stands next to the "silver" pavilion.

## 3. THE BUILDINGS

a. LATER BUILDINGS. The tile-roofed Kuri (Priests' Quarters), standing to the left of the entrance, was rebuilt in 1837. Beyond it is the shingle-roofed Hon-do (Main Hall), which is said to be a faithful copy of the original Hon-do. There is a curved-gable gate (Kara-mon) between Kuri and Hon-do. The present Hon-do and the gate are said to date from the Kanei era (1624–44).

The Hon-do is designed in *hojo* style. Its eight-mat west room has *fusuma* depicting birds and palms by Taniguchi Buson (1716–83), a famous painter and poet. The center and east rooms, ten and eight mats respectively, are decorated with paintings of sages which are by Buson's contemporary and sometime partner, Ikeno Taiga (1723–76). Behind the center room is a small altar room whose main image is Shaka. The altar cloth is decorated with the *kiri* crest of the Ashikaga.

Ashikaga
*(kiri)*

Rosei-tei, a building of two rooms just north of Togu-do (see below), is an exact reproduction of the original building of that name, which Yoshimasa used for his incense parties.

b. TOGU-DO (東求堂 East Request Hall). One of the two remaining original buildings, this one was built in 1486–87 and stands east of the Hon-do. Between them is a small court that contains a fragrant olive tree *(mokusei)* and a large square stone basin whose unique grill design is famous.

Essentially Togu-do consists of two rooms. The front room, in which Yoshimasa is said to have lived, is dominated by a statue of the man in priest's garb which he himself is reputed to have carved. The statue is black with age, and its glowing crystal eyes make it surprisingly lifelike. The room in back is a 4½-mat tearoom called Dojinsai ("comradely abstinence"), famous as the prototype of this size of room which later became the standard for tea-ceremony rooms everywhere. It was here that Yoshimasa's famous tea masters Shuko and So-ami brought their art to its zenith. The faded and time-worn screens were painted by So-ami and others but barely show traces of the original work.

The room also contains an early example of shelf alcove and tokonoma, a combination which later became an indispensable part of Japanese room design. While the shelf alcove contains the usual offset shelves, the tokonoma is still experimental: it has sliding screens instead of a solid wall at its back. It is in reality a kind of *sho-in* bay, although it does have "space for a bed" *(toko-no-ma)*, a qualification that later alcoves generally abandoned.

c. GINKAKU (銀閣 Silver Pavilion). Unlike its rival Kinkaku, this pavilion was never actually coated with foil. Perhaps because he was busy erecting other buildings, Yoshimasa did not find time to do this before he died. The pavilion is simple and refined, of two stories, the upper smaller in area than the lower. Upstairs there is a gilt image of Kannon said to be the work of Unkei, a famous Kamakura-period sculptor, while downstairs there is an image of Jizo. The screens which divide the ground floor into rooms can be manipulated to make rooms of different sizes or taken away altogether, leaving a single large room. The upper windows are in the cusped-arch shape associated with the Zen sect, and the building is topped by a bronze phoenix. The only purely decorative touch in the restrained design of the building appears in the edge of the shingled roof, which is notched in front near the corners. In design this building shows a refinement even greater than that of the Kinkaku, which preceded it by about seventy years.

## 浄土院 Jodo-in
## Pure Land Temple

THE SMALL Tendai temple to the left of Ginkaku-ji's entrance, Jodo-in, as it stands has little history outside being remotely connected to the legend related in chapter 9. The temple possesses a charred Amida which it claims is the original of the legend, and its main hall is dominated by an image of Kobo Daishi (774–835), the famous priest who is also connected to the legend. Oddly enough, this priest enshrined in a Tendai temple was the founder of the rival Shingon sect.

# 竜安寺 Ryoan-ji
# Dragon Peace Temple

1. HISTORY. The estate which is now Ryoan-ji was originally established in the Heian period by a nobleman of the Tokudaiji, a powerful branch of the Fujiwara family. The temple's great relic from that period is its large pond.

The estate passed through various hands to the Hosokawa family and was eventually inherited by Hosokawa Katsumoto (1430–73). This man had the misfortune to become a leading general in the Onin War. He died in the war and was buried on the grounds of his estate, which, according to his wishes, was made into a Zen sect temple.

The new temple was patronized by the nearby monastery Myoshin-ji, whose abbot, Giten, became the first abbot of Ryoan-ji. Ryoan-ji thus entered the Rinzai branch of the Zen sect, Myoshin-ji wing. Both temples burned in the Onin War and were reconstructed by the end of the 15th century. It was about 1500 that Ryoan-ji's rock garden appeared.

For approximately 300 years the temple existed without disaster. As regards the number and size of its buildings, Ryoan-ji probably reached its peak in the 18th century. In the 1790's it burned, and when it was rebuilt, some of its halls were not replaced. The temple now formed a tighter cluster about the rock garden, which had of course survived the fire.

This is the temple as we see it today. It has not changed significantly since the beginning of the 19th century, except to become famous for its rock garden. What was an almost unnoticed part of the new Zen temple has with the passage of time become its chief attraction.

2. GROUNDS AND MINOR BUILDINGS. The great pond, Kyoyo-chi (鏡容池 Mirror-Shape Pond), retains its Heian character. Its size, openness, simplicity, and refinement all recall that long-past age when ponds like this one and the one at Shinsen-en were the height of style. Of the two islands, the larger, Benten-jima

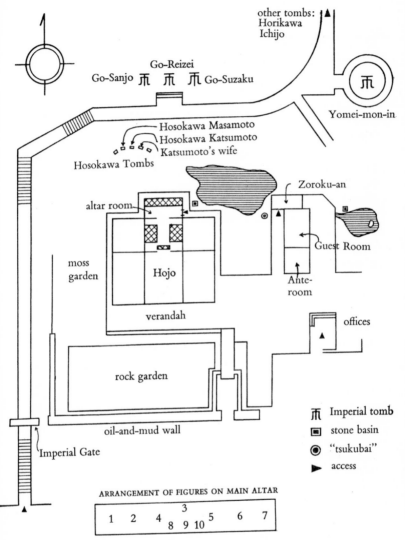

other tombs:
Horikawa
Ichijo

Go-Reizei

Go-Sanjo 禾 禾 禾 Go-Suzaku

Yomei-mon-in

— Hosokawa Masamoto
— Hosokawa Katsumoto
Katsumoto's wife

Hosokawa Tombs

Zoroku-an

altar room

Guest Room

moss
garden

Hojo

Ante-
room

verandah

offices

rock garden

oil-and-mud wall

Imperial Gate

禾 Imperial tomb

◼ stone basin

◉ "tsukubai"

▶ access

ARRANGEMENT OF FIGURES ON MAIN ALTAR

|   |   |   | 3 |   |   |   |
|---|---|---|---|---|---|---|
| 1 | 2 | 4 | 8 9 10 | 5 | 6 | 7 |

MAP EIGHT
Ryoan-ji

竜安寺

1. Statue of Hosokawa Katsumoto
2. Family tablet of Giten, First Abbot
3. Image of Shaka
4. Minor image: Monju
5. Minor image: Fugen
6. Statue of Giten ⎫ abbots of temple
7. Statue of Chuko ⎭
8. ⎫ Ihai or ⎧ for protection of temple
9. ⎬ prayer ⎨ for well-being of Hosokawa family
10. ⎭ tablets ⎩ for well-being of present emperor

(弁天島), is reached by a small causeway and bridge that contributes to the pond's serenity. The island has a Shinto shrine to Benten, the only female among the seven Shinto gods of luck, whose shrine is usually placed on an island. There is also a giant old red pine *(akamatsu)* that is propped up from falling into the pond. The smaller island is called Fushidora-jima (伏虎島 Hiding Tiger Island).

The building west of Benten-jima is a hall of the temple named Daishu-in (大珠院 Big Pearl Temple), and beyond it is another building called Seigen-in (西源院) which is a resting and eating place.

There are three hills behind Ryoan-ji upon which are the tombs of several emperors, discussed in detail below. From east to west the hills are called Kinugasa-yama (衣笠山 Cloth Hat Mountain), Shu-zan (朱山 Vermilion or Cinnabar Mountain), and O-uchi-yama (大内山 Great Inner Mountain). The name of the first is explained as follows: "This name...was given in allusion to the incident of the ex-Mikado Uda having ordered it [the hill] to be spread with white silk one hot day in July, in order that his eyes at least might enjoy a cool, wintry sensation."[1]

The grounds of Ryoan-ji cover about 123 acres.

3. HOJO (方丈 Superior's Quarters). The main building of the temple, this structure dates from about 1797 and characteristically consists of five connecting rooms that surround a sanctum and altar room at the center back. The *fusuma* of all these rooms were painted by the contemporary artist Satsuki Kakuo, between 1954 and 1958.

On the west side of the building, the front room (20 mats) has screens showing the Kongo, or Diamond, Mountains of Korea[2] in the winter, and the room behind it (12½ mats) has scenes of the same mountains in the fall. These rooms are used during ceremonies to accommodate attending priests.

On the east side the screens in the front room (20 mats) show

1. B. H. Chamberlain and W. B. Mason, *A Handbook for Travellers in Japan,* London, 1894, page 303.
2. The Kongo-san is one of the most prominent of the mountain groups sacred to Buddhism in the Orient. Historically it was the site of many of Korea's foremost Buddhist temples and monasteries. The scenery of its jagged peaks and vertical drops is famous in its own right.

Hosokawa

the Kongo Mountains in summer, and those of the back room (12½ mats) show them in spring. These rooms accommodate parishioners, and the back one is also used as a waiting room.

The front center room (24 mats) is the Hojo proper. The side screens depict ascending and descending dragons, and those at the back of the room a plum tree done to resemble a dragon. The large wooden gong *(mokugyo)* in this room is rung during ceremonies.

The room at the center back of the building is a kind of fore-hall to the altar room proper. It contains numerous memorial tablets *(ihai)*—most of them for former abbots—and small statues. Two panels visible from the front on either side depict fabulous beasts in green and blue. The curtain hanging between the front and back rooms is decorated with Hosokawa Katsumoto's family crest.

The main altar is in a narrow room projecting out from the back of the building which may be reached from the outside (see map 8). It contains large statues of Hosokawa Katsumoto (see photo) and two former abbots, Giten and Chuko, as well as religious images and *ihai* (see map). There is a dragon on the ceiling, painted by Cho Densu (1352–1431) on paper nailed up in sections. Although it is getting dilapidated, the dragon's wild-eyed look commands attention. The statue (1470?) of Katsumoto, which is carved from a single block of wood, is particularly noteworthy. This room may be closed but the sentence in appendix III should help open it, and it is worth the effort.

West of the Hojo there is a small moss garden which contains a stone lantern designed after the style of the Kamakura period.

4. THE ROCK GARDEN. The rock garden is generally attributed to So-ami (1472–1523), more on the basis of its quality than of its history, the latter being very uncertain. It is thought to have been made around 1500 or a little earlier. It is almost a rectangle—a notch is built into its east side—and measures approximately 102 by 50 feet.

The stones—fifteen of them—which make up the garden are all from the Kyoto area except one. The exception, the long low one nearest the far wall, came from Shikoku and has two men's names etched on its far side, Kotaro (小太郎) and (Sei?)jiro (?二郎)

This stone has contributed to speculation on the garden's history. Were the two men So-ami's assistants? Did they bring the stone to complete the garden, or was the stone already here? Was the garden based on this stone? No one knows the answers to these and similar questions, and indeed it may well be that this stone had been brought from Shikoku for some other purpose and was simply selected like the others as fitting the garden plan.

The wall around the garden is made of oil and mud. It was originally brown but has become streaked with age. Its roof was originally thatched but in recent times the thatch has given way to tile. It is worth noting that the west section of the wall has a built-in perspective: near the Hojo it is 6 to 8 inches higher than it is at the far corner, thus strengthening one's impression that the far side of the garden is distant. The east section of the wall is only a few years old and ends at the formal entrance to the temple, a Momoyama-style corridor with a curved gable at either end.

Outside the garden one sees tall trees now, but originally this garden was of the "borrowed scenery" type, using as its own such exterior sceneries as the then visible distant ridge of Higashiyama.

Numerous interpretations have been placed on this garden in an effort to pin down its meaning. Among the most common are that (1) it shows mountains poking through a layer of clouds, (2) it shows rocks in a river, or islands in a sea, (3) it shows a mother tiger and her cubs fording a river—they being represented by the central group of stones, and (4) it represents the five "great temples" of the Zen sect. Other interpretations have the rocks a stylized representation of the character *shin* (心 heart, mind) or the outline of a dragon, whose head is at the east end and whose body curves through the center, northwest, and southwest stones back to a tail ending at the long low stone from Shikoku. It is generally agreed, however, that the garden defies such concrete analyses.

5. KURI (庫裡 Priests' Quarters). This building is attached to the Hojo by a wide corridor that has a small bell *(densho)* hanging up under its eaves. The bell is for calling assemblies.

At the back of the building is a tearoom called Zoroku-an (蔵六庵 Tortoise Arbor). Near the entrance to the tearoom is a round stone basin *(tsukubai)* that is for washing one's hands prior to receiving tea. It dates from the Edo period, being the gift of Tokugawa Mitsukuni (1628–1700), a famous scholar and, curiously, foe of Buddhism, who gave it in thanks for some scholarly assistance the temple had given him.

The *tsukubai* is decorated with four characters (五, 隹, 止, 矢) around its edge, and the square basin represents a fifth (口). This fifth one is combined with the other four in the appropriate relationship in the phrase 吾れ唯だ足ることを知る, where it is common to each of the four Chinese characters used (the rest being syllabics). The phrase can be translated "we know only satisfaction," or "we are satisfied with what we have," which is an expression of humility appropriate to both the tea ceremony and the Zen sect. Thus this seeming decorative design is in reality a clever calligraphic pun which places the four characters about their common element.

The camellia tree in the small garden between Hojo and Kuri received its name, Wabisuke-tsubaki (侘助椿 Misery-Helping Camellia), indirectly from Toyotomi Hideyoshi, who applied the nickname Wabisuke to the man who transplanted the tree from Korea.

The anteroom (see map 8) to the guest room in the Kuri has a portable screen of the Edo period, done by a member of the Unkoku school founded by the famous painter Sesshu (1420–1507). The outer hallway of the building also contains decorative—if not historic—screens.

East of the wing containing the tearoom there is a stone basin for drawing tea water and a small pond that has metal dragons on a miniature stone island.

6. TOMBS AT RYOAN-JI. Tombs of the Hosokawa family stand on the hill north of the Hojo. There are five in the open space there, with Katsumoto's at the center (see map).

The "Ryoan-ji Seven Imperial Tombs" stand on the three hills behind the temple in pleasant surroundings. There is also the tomb of one imperial consort near the temple. The tombs are as follows:

| EMPEROR AND NO. | BORN | RULED | DIED | HILL |
|---|---|---|---|---|
| Uda (59) | 867 | 887–97 | 931 | O-uchi-yama |
| Kazan (65) | 967 | 984–86 | 1008 | Kinugasa-yama |

| | | | | |
|---|---|---|---|---|
| Ichijo (66) | 980 | 986–1011 | 1011 | Kinugasa-yama |
| Go-Suzaku (69) and consort Teishi Nai-shinno (1013–94) | 1009 | 1036–45 | 1045 | Shu-zan |
| Go-Reizei (70) | 1025 | 1045–68 | 1068 | Shu-zan |
| Go-Sanjo (71) | 1034 | 1068–72 | 1073 | Shu-zan |
| Horikawa (73) | 1078 | 1086–1107 | 1107 | Kinugasa-yama |

Uda was the first retired emperor to become a Buddhist priest (*ho-o*) and lived out his days at the nearby temple Ninna-ji, which thus became the first *monzeki* temple. Ichijo's consorts gathered a famous literary court around them which included the authoresses Sei Shonagon and Murasaki Shikibu. Go-Sanjo was one of the greatest emperors in the history of Japan.[3] Teishi Naishinno was the daughter of the Emperor Sanjo (67th emperor) and the mother of Go-Sanjo. She later became a nun and is known to history by her later name Yomei-mon-in. Go-Reizei was the emperor whom Fujiwara Yorimichi entertained at the Byodo-in in Uji in the year 1067.

Many of the emperors entombed here were related in one way or another to the famous Fujiwara minister Michinaga.[4] All lived in the period when the Fujiwara were powerful and when Buddhism held an unusual sway over the imperial house. As in the case of Reizei (q.v.), their tombs must have been humble— all but non-existent—at the times of their deaths and probably reached their present state in the 19th-century restoration of imperial tombs instigated by the Emperor Meiji.

3. See chapter 4.
4. See genealogical chart, chapter 4.

# 醍醐寺 Daigo-ji

1. ITS NAME. Buddha's teachings are generally divided into five periods beginning with his early efforts to ascertain what those around him were capable of understanding and culminating in a period of eight years during which "he expounded the ultimate truth of his doctrines, leaving nothing out." The teaching of this last period was based on the Lotus Sutra, and at the end of it, convinced that he could do no more to increase the understanding of his disciples, Shaka (Buddha) passed into Nirvana.

These five periods are compared to the "five flavors" of milk prepared in India: milk, coagulated milk, fresh butter, clarified butter, and milk extract, the ultimate essence. The last one, which is said to have "the finest flavor of all eatable things," is called *daigo* (醍醐) in Japanese.

It is said that the priest Shobo, in the year 874, prayed that a location for a temple would be shown to him. "Then he saw the clouds of 5 colours, spread about in the air over the top of the hill, whereby the present temple [Daigo-ji] is situated. He at once climbed the hill, and rested for a little while at the place, where there is at present a well of the Aka.... At that time an old man of the white-hair appeared suddenly, making his way by pushing the fallen leaves to each side, and dipped the water with both hands and drank it, saying: 'Ah it is the taste of Daigo.'"[1]

The old man turned out to be a deity who was "landowner of this hill." He presented the hill to Shobo for his temple and disappeared. Shobo then "went to the place where the old man took a drink, and found the water gushing forth from the ground as pure as an emerald...."

This was the beginning of Daigo-ji; and the name of the temple has not only its literal meaning but also implies the final great period of Shaka's teaching.

1. *A Brief History of the Daigo-ji,* a small pamphlet published by the temple about thirty years ago, page 2.

2. GENERAL HISTORY. Daigo-ji was founded in 874 by the priest Shobo (832–909, posth. Rigen Daishi). During the 10th century it grew quickly: its first permanent building was the Shaka-do (926), and the complex of Lower Daigo was completed with the building of the five-storied pagoda in 951. By the 13th century the temple was vast in precinct and structures, but in 1260 and 1295 there were fires. Although the buildings that burned were replaced, the temple had entered a period of disasters. There was another fire in 1336, and finally, in 1470, the Onin War destroyed every building in Lower Daigo except the pagoda.

During the 16th century the temple remained in ruins. Then, near the end of the century, Toyotomi Hideyoshi (1536–98) undertook the reconstruction of Daigo-ji and of Sambo-in.

In 1585, the monks of a powerful Shingon temple named Negoro-dera in the Kii peninsula (Wakayama Prefecture) had risen up against Hideyoshi, and he had successfully besieged their temple. He awarded the remains of Negoro-dera to Daigo-ji's re-building. At the height of its power in the time of the Ashikaga shoguns Negoro-dera controlled about 2700 temples.

Hideyoshi died in 1598, and his son saw through the remainder of the work at Daigo-ji. The present Kon-do and Nio-mon were transferred from Negoro-dera in 1598 and reopened in 1600, and other buildings were rebuilt during that time. Simultaneously Sambo-in was enlarged and put in its present magnificent state.

In 1930 the temple celebrated the 1000th anniversary of the Emperor Daigo, one of its great patrons whose posthumous name was taken from the name of the temple. In 1935 the Reiho-kan, a new museum for the temple's outstanding collection of priceless relics, was first opened. Finally, from 1955 to 1960 the old pagoda was restored; its condition now is so perfect as to belie its age of over a thousand years.

Formerly, as at Mt. Hiei and the Shingon headquarters, Mt. Koya, women were not allowed in the precinct here.

Daigo-ji is subdivided into upper and lower sections, the former being on top of the hill and the latter at its western foot. There are many smaller temples within these precincts. All are of the Shingon sect, which was founded by the priest Kukai

(Kobo Daishi, 774–835) and was one of the two great sects of the Heian period.

### 3. LOWER DAIGO BUILDINGS.

a. NIO-MON (仁王門). This huge gate, which is said to be bigger than the one that preceded it, probably came from Negoro-dera. It contains two Deva kings or Nio, guardians of the temple, who may have been transferred with it. The Nio are sculptured after the style of the famous Kamakura sculptors Unkei and Tankei, but they are indications rather than good examples of the work in this style.

"The one on the left (from the temple), with its mouth opened to pronounce the Sanskrit vowel 'ah' is a positive image, which invites every good to come in, while the other, on the right, with its mouth closed to pronounce 'um,' is a negative image for shutting evil out."[2]

The gate and statues are said to date from the Kamakura period, but their history is very uncertain.

b. KON-DO (金堂 Golden or Main Hall). This hall was definitely brought from the ruins of Negoro-dera and rebuilt here. It was first built early in the Kamakura period (1185–1392) in the national style continuing from that of the Heian period, although its exact age is uncertain. It was brought here to replace the Shaka-do, which had first been built in 926 but had burned in 1295.

The central image of the Kon-do is Yakushi Nyorai. The figure was made in the late Heian or early Kamakura period, but it is in the style of the earlier Jokan era (859–77). It is made of sectioned wood. With the two lesser Buddhas Nikko and Gekko it forms a trinity; all are of the same date and are believed to have been in the hall when it was at Negoro-dera.

The trinity is guarded by the Shi-tenno. These fall into two pairs: the ones in front—to the outside—are also in the Jokan style. The two central figures, at the back, date from the Fujiwara period (10th–11th century).

*Ihai* (memorial tablets) in front of Yakushi are to (left to

2. Fujiya Hotel, Ltd., *We Japanese,* Yokohama, 1950, page 332.

right): the Emperors Suzaku and Daigo; Daigo's consort Onji Kogo, who initiated the building of the pagoda after his death; and the Emperor Murakami, under whom it was completed.

c. FIVE-STORIED PAGODA. It was begun in 936 and completed in 951 as described above. It has been said that the design of this pagoda followed that of a pagoda at Fuko-ji in Nara which no longer exists. If this is true, the Daigo pagoda is as important to students of the Nara period as it is to those of the Heian. Only two Heian five-storied pagodas now survive; the other is at Muro-ji near Nara.

The pagoda is 121 feet tall and is distinguished by its structural balance and the large size of its spire *(sorin)*. Its interior is decorated with *mandala* paintings of the Kongo-kai and Taizo-kai (Diamond and Womb worlds central to Shingon philosophy) which may be the oldest such paintings in color that now exist. They are a famous example of this type of painting. Although one damaged section has been removed to the Reiho-kan, the others remain inside the pagoda, where, unfortunately, visitors are not usually allowed.

The pagoda was damaged in an earthquake in 1596 but was repaired at the time of Hideyoshi's restoration. Its most recent restoration was completed in 1960.[3]

Perhaps it is appropriate to interject a word here about pagodas in general. They are found in different shapes throughout Asia—in India, Southeast Asia, China, Korea, Japan. Originally made to house the remains of Buddha, they later came to be used for other purposes: markers for holy places, offerings to the dead, tomb markers.

Pagodas came to Japan in the 6th century not long after Buddhism itself. In Japan they have as few as no stories (Enryaku-ji) or as many as thirteen (Danzan Shrine near Nara). It is interesting that this Buddhist building was used at Shinto shrines, including the great Tosho-gu at Nikko.

The spire usually has nine metal rings, often with bells hanging from them, whose significance varies among the different sects. Generally speaking the rings represent Buddhist deities.

---

3. When the pagoda was taken apart the last time, coins minted in the 9th and 10th centuries were found under the main column, confirming the date of its construction.

In Japan pagodas are more common to temples of the older sects, being unusual in Jodo and Shin temples, and unused by Zen temples, except in miniature forms.

d. SEIRYU-GU (清滝宮 Clear Waterfall Shrine). This Shinto shrine, directly west of the pagoda, was first built in 1097. It burned in 1470, and its main hall (Hon-den 本殿) now dates from 1517.

e. OTHER BUILDINGS OF LOWER DAIGO. The Fudo-do (不動堂), which houses the deity of that name, is a small hall east of the Kon-do. Formerly it stood uphill from the Benten-do, overlooking the ponds, but it was recently moved to its present location. East of Fudo-do are the priests' quarters. Next is the Dai-ko-do (大講堂 Great Lecture Hall), a building of this century. Built in 1930, it stands on the west bank of the large pond uphill from the pagoda and houses an image of Amida which is old but of uncertain date. The Benten-do (弁天堂) is a small Shinto shrine to Benten which stands at the far side of the small curved bridge over the pond. The simple garden of informal terraced ponds is not only beautiful but is also an interesting contrast to the intricate garden at Sambo-in. Where Fudo-do once stood there is now a small arbor.

4. UPPER DAIGO BUILDINGS. There are many valuable buildings and statues in the upper section of Daigo-ji. The most valued are the Seiryu-gongen Haiden (清滝権現拝殿), a Shinto building dating from 1434, and the image of Yakushi Nyorai in the Yakushi-do, which dates from about 907—a time, however, not noted for its sculpture.

Other important buildings at Upper Daigo include the Yakushi-do (薬師堂), a building dating from 1211 whose curved interior bracketing was the first such used in Japan, and whose interior grillwork partition is particularly characteristic of its period; also, at the top of the hill, the Miei-do (御影堂 or Kai-san-do 開山堂)[4] and Nyoirin-do (如意輪堂), both of which burned in 1260 and were rebuilt in 1608. The image in the latter is Nyoi-rin Kannon, estimated to date from 1089.

4. *Kaisan:* lit., "mountain-opener," hence the founder of a Buddhist temple, hence Kaisan-do = Founder's Hall. This one houses a statue of Daigo-ji's founder which dates from 1261.

This Kannon, with its jewel granting all wishes, is typically seated in an utterly relaxed position, two of its six arms propping it up and the other four holding symbolic objects: wheel, rosary, lotus, and jewel.

The Kyo-zo (経蔵 Sutra Storehouse) of Upper Daigo is noteworthy as one of the three remaining buildings in the "Indian style" of the Kamakura period, a style marked by vertically piled two-dimensional bracketing under the eaves. It was built about 1198.

The other two buildings in this style are the Great South Gate of Todai-ji at Nara and the Jodo-do of Jodo-ji in Hyogo Prefecture. All were built under the influence of a single priest, one Chogen, and the style rose and fell with his life and death. Chogen apparently brought it with him from China, but it did not take root in Japan and was quickly forgotten after he died in 1205. The famous Dai-Butsu-den of Todai-ji, once built in this style but since burned and eclectically restored, retains its "Indian-style" bracketing.

5. REIHO-KAN (霊宝館 Sacred Treasure Hall), first opened in 1935, houses innumerable treasures including calligraphy, writings, paintings, and screens, and is open twice a year, in April-May and in October-November. The rest of the year it is closed. Its contents truly make it a Sacred Treasure Hall. It is located opposite Sambo-in, south of the main path in to Daigo-ji from the road.

# 三宝院 Sambo-in
## Three Treasures Temple

1. ITS NAME. It is said that at the time of Shobo's encounter with the old man and the water that tasted of Daigo, he saw a large oak tree on the hill where the singing of a peculiar bird was heard. "The bird was called Sambo-cho or 'the bird of three treasures,' for when it sang, the sound was like that of Buppo-so, i.e. Buddha, Dharma or Law, and Samgha, or priesthood."[1]

These are the three treasures referred to in the name Sambo-in. Generally speaking, they are the object of faith and devotion in Buddhism, although they are interpreted differently by different sects—the Jodo, for instance, seeing all three embodied in the personality of Amida.

2. GENERAL HISTORY. Sambo-in was founded in 1115 as a sub-temple by Shokaku, 14th abbot of Daigo-ji, and was appointed to *monzeki* rank in 1143. With four similar temples there it became famous as one of the "five *monzeki* of Daigo." Sambo-in, which has had sons of emperors among its abbots, still holds its rank, one of the symbols of which is the high white wall around its precinct.[2]

Through fortunate political alliance Sambo-in flourished until 1470, when it was destroyed by the same fires that burned Daigo-ji.

When Hideyoshi agreed to restore Daigo-ji and Sambo-in in 1598, he planned the work on the buildings and gardens of Sambo-in in great detail, but he died before it could be carried out. Nevertheless, Sambo-in was rebuilt following Hideyoshi's plan; the work was finished about 1601. So strong was the influence of the Toyotomi family that for the purposes of history Sambo-in is now a relic of their period rather than the earlier one in which it was founded.

---

1. *A Brief History of the Daigo-ji,* page 3.
2. The wall is six horizontal sections, or layers, high, instead of the more conventional four seen elsewhere.

Over the years since its restoration, Sambo-in, no longer a sub-temple, has added two or three period structures but has not changed greatly. It now preserves with greater integrity than any other place the style and appearance of a pleasure mansion planned and built by the flamboyant and short-lived Toyotomi family.

3. ARCHITECTURAL COMMENT. The buildings of Sambo-in are stylistically interesting as examples of Japanese secular architecture. In Japanese architecture whole styles turn on small points of detail which would seem trivial or secondary to the foreigner. Because of this, and because Sambo-in is a combination of styles, its architectural character is difficult to define briefly.

Three styles influenced Sambo-in: *buke-zukuri, shinden-zukuri,* and *sho-in-zukuri.*

The influence of *buke-zukuri*—warrior architecture—is the least potent of the three. Details which hint at it are the outside entrance followed by a long corridor which could serve as a guard post; the building plan, which makes access to the important personage within difficult; other details which tend to "fortify" the place from unwelcome visitors or strangers. But *buke-zukuri* only came into its own as a distinctive style in castle architecture; its influence here is more in the mood of fortification than in actual elements of design.

*Shinden-zukuri* is the oldest of the three styles. It flourished in the Heian period, particularly in palace architecture. Among its general characteristics: an oblong central building opens along its long south side onto a garden. The garden contains a pond fed from two sides—by a stream at one end, a waterfall at the other. Often these waters have the same ultimate source, split somewhere out of sight to feed them both. The pond has islands and bridges, and is backed by trees and stone arrangements. Connected to the central building by corridors are other buildings, living quarters to east and west, and possibly also to the north.

These details are adhered to faithfully in the central building, Omote Shinden, of Sambo-in and those around it.

*Sho-in-zukuri* appeared in Japan in the Kamakura period, originally in the studies *(sho-in)* of Buddhist priests. In *sho-in-zukuri* a bay, or bay window, projects south from the building, usually containing a wide window sill or desk, to give more light to the study. The room with the bay opens to other rooms, culminating in a room backed by an alcove (tokonoma) and a niche with shelves *(tana)*. Quite often the building complex has an outside entrance porch surmounted by a Chinese (curved) gable.

These details too appear at Sambo-in. The entrance has the porch and gable, and the Omote Shinden has a small bay which projects into the garden in a way reminiscent of *sho-in-zukuri*—although the bay is not part of the interior and has no sill or desk. Further, the rooms of all buildings culminate in the single room with tokonoma and *tana*.

Added to these architectural styles is that of *cha-shitsu,* the astringent distillation of nature which accompanies the tea ceremony and its houses, two of which are here.

Thus it is legitimate to call the Sambo-in buildings eclectic, yet fortunately this mixture of styles has not obliterated the features of any one of them.


4. THE BUILDINGS. These are taken here in the order in which they are usually shown (see map 9).

a. One enters through a courtyard west of the garden. It contains a circular plot of small pines, a large old white fir, and a weeping cherry tree of considerable size and fame. This last rivals the cherry tree avenue of Daigo-ji, just outside these grounds, for visitors in the spring.

The buildings are reached through a gabled porch, which leads inside and passes through a protective wall to the interior. Since there is no outside entrance to the place and one can only pass through the wall via this hallway, the privacy of those inside is easily maintained.

b. FIRST BUILDING.

(1) The first room is called Aoi-no-ma, after the annual Aoi festival of Kyoto, the procession of which is depicted on the walls of the room. It was painted by Ishida Yutei (d. 1785), who is famous as a teacher of the noted painter Maruyama Okyo (1733–95).

(2) The second room is called Akigusa-no-ma, Autumn Grass Room, because its screens depict the "seven grasses of autumn." The painter: Kano Sanraku (1559–1635). This 15-mat room looks out on another weeping cherry tree.

(3) Chokushi-no-ma, or Imperial Messenger Room, 10 mats.

Koto-hiki
path

4a
4b1
4b2
4b3
4c
5a
5a
5b
5b
4d1
4d2
4d3
5a
5c
4e
4k
4f
4j
5d
4f
4i
4g
4h

MAP NINE
Sambo-in

三法院

Imperial Crest
(*kiku*)

Imperial Crest
(*kiri*)

The messenger entered the grounds through the Chokushi-mon (see below) and waited for his audience here. The screens, again by Kano Sanraku, depict *ka-cho-san-sui,* or "flower-bird-mountain-water," a conventional combination of elements. There is a tokonoma in the east wall of this room which has the unusual feature of being backed by sliding screens instead of solid wall. In this case the reason is to permit emergency access or escape, something often needed in the time of military rule and uncertain alliances.

c. CHOKUSHI-MON (勅使門 Imperial Messenger Gate). This gate was for the use of the imperial messenger only, and is said to have been transferred here from Hideyoshi's Fushimi Castle. Old plans of Sambo-in locate it in the west wall near its present position, which is in the south wall at the southwest corner of the grounds.

The gate is emblazoned in bold relief with the two imperial crests, *kiku* (chrysanthemum) and *kiri* (paulownia). The latter was the crest adopted by Hideyoshi, so the juxtaposition was probably important to this man whose low birth prevented him from becoming shogun.

Originally the crests were gold-lacquered and the rest of the gate was done in black. Traces of the gold lacquer still cling to the undersides of some of the chrysanthemum petals. Other streaks on the gate are the remains of the undercoat. The hooks on the beams above the crests are for hanging festive curtains. A close examination of the gate, which is permitted on request, can only be made from the outside.

A stone west of the path from Chokushi-mon is called Koto-hiki—a seat where one can play the *koto.*

d. OMOTE SHO-IN (表書院) or OMOTE SHINDEN (表宸殿).

(1) The first room is the *omote sho-in* (outer study) proper, and the bay which projects into the garden from it, called Sen-den, reflects the influence of *sho-in-zukuri.* The north and east walls of this room are painted with palm and birch trees by Ishida Yutei. There is also a portable screen depicting a white eagle on

a gold ground, by the same painter. When this room is furnished in Japanese style, the mats may be raised to uncover a fine wood floor which can be used as a stage for Noh plays.

(2) *Omote sho-in chu-dan-no-ma,* the middle room of the *sho-in,* 18 mats. The screen paintings, of bamboo and pine trees and grasses in springtime, are by Kano Sanraku.

(3) *Omote sho-in jo-dan-no-ma,* 15 mats. This is the "upper" room of the three. It contains the tokonoma for all three rooms, and an alcove with *chigai-dana,* or shelves of different levels, which fills out the east wall next to the tokonoma. The walls of the room depict willows in the four seasons, from which it gets another name, Yanagi-no-ma, Willow Room. The paintings are by Kano Sanraku.

An unusual feature of this room is that the beams of the ceiling are set at right angles to the "lines of the room." This arrangement is unorthodox and reflects Hideyoshi's irregular ideas about architectural style. Hideyoshi was proud of his numerous idiosyncrasies of taste, which he incorporated into many of the buildings he built.

e. Between the second and third buildings there is a maple tree and a small thicket of bamboos.

f. JUNJO-KAN (純浄観 very pure view). This is essentially a party building, and it is said that Hideyoshi entertained the wives of soldiers he sent to his Korean campaign in it, but probably not here, for conflicting dates and the absence of Junjo-kan from early plans of Sambo-in make that impossible. The building may have been a part of Hideyoshi's Fushimi Castle, brought here some time after his death. It was damaged by a typhoon in 1934 and extensively restored in 1936. It has two rooms of 20 and 15 mats surrounded on three sides by matted corridors. The screens were painted by Domoto Insho (b. 1891) in 1936.

g. East of Junjo-kan runs A NARROW STREAM that feeds the pond. Tradition is that one could float a cup of saké down it to someone else. Beyond it are large patterns in cedar moss, of circles and gourd *(hyotan)* shapes, meant to represent saké cups and bottles and to reflect the festive mood. The gourd shape is also associated with Hideyoshi as a kind of crest.

h. HON-DO (本堂) or MIROKU-DO (弥勒堂). It contains an image of Miroku Bosatsu, the "future" Buddha, who will be born

5000 years after Shaka, the "historical" Buddha, attained Nirvana. The exact age of this image is unknown, but it is the work of Anami Kaikei (12th–13th century).

Kaikei, his master Kokei, and the latter's son Unkei (the last two descended from Jocho) formed the nucleus of the group of sculptors responsible for the bold sculpture of the Kamakura period. But where Unkei tended toward the grotesque, Kaikei's work was quieter, as this figure, particularly if it is compared with any of Unkei's Nio, reveals.

Miroku-do is the principal religious hall of Sambo-in. To the left of Miroku Bosatsu is an image of Shobo (Rigen Daishi), founder of Daigo-ji, and to the right is an image of Kukai (Kobo Daishi), founder of the Shingon sect.

i. CHINRYU-TEI (枕流亭 Pillow-on-the-Stream Teahouse). This teahouse is of a later date than the other buildings and was restored in 1950. It has three rooms, all unusually small, two of three mats and one of only two. The room to the left of the entrance is for tea drinking, the center room is the "entrance room," and the two-mat room on the right is a pantry. The house is surrounded by a small garden within the main garden which is of the *karesansui* type.

j. SHOGETSU-TEI (松月亭 Pines-in-the-Moonlight Teahouse). This house was probably brought to its present location early in the 19th century, but it was made in the late 15th or early 16th century. Among its peculiarities of design are that one corner of the building is supported by a post resting on a stone in the stream, and that the stone basin also stands in the stream instead of on land. In former days a boat might be kept here which could go under Junjo-kan and out into the pond for pleasure boating. The east wall of the tearoom ($4\frac{1}{2}$ mats) is a round moon window. The bridge of staggered walnut planks and the general surroundings and materials used are all typical of the tea-cult style.

k. SHINDEN (宸殿). The Shinden consists of four rooms, two outer and two inner, surrounded by a matted corridor. The inner rooms are the more important pair, the one to the northeast being for the "person with most authority" and the one to the northwest, connected to it by decorated sliding panels, for bodyguards to be posted in case of emergency.

The paintings are by Hasegawa Tohaku (1539–1610), an outstanding painter of the Momoyama period.

The raised mat in the center of the main room is for the master of the house, presumably Hideyoshi. Only shoguns, persons of imperial rank, and the like used such raised mats.

The offset shelf *(chigai-dana)* in this room is considered to be one of three famous shelves of its type in Japan, the other two being at the Katsura and Shugaku-in imperial villas. It is nicknamed Daigo-dana, and its uniqueness lies in the fact that the back of the shelf does not touch the wall behind it, but has its own back. The gap of about 30 cm. allows the palm design cut out of the shelf-back to cast a shadow on the wall. To the sparely furnished Japanese room the presence of a shelf is important, and every detail of its design is significant to the sensitive observer. Shelves like Daigo-dana have a national fame all their own.

5. THE GARDEN. Most of the buildings overlook the large garden. It is typical of the Momoyama period, except that it is on a grander scale than anyone except Hideyoshi could afford. The Momoyama garden, like the buildings of that time, shows a flamboyancy, color, and vigor that distinguishes it from all others. Stones are ubiquitous and there is little restraint in the design, which is complex and massive.

The garden of Sambo-in is a prime example of all the qualities that went into its lesser contemporaries. The amount of stones used here and their individual quality are without equal. Background foliage is both deciduous and evergreen to insure prominent colors in all seasons. The pond is fed by a stream and a waterfall, both coming from the same source in the southeast corner of the grounds. Tortoise, crane, and *horai* islands, any or all conventionally used in gardens of this kind, are all here. Bridges are of different materials: small stone ones near the buildings; a finished wood one at the west side; and earth bridges, including the large one in the center of the pond. The earth bridges are built high to allow pleasure boats to pass beneath them.

Some details of the garden follow:

a. The three islands in front of the Omote Sho-in are, east to west, tortoise, crane, and *horai*. The first two are longevity symbols, while *horai,* the most distant, is a traditional imaginary paradise, the concept of which comes from China.

Here it is not actually an island at all, but the semi-peninsular west shore of the pond, meant to be accepted mentally as an island.

The complicated pine shape on the tortoise island represents the shape of that reptile.

b. A small *karesansui* garden lies next to the Omote Sho-in, between it and the pond. It consists of a gravel area containing three stones which were selected to express different moods of river water.

They are called Kamo-no-san-seki (Three Stones of the Kamo River). The one to the east represents rapids and whirlpools; the one in the center, a slow heavy stream; and the one to the west, churning water and foam. The representations are clever. The last stone was brought by a lord from Shikoku, while the other two actually came from the Kamo River in Kyoto.

Another stone near these three (see map 9) is called Gyu-ga-seki (Cow Stone) because it is thought to resemble a cow.

c. FUJITO. There are about 800 stones in the garden, about eighty of which were brought from the various provinces of the country by their respective lords in homage to the Toyotomi. Many of the rest Hideyoshi himself supplied from his former palace at Juraku-dai in Kyoto.

One from the latter group and the most famous stone in the garden is named Fujito-no-ishi (藤戸石), after the place where it originally stood. It is easily located, being the largest upright stone, rectangular in shape, standing across the pond to the left of the large earth bridge (see map 9).

Originally this stone was at Fujito, near modern Kojima city, Okayama Prefecture, in western Japan. It stood in water that just covered it at high tide, and so came to be called "the floating rock" *(ukitsu-no-iwa).* In 1184 there was a battle at this place between the Taira and the Minamoto. The Minamoto general, Sasaki Moritsuna, needing to ford the strait of Fujito, is said to have hired a fisherman as a spy, and, having learned from him the secret of the ford and "the floating rock," to have killed him to keep the information secret. According to legend, the fisherman's blood was spilled upon the stone.

Moritsuna then successfully forded the strait and won his battle, and in due course was given the nearby lands as a reward.

The occasion of his return to take possession of this land and his confrontation by the fisherman's mother is the subject of the Noh play *Fujito*. The dead man's mother persuades him to admit and repent the murder. Moritsuna prays for the soul of the fisherman, and the play concludes with the appearance of the fisherman's ghost, which has been released from hatred by Moritsuna's prayers.

Some centuries after Moritsuna's time the famous stone was brought to Kyoto, to the garden of the 16th-century general Hosokawa Ujitsuna, and from there it went to other places, eventually being donated to Hideyoshi's garden at Juraku-dai. They say that Hideyoshi offered the priest Gien, abbot of Daigo-ji, his choice between 1000 *koku* of rice (one *koku* is about five bushels) and the stone. Gien took the stone, and thus it came to its present location in front of the camellia tree at Sambo-in. During all of its many travels the stone Fujito was always splendidly clothed and conveyed in great dignity with numerous attendants because of its importance and great value.

d. The waterfall is arranged in three drops calculated to produce a pleasing sound.

# 二条城 Nijo-jo
# Nijo Castle

1. GENERAL HISTORY. Nijo Castle was started by Ieyasu (1542–1616), the first Tokugawa shogun, in 1602. The site was in the center of the city: lately it had held a mansion of the Ashikaga shoguns; originally it was at the southeast corner of the old Imperial Palace enclosure.

Ieyasu's first visit to his castle came in 1603, but its expansion and development continued through 1625 under the third shogun, Iemitsu (1603–51), who added buildings from the Fushimi Castle of Hideyoshi. Ieyasu visited Nijo again in 1611 and in 1614–15; the second shogun, Hidetada (1579–1632), and his son Iemitsu came in 1623 and 1626. In 1626 the Emperor Go-Mizu-no-o was received at the castle; and the final appearance of the early shoguns was in 1634, when Iemitsu "appeared at Nijo at the head of 300,000 troops." After that the Tokugawa apparently decided they could afford to ignore Kyoto, for they stopped coming there and had certain buildings in the castle dismantled and taken elsewhere.

After Iemitsu's last visit Nijo spent about 230 years without seeing a shogun. In the meantime more buildings disappeared. The Hon-maru (本丸 the central building) and the main keep, both of them relics of Fushimi Castle, burned late in the 18th century and were not replaced.

The present Hon-maru was the town mansion of Prince Katsura before being given to Nijo (then an imperial villa) in the 1870's. The keep has never been replaced.

This left little more than the halls of the Ni-no-maru(二之丸 the secondary ring) standing within the castle's great stone walls, but the shoguns did not do any rebuilding.

In 1863 the fourteenth shogun, Iemochi (1846–1866), came to Kyoto to confer with the emperor on the growing problem of foreign visitors to Japan, a problem which he was not strong enough to handle. The emperor told him to send the foreigners away, but Iemochi was unable to accomplish this. His visits to Kyoto became more frequent. In 1866 he died and was succeeded by Tokugawa Keiki (1837–1913). The latter lived most of his brief rule at Nijo Castle. The combination of a weak economy, foreign intervention, and pressure from the barons of western Japan forced Keiki to resign in 1867, and early the following year the shogunate was abolished by an imperial edict issued from the main audience hall of Nijo Castle, and then the capital was removed from Kyoto to Edo.

Nijo Castle now entered a period of varied careers. From 1871 to 1884 it was the Kyoto Prefectural Office, and it suffered heavily from thoughtless vandalism. The government employees who worked there, caught up in the craze for foreign things and reaction against the shogunate, used Nijo's paintings for such purposes as posting signs and generally abused their priceless surroundings. Fortunately, the castle was taken over by the imperial house in 1884 and restored and carefully maintained for 55 years. As a detached palace Nijo was used for banquets and other functions during the enthronement ceremonies of both the present emperor and his predecessor, the Emperor Taisho.

In 1939 the castle was turned over to the city of Kyoto, in whose care it remains today.

2. ENTRANCE AND KARA-MON (唐門). The entrance gates are arranged in castle style, so that they lead to blank walls, forcing the intruder to slow his advance and turn before proceeding farther.

Visitors are admitted to the castle by the east gate, and after turning left and then right arrive at the Kara-mon, or Chinese-style gate. This gate is said to have come from Fushimi Castle, and except for parts of the Ni-no-maru it is the only relic of Fushimi still standing on the grounds. It is typical of the fine Momoyama gates patronized by Hideyoshi and carved by Hidari Jingoro. Its roof follows the contour of the curved gable that gives it its name and shelters an intricate bank of carvings which are attributed to Jingoro.

Beyond the Kara-mon is the "carriage approach," which is the single entrance to the halls of the Ni-no-maru. Its ornate carvings of phoenixes and peonies are often attributed to Jingoro and said to come from Fushimi Castle.

3. GENERAL ASPECTS OF THE NI-NO-MARU. The Ni–no–maru consists of five buildings connected by interior passages or covered corridors. An idea of their arrangement and purpose may be helpful.

The buildings were placed in a staggered pattern with each one connected to the next.

The first building was for receiving the imperial messenger and also contained outer waiting rooms.

The second building was a minor hall for the reception of lords by ministers of the shogun. There were also ministers' offices in this building.

The third building was for the reception of "outer" lords (those who had initially sided against the Tokugawa) by the shogun.

The fourth building was for the reception of "inner" lords (Tokugawa allies from the beginning) by the shogun.

The fifth building was the shogun's own quarters.

The buildings are made of Japanese cypress *(hinoki)* and zelkova *(keyaki)* woods. They are independent units, each containing a complete series of rooms, arranged in "lower to upper" style. In each building an outer waiting room connects to more important chambers which in turn eventually admit one to the audience hall. For his audience the visitor remained in the penultimate room of the series, while the raised final room sheltered the shogun. This last room always has a large tokonoma and shelf alcove across its back.

Additional characteristics common to these halls are as follows:

All rooms lock "upper to lower," so that one cannot pass to a more important room unless the screen is unlocked on the other side.

The ornate carvings which appear in the transoms between rooms have two faces depicting different scenes. The less ornate side—usually that lacking peacocks—faces into the less important room.

Each building has hidden rooms which are built into its center, surrounded by the visible rooms. These were for bodyguards and were always connected by panels to the raised room of the shogun. They could also be used for the interrogation, incarceration, or even the disposal of prisoners. As they had no windows they acquired such names as "room of darkness," etc.

Tokugawa
*(aoi)*

Imperial Crest
*(kiku)*

The corridors, with their built-in squeak to warn of intruders, were closed off here and there by mounted wooden screens which increased the safety and privacy of those beyond them. (Most of these have been moved and are now displayed along the wider halls.) These decorated sliding doors are made of cryptomeria *(sugi),* and many of them were used as signboards and badly damaged when Nijo was used for prefectural offices in the 19th century.

The ceilings in some cases have been damaged beyond repair. Where a ceiling retains its original decoration, the ornateness of the design makes this obvious. Elsewhere simple restorations have been attempted, or the ceiling has been painted over plain—but originally all the ceilings were ornately decorated.

The paintings on walls and doors are all by members of the Kano school.

Because each building had to be progressively less bold than its predecessor, a different painter from a different sub-school of the Kano dominated each main hall. The painters were as follows:

| BUILDING | PRINCIPAL PAINTER, HIS SUB-SCHOOL |
|---|---|
| First | Kano Sanraku (1559–1635), Kyoto school; also unknown painters |
| Second, third | Kano Tanyu (1602–74), Kaji-bashi (Edo) school |
| Fourth | Kano Naonobu (1607–50), Kobiki-cho (Edo) school |
| Fifth | Kano Koi (c.1569–1636), Naka-bashi (Edo) school |

Tanyu and Naonobu were brothers, and the latter studied under Koi for some time. Sanraku and Tanyu rank among the greatest masters of the Kano school, which reached its peak in this period.

There are indications that these painters treated their work more like a craft than a medium for individual artistry. None of the paintings is signed, so that in many cases the artist is unknown. On some paintings artists apparently combined their efforts. The paintings are all done against backgrounds of gold leaf, a product of the craftsman rather than the artist.

Finally, the large metal nail covers in the corridors and elsewhere should be noted. Each is slightly different from the rest

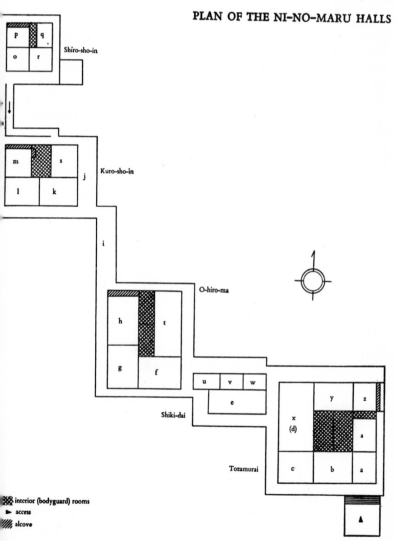

MAP TEN
Nijo Castle

二条城

**PLAN OF THE NI-NO-MARU HALLS**

Shiro-sho-in

Kuro-sho-in

O-hiro-ma

Shiki-dai

Tozamurai

interior (bodyguard) rooms

access

alcove

and all have the Tokugawa crest at their centers. When the castle became imperial property, the imperial crest was substituted in many places for that of the Tokugawa, especially on the metal inserts of door slides. The greatest part of this replacement was done in the fifth building.

4. THE ROOMS OF THE NI-NO-MARU. The rooms are discussed in the order they are usually shown the visitor, beginning and ending at the "carriage approach" at the south end of the first building (see map 10). For brevity the basic facts about each room are listed in the order name, number of mats, subject of painting, and painter. The number in parentheses indicates the building in which the room is located.

a. (1) YANAGI-NO-MA, Willow Room, or inspector's office. 24 mats. Willow trees, painter unidentified. Beyond this room one can see a 24-mat anteroom called Wakamatsu-no-ma, Young Pine Room, after its paintings, and screens in the latter's west wall lead to an inner room called Fuyo-no-ma, Lotus Room.

b. (1) RETAINER'S ROOM, 40 mats. Leopards, tigers, and bamboos, painter unidentified.

It is said that the painters of these beasts, having never seen them in life, thought that their spots and stripes indicated their sex, which may account for some combinations of leopards and tigers. The beasts symbolize strength and courage, the bamboos moral rectitude.

c. (1) WAITING ROOM OF GREATER IMPORTANCE, 36 mats. Paintings similar to those of room (b). Carvings.

d. (1) This large room is discussed in (x) below, for it is better seen on the return trip.

e. (2) SHIKIDAI-NO-MA, Reception Room, 45 mats. Giant pine by Kano Tanyu. Used for the reception of feudal lords by ministers of the shogun.

f. (3) ANTEROOM, 44 mats. Pines by Kano Tanyu. A waiting room for "outer" feudal lords.

g, and h. (3) OHIRO-MA, Grand Audience Chamber. The lower room, 44 mats, the upper 48. Giant pines and peacocks by Kano Tanyu. Doors in the east wall of the upper room connect to bodyguard rooms. The bird on one of them is a golden pheasant. Double coffered ceilings, and large tokonoma and shelf alcove across the north wall. (The shelf of this tokonoma is a single piece of zelkova wood 18 feet long and 7 inches thick.)

This is the largest audience hall of the castle, and was for the reception of the "outer" lords, who were kept to the lower room, the shogun occupying the upper one. The ornate use of lacquer and gilt reaches a climax in this hall. It was here that the Emperor Meiji pronounced the shogunate abolished in 1868.

i. (3–4) SOTETSU-NO-MA, Cycad Room, a hallway between buildings. Badly defaced in the 1870's, the walls of this hallway have been restored in plain gold leaf. Some cedar hallway doors are displayed here.

j. (4) BOTAN-NO-MA, Peony Room, a wide hallway whose coffered ceiling luxuriates in red and gold peonies. Undoubtedly the Sotetsu-no-ma was once equally well decorated.

k. (4) HAMAMATSU-NO-MA, Pine-Beach Room, a waiting room of 35 mats for "inner" lords. Pines and heron by Kano Naonobu. Note the conservative grillwork in the west transom and the mildness of these pines compared with those of room (f).

At the southeast corner of this room, a partition extending into the hallway is decorated with a famous painting of a heron on a boat in the rain, which is also attributed to Naonobu.

l, and m. (4) KURO-SHO-IN (lit., "black parlor"), audience chamber for receiving "inner" lords. Lower room, $31\frac{1}{2}$ mats, upper $24\frac{1}{2}$. Cherry blossoms, trellises, and pine by Naonobu. The arrangement is similar to that of the previous audience hall, but here everything is milder, even down to the pheasant on the second bodyguard panel—here it is a hen! There is an unusual double shelf alcove in the northeast corner of the upper room, and this room is also equipped with a small *sho-in* bay that projects into the hall.

The last Tokugawa shogun, Keiki, is said to have made his decision to resign in this chamber, in 1867.

n. (4–5) A simple narrow HALLWAY that increases the privacy and protection of the shogun's personal quarters.

o, and p. (5) SHIRO-SHO-IN (lit., "white parlor"), the shogun's own parlor, the lower room (for attendants) 18 mats, the upper 15. Scenes of China in near monochrome by Kano Koi.

Although only female attendants were allowed in these apartments, the shogun's room is still equipped with access to inner bodyguard spaces. The flower paintings in the coffered ceiling may have been supplied by the various feudal lords. Note that the imperial crest has been substituted in various places here.

q. (5) NEMURU SUZUME-NO-MA, Sleeping Sparrow Room, 12 mats. The famous painting of sparrows sleeping in a snow-covered bamboo grove is by Kano Koi and gives this anteroom its name.

r. (5) SANSUI-NO-MA, Mountain-Water Room, a name also applied to room (o). Servants' anteroom, 18 mats. Paintings similar to those of the main rooms, by Kano Koi. In the hallway corner here there are paintings of geese.

s. (4) KIKU-NO-MA, Chrysanthemum Room, 28 mats. Trellises and open fans by Naonobu. I believe the flowers on them are, however, peonies *(botan)*.

t. (3) YARI-NO-MA, Spear Hall, or TAKA-NO-MA, Hawk Room, $52\frac{1}{2}$ mats. Massive pines and hawks attributed to Kano Tanyu. This room was the shogun's armory. Note that not all of its west wall is solid—the sliding sections open to the inner bodyguard rooms.

u, v, and w. (2) THREE SMALL MINISTERS' OFFICES of 14, 12, and 12 mats respectively. The first two have paintings of geese, and the third of willows and cranes, all attributed to Tanyu. As they face north, these rooms are dark. Like all rooms not expressly for the use of the shogun, they have no alcoves.

x. (1) IMPERIAL MESSENGER'S WAITING ROOM, $76\frac{1}{2}$ mats. Jungle beasts and bamboos by unidentified Kano artist(s). Ornate carvings seem to float in the transom on the east wall.

y, and z. (1) CHOKUSHI-NO-MA, Imperial Messenger's Audience Hall, two rooms in the usual upper-lower arrangement. Lower room, 35 mats, upper 21. Maples by Kano Sanraku. The hallway along this room runs to a dead end. There are several interior spaces that connect to the inner walls of these two rooms.

All together, counting the two wide hallways, there are 35 rooms (about 800 mats), of which the 24 or 25 principal ones are shown to visitors.

5. NI-NO-MARU GROUNDS. The buildings north of the Ni-no-maru are the kitchen complex of the castle, consisting of two kitchen buildings—one was reserved for the shogun—and a rice granary.

West of the Ni-no-maru is a garden built around a large pond. The garden is thought to have been designed by Kobori Enshu (1576–1647) about 1626, the time of the Emperor Go-Mizu-no-o's visit here. It has numerous fine stones and a general appearance of strength and solidity in keeping with the impression that the shogun wished to make. It has a central *horai* (mythical paradise) island, flanked left and right by "tortoise" and "crane" islands, respectively. It is said that this garden was originally designed without trees because the shogun did not wish to be reminded by their falling leaves of the transitoriness of life.

# 修学院　Shugaku-in Rikyu
# 離宮　Detached Palace at Shugaku-in

1. HISTORY. The name Shugaku (learning, scholarship) is said to go back more than a thousand years to the time when a Tendai temple to Fudo Myo-o was erected here by a man grateful to a priest who had secured him a governorship. The temple was named Shugaku-ji. It flourished in the years prior to 1000 but, after continuing to exist into the 15th century, it was destroyed in the Onin War and never rebuilt. The name lived on as Shugaku-in, the hamlet which had grown up around the temple.

The Emperor Go-Mizu-no-o (1596–1680, reigned 1611–29) was the man behind the founding of Shugaku-in Rikyu. After his abdication in 1629 he began searching out a site for a villa. For several years he examined the northern environs of the city, and finally he decided on Shugaku-in. He himself designed much of the villa which was made there. The project was supported by the Tokugawa, who had become friendly towards him after he retired, and the villa was completed in the 1650's. Thereafter Go-Mizu-no-o visited it at least twice annually.

When Go-Mizu-no-o died in 1680, the villa was abandoned and went to ruin. It was restored beginning in 1716 for the use of the retired Emperor Reigen, the last of Go-Mizu-no-o's reigning children. Reigen visited the villa regularly between 1721 and 1732, the year he died. Again, this time for ninety years, the villa was abandoned. In 1822–26 it was restored again, for the retired Emperor Kokaku, who used it for ten years until he got too old to come, and after his death in 1841 Shugaku-in entered its third period of neglect.

The Emperor Meiji took it over after the Restoration and in 1883 it was thoroughly repaired into its present condition.

It is from this last restoration that the tree-lined avenues between the three sections of the villa date—they replaced narrow trails among the rice fields in 1890. Even today these rice fields that separate the parts of the villa are privately farmed land.

The beauty of Shugaku-in Rikyu lies in its naturalness, for all the human creations here have been designed not to intrude on the beauties of the natural scenery. In this respect the villa may be contrasted with Katsura Rikyu, where the artfulness of the human creator, particularly in the field of architecture, is emphasized. Lacking Shugaku-in's spectacular site, Katsura depends for its effect upon the skill of those who made it. Because of this differing emphasis, Katsura's basic strength lies in its architecture, while that of Shugaku-in lies in its gardens.

2. THE LOWER VILLA. Visitors enter Shugaku-in Rikyu through a small door set in the west gate of the Lower Villa; the gate itself is not opened for ordinary visitors. Inside, a wide path leads to the left past the closed Miyuki-mon (御幸門 Imperial Gate), opposite which is the site of the former temple Shugaku-ji. The path doubles back through a side entrance and crosses behind Miyuki-mon.

The garden surrounds a single building which hangs out over it. Each wing of this building has its own name: the small, pink-walled wing which one sees first is Mikoshi-yose (御輿寄 Imperial Palanquin Approach); the southern wing, around which one walks, is Zoroku-an (蔵六庵 Tortoise Arbor); the eastern side—the heart of the building—is Jugetsu-kan (寿月観 Felicitous Moon View).

The present structure is a restoration of Go-Mizu-no-o's original building; it dates from 1824. It contains seven rooms of 15, 12, 10½, 6, 5, 4½, and 1½ mats respectively. The most important of these is Jugetsu-kan's central room of 15 mats, three of which are raised to indicate imperial use. The room has a tokonoma and shelf alcove, the latter having cupboards whose doors are decorated with flowers on gold by Hara Zaichu. Between the alcoves is a third one, tall and narrow, which was specially built in to house Go-Mizu-no-o's *biwa* (large lute). The screens on the side wall depict the "Three Laughing Sages of Kokei" and were painted by Kishi Ganku (1749–1838).

Formerly there were two additional structures here. A wing extending to the north was called Zoroku-an—its name plaque was apparently transferred to the present Zoroku-an—and a separate structure in the southeast corner of the garden was called Wankyoku-kaku. Both of these are gone, as is the path to the latter, which was lit by the stone lantern which still stands in that part of the garden. The name plaques of Zoroku-an and Jugetsu-kan are said to have been written by Go-Mizu-no-o himself.

The garden was designed by Go-Mizu-no-o, although the island in the small pond apparently came later, perhaps through the continued deposit of sand by the stream. There are three stone lanterns in the garden. The one mentioned above is called "turret shape." The primitive one on the island is known as "sleeve shape" (i.e., kimono sleeve) or "alligator's mouth," and the last one, next to the path, is called "Korean lantern." The water in this garden comes from the garden of the Upper Villa. The garden is small and offers no distant perspective; one is rather surrounded by it and its maple trees.

3. THE MIDDLE VILLA. It is this section that has undergone the most change over the years. It was built somewhat after the others and was first used by Go-Mizu-no-o's eleventh daughter. When she became a nun in 1680, the temple Rinkyu-ji (林丘寺) was founded and erected next to this villa, which she used as an abbess's residence. She started a line of royal abbesses that continued until the Meiji Restoration. At that time the temple was disestablished and its buildings taken to enlarge the Middle Villa, but in 1872 the temple was recreated and the buildings returned to it, with the exception of the two which stand in the Middle Villa today. One of these, Rakushi-ken (楽只軒 lit., "free-ease eaves"), was formerly the abbess's residence. The other, Okesho-den (御化粧殿 lit., "toilette palace"), was once the dressing room of Tofuku Mon-in (1607–78), Go-Mizu-no-o's Tokugawa consort, brought here after her death. Today the villa and Rinkyu-ji stand side by side; the temple is not generally open to visitors.

The grounds of the Middle Villa are entered from the northwest. There are two gates and three wide flights of stone steps. A third gate, which has a tile roof and stands to one side between the other two, formerly belonged to Rinkyu-ji.

The garden is dominated by a low flat pine tree which, because of its enforced shape, is called *kasa-matsu*, umbrella pine. At its highest it is about two feet tall. There is also a stone lantern of interest in this garden. It is said to contain disguised Christian symbols dating from the time when Christianity was forbidden in Japan. A Jizo-like image in relief near the base is said to be Mary; two lines cut out of the pedestal are said to be an "undone" cross.

Okesho-den (now often Kyaku-den, Reception Hall) is the upper building. It is the most ornate building at Shugaku-in, a reminder that it was not originally designed for this villa. The Tokugawa crest which appears here and there also testifies to this hall's earlier days as Tofuku Mon-in's dressing room. It opens wide on the garden, and is surmounted by a heavy hip-and-gable roof.

The central room is Okesho-no-ma, Dressing Room, 12½ mats. At its center back is a shelf alcove called *kasumi-dana* ("shelves of mist") which ranks with the shelf alcoves at Katsura Rikyu and Daigo's Sambo-in as one of the three most admired in Japan. The walls of this room are decorated with poems by various nobles and scenes of the "eight views" of Shugaku-in, pasted up against a background of gold dust clouds. The cupboard panels have sectioned paintings attributed to Yuzen. The screens and walls of this room have a lower border of blue and gold diamonds.

There are four cedar doors in the corridors about this room. Two flank the outer corridors and depict carp, attributed to Sumiyoshi Gukei (1631–1705)—it is said that the painter Maruyama Okyo (1733–95) found these carp so lifelike that he added the netting now over them to keep them in at night, but others attribute the whole painting to Kano Hidenobu (1775–1828); so the story is in doubt. The other two doors, at the back of the west corridor, depict carts of the type still used in the annual Gion Festival. On the back of these doors is a third cart, a sort of warship on wheels filled with tiny men. All are said to be the work of Sumiyoshi Gukei.

East of the main room is Shiki-no-ma, Four Seasons Room (10 mats), so named because its screens have paintings of the four seasons, one season to each wall. They are by Kano Hidenobu.

Both of these rooms have notable cloisonné beam ornaments—in the main room they are flower carts, in this one bamboo leaves. The door slides of Shiki-no-ma, shaped like cocks, are also interesting.

There are two other rooms at the back of Okesho-den, the

San-no-ma (Third Room) of 10 mats and the Butsu-no-ma (Buddha Room) of 6. The latter has an altar, but no image, and is said to have been added when the building was part of Rinkyu-ji. Its cupboard doors are decorated with fan-shaped paintings of the seasons. The railing on the verandah here apparently encircled the building at one time.

Rakushi-ken is a pink-walled building that dates from 1668. In the Rinkyu-ji period it was used by the abbess and called Shosho-in. Of its six rooms the visitor is usually shown only the outer two. The first (6 mats) has alcove paintings of the cherry trees at Mt. Yoshino, south of Nara, and the second (8 mats) has a badly blackened painting of the famous maples of the Tatsuta River, near Yoshino. Both are by Kano Tanshin (1653–1718), a son of Tanyu. Between the two rooms hangs a tablet with the name of the building on it, written by Go-Mizu-no-o. It is decorated with cloisonné bamboo leaves.

The two buildings are connected by a flight of steps which have risers of differing heights.

4. THE UPPER VILLA. Here the varied and natural beauty of the Shugaku-in gardens reaches its climax. The combination of luxuriant foliage of all kinds and distant sceneries—the mountains to the northwest, the city to the southwest—is probably unequaled in any other Kyoto garden.

The garden is built around a large pond (Yokuryu-chi 浴竜池 Bathing Dragon Pond) which is supported on its west bank by a massive dam. The dam is hidden under a broad, flat-topped hedge, from the surface of which maple trees emerge. Another mass of hedge rises up a hill at the south end of the pond. It is made of dozens of different plants that provide a constantly changing pattern of color. Because of its width and varied consistency it can only be trimmed by an enormous razor-sharp scythe specially made for the purpose.

Upon entering the villa, one climbs a path through this hedge and emerges at the highest point on the grounds. There is an excellent view back to Kyoto from here. The building perched here is Rinun-tei (隣雲亭 Pavilion in the Clouds); it is an 1824 reconstruction—changed somewhat in back—of the original pavilion.

Rinun-tei has two sets of rooms. In back there are three of 8, 6, and 6 mats respectively. In the front, separated from them by a breezeway, are two more, of 6 and 3 mats, and a porch called Senshi-dai (洗詩台 Poem-Washing Platform). The breezeway permits the front rooms to be opened on all four sides, making Rinun-tei a cool paradise in the hot summer. This part of the building is surrounded by a paved court embedded with fine stones in groups of one, two, and three. On the northeast side there is a stone lantern nicknamed *yama-dera,* "mountain temple."

The second building of the Upper Villa is at the opposite end of the grounds, standing on the pond's largest island. It is called Kyusui-tei (窮邃亭), and has stood unchanged since the 1650's. It has a large ornament at the apex of its roof that is decorated with the imperial crest, and a fancy name plaque under the southwest eaves written by Go-Mizu-no-o, but otherwise it is quite plain.

Inside Kyusui-tei a single space has been divided into three "rooms." The outside "room" is 12 mats, two of them oversize, ranged about the *jo-dan* (upper level) which consists of 6 raised undersize mats in the north corner overlooking the pond. The different levels of the two areas and a sort of hanging cornice between them give them the quality of being two separate rooms. The third "room" is a wooden-floored tea pantry about 6 by 6 feet in size. There is a "humble entrance" to the pantry through its outside wall—humbling because one must bend double to get through.

The large sliding screens in the windows overlooking the pond have the unusual feature of swinging out from the bottom. Like Rinun-tei, Kyusui-tei has a paved court around it, in this case embedded with single stones.

There are two other sizable islands in the pond besides the one under Kyusui-tei. Miho Island, at the northern end of the pond, is so named because its pine trees are meant to remind one of the famous pine-clad sand bar of the same name in eastern Japan. Bansho-u (万松塢 Myriad Pines Landing), the overgrown island south of Kyusui-tei, was once a barren, rocky "dragon's back." Its boat landing and small pavilion date from a visit by the Emperor Meiji. The island is reached by a handsome, asymmetrical bridge called Chitose-bashi (千歳橋 Bridge of Eternity) that stands on two stone piers.

This bridge was donated by the governor of Kii Province in 1824, when the villa was being restored. His name was Naito Nobuatsu, Kii-no-kami, and it is said that the shogun disapproved of his handsome gift to the imperial house and ordered him to commit suicide. There had been no bridge to Bansho-u before this one was built.

There are two other bridges from Kyusui-tei's island. Kaede-bashi (楓橋 Maple Bridge), on the east side, is so named because it affords a view up into the "maple valley" at the north end of the pond. Do-bashi (土橋 Earth Bridge) is a long span on the northwest side of the island. From it one sees Miho Island and the maple valley on his right, and the flat hedge on top of the dam and distant mountains on his left.

There is a boat landing in the western corner of the pond.

Originally a large building called Shishi-sai (止々斎) stood near this landing, but it was removed from the villa in 1709, and later it burned (1788).

The pond is fed from several sources, among which are two waterfalls with the same ultimate source. O-daki (雄滝 Male Waterfall) has a drop of about thirty feet and is northeast of Rinun-tei. The same stream feeds Me-daki (雌滝 Female Waterfall), a small, gurgling opening at the southern end of the pond near the villa gate.

Shugaku-in owns the paths linking the three villas and the two low hills behind it to the east. The total property is about 70 acres.

# 二条 Nijo Jinya
# 陣屋 The Encampment House at Nijo

1. HISTORY. The family which built Nijo Jinya descends from a man who worked at the Kasuga Shrine in Nara and lived in a nearby village called Ogawa (小川); he took the name of his village. A descendant of this first Ogawa was a retainer to Oda Nobunaga and Toyotomi Hideyoshi. Under them he held a castle at Imabaru, but after Hideyoshi's death he lost his holdings and drifted for a while, eventually buying the land where Nijo Jinya now stands. He started a rice dealership and won the trade of the imperial court, which gave him access to the palace and brought him in contact with various *daimyo* (feudal lords). Some of these lords began to stop over at Ogawa's house when they were in Kyoto, and thus the house began to fill the position of a hostelry.

Ogawa eventually acknowledged that his home was an inn and set about enlarging and fortifying it to suit it to the requirements of his guests. Good taste and the best available materials were used in this enlargement, which took about thirty years. The result, about the middle of the 17th century, was a building of 24 rooms that was characterized by concealed fortifications, amazingly comprehensive fireproofing devices, and revolutionary structural materials. The last were used both for fireproofing and for ornament. As an example of the ingenuity that went into this building 12 wells were drilled, all of them interconnected so that water would never be lacking. Another noteworthy achievement was that the *jinya's* fireproofing devices—earthen doors and window slides, narrow windows, plastered and metal-sheathed roof sections, and the like—were installed without damaging the artistic appearance of the rooms or making their interiors seem oppressive. A fine balance was struck between practical and aesthetic requirements.

The building appears disorderly in arrangement, but the disorder is deceptive: many elements which contribute to this im-

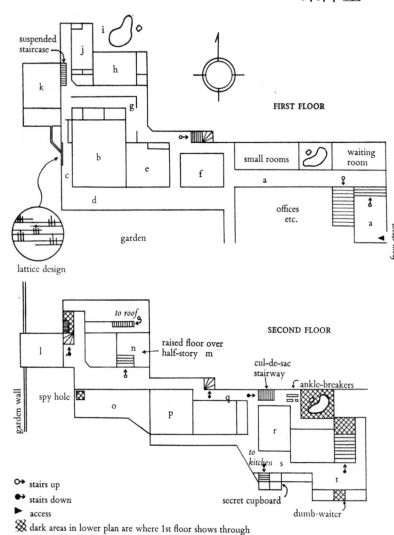

MAP ELEVEN
Nijo Jinya

二条陣屋

**FIRST FLOOR**

suspended staircase

i

j

h

k

g

b

e

f

small rooms

waiting room

a

c

d

offices etc.

a

a

garden

lattice design

from street

**SECOND FLOOR**

to roof

l

n

raised floor over half-story  m

cul-de-sac stairway

ankle-breakers

garden wall

spy hole

o

p

q

r

to kitchen  s

secret cupboard

t

dumb-waiter

stairs up

stairs down

access

dark areas in lower plan are where 1st floor shows through

Ogawa
*(kuyoboshi)*

Ogawa
*(kuyoboshi)*

pression have ingenious hidden purposes. The rooms are spread over three stories (the third has only one room), but the roof was originally arranged so that the building would appear from the street to be a one-story structure. From the beginning the intention was to disarm the outsider, and the skill with which the *jinya's* fortress nature was built into it leads one to believe that this intention was successfully carried out.

Because Nijo Jinya is still privately owned by the Ogawa family, it is shown only by appointment (see Part III).

2. THE BUILDING IN DETAIL. As it is difficult to describe otherwise the items following are keyed to the accompanying plan (map 11).

a. The outside entrance to the building was originally done in Kyoto fashion, with a narrow-lattice door of the type one still sees everywhere in the city. It was fixed so its place could be taken by an earthen door if fire threatened.

The entrance hall contains a wooden sign that is an old advertisement for an apothecary shop—besides its rice business, the family dealt in pharmaceuticals from time to time. The flooring of the hallway has a built-in squeak to warn of intruders. To the right of this hallway there is a small interior court containing a shrine to Benten.

b. O-ZASHIKI (大座敷 Great Parlor). This is the largest room in the building: 15 mats. It is the principal room for receiving and entertaining. Along its north wall are an incense chamber, a tokonoma, and a shelf alcove. The painting of a seated man on the panels of the incense chamber, which has raised contours and is inlaid with pearl, was done by Ogawa Haritsu, an artist who belonged to a branch of the *jinya's* family. It also has some inlaid glass, noteworthy because at that time glass was rare and considered precious. There is a wooden roof "tile" on the shelf of this chamber, an ancestor of the roof tiles used today.

The cupboard over the shelf is decorated with a charcoal drawing by Kano Eishin (or Yasunobu, 1616–85). The pulls on the cupboard doors are patterned to be an abbreviated form of the *kuyoboshi,* the Ogawa crest.

The sliding screens on the east side of the room, depicting dogs, were painted by a member of the Maruyama school. The screens here are fitted with clever flush locks and keys for security, as they are in many places about the building.

On three sides of this room the lower borders of the screens are decorated with a panorama of the 36 mountains of Higashiyama, the eastern horizon of Kyoto. Many temples are shown which no longer exist. "North" on this pictorial map is in the northeast part of the room, and the picture circles the room to "south" at the north end of the west wall.

Some of the more readily discernible landmarks in the long picture are (from "north"): Shimogamo Shrine (first screen); Nanzen-ji, Chion-in, Yasaka Pagoda, and Kiyomizu-dera (second); Tofuku-ji and the Inari Shrine (fourth); Uji Bridge and the Byodo-in (tenth).

The part of this picture along the east wall was painted about 1700 by Toda Shorei; the remainder is about a century younger, and is the work of one Higashiyama Yoshiaki.

The decorative nail covers on the beams of this room are made of china rather than the usual metal; they date from the early part of the 17th century. They are Kutani ware, one of Japan's more famous older chinas, made on the coast of the Japan Sea north of Kyoto in what is now Ishikawa Prefecture. The plaque on the east wall was written by Sanjo Sanetaka in 1501 by order of the emperor, and concerns the eight views of Lake Biwa.

The sheet paulownia-wood ceiling has a square hole in it which appears to be solely for access to the skylight window above it. However, this hole also leads to a hidden, soundproof guard post built into the floor above. The trap is situated directly over the residing baron's visitor (in the normal seating arrangement), so that the guard above could drop right on him should this prove necessary. The hole is designed, however, so that one cannot see anything above it except the innocent skylight window. It has acoustic qualities which enable the guard to hear everything spoken below.

c. WEST HALLWAY. Screens in this hallway have a lattice design that forms a pun on "Ogawa" (see map). The vertical lines represent 小 (O), while the horizontal lines form the caricature of an ambling river (*gawa*, river).

d. SOUTH HALLWAY. The outside screens here have paintings of pines that date from the 17th century and are associated with an old song for the *koto*. These screens are built on different levels so that, at night, one can distinguish their rattling in the wind, etc., from the sounds made by an intruder trying to move them.

The hooks up under the eaves of the roof are for hanging wet mats to protect the building from neighborhood fires. As a similar precaution the edge of the roof was sheathed in sheet brass.

Visitors are advised that the garden is meant to be viewed from inside the main room near the tokonoma, and not from the edge of the hallway. To sit on the edge of the hallway and look at the garden is considered a serious misunderstanding.

e. O-NOH-NO-MA, Noh Room, 8 mats. In this room the mats can be raised to reveal a fine floor usable as a Noh stage. Beneath the floor there is a deep open space and strategically placed great jars to swallow the noise made by shoes and feet. The pine tree painting usually found on Noh stages is in the adjoining hall. The screens on both the west and east walls have soundproof panels which can be dropped into place to contain the Noh noises—or to prevent eavesdropping between rooms. Around the base of these screens there are paintings as follows: west: Hozu Rapids by Toda Shorei, ca. 1700; south: the Seta River to Yodo by Higashiyama Giryo, 18th century; east: Hokoku Jinja festival by Nagazawa Roho, 18th century. (The Hokoku Jinja was patronized by Toyotomi Hideyoshi and stands near the National Museum in Kyoto.)

The *fusuma* of cranes on the north wall is believed to be a work of the Kano school. The hanging post at the corner of the tokonoma is hollow and gives a resonant sound when its end is struck.

f. A SIX-MAT GUEST ROOM.

g. A HALLWAY running north and then west. Where it turns, the corner beams are built out so that a man can scale them and escape to a concealed half-story above by means of a small triangular hole near the ceiling. At waist level in this corner there was originally a copper mirror with a miniature stone garden at its base. The stones could be used as emergency weapons.

The east-west part of this hallway is divided into two corridors, so that traffic can be directed down the side away from the occupied room, again to prevent eavesdropping.

h. KASUGA-NO-MA (春日の間), a six-mat room looking out on a garden. It is named after the Kasuga Shrine in Nara, honoring the Ogawa ancestor who worked there. The tokonoma contains a scene of Mt. Mikasa in Nara. The gourd shape cut out there is a symbol for Nara's Sarusawa Pond. The cupboard panels on the east wall are painted with a view of Nara's Todai-ji, showing two gates, the Daibutsu-den, and the Nigatsu-do with its famous cedar tree.

Above the south doorway to this room there are painted gold lacquer bats, and a fan design with a fish on it. The panel in the floor of the room lifts to become a hearth.

i. The small GARDEN is intended to represent Sarusawa Pond and its lantern a small Kasuga-type shrine. Small wells dug in this garden provided hiding places for valuables and documents in case of fire or siege.

j. KAINYO-AN (皆如庵), a small tearoom. The natural grain of its ceiling is much admired. Bamboo uprights on the north wall form a symbolic tokonoma. A panel in the far corner lifts to make a hearth. Two others conceal china storage shelves. The closet at the south end of this room has a "back door" into the hallway, so that someone hiding there can escape if necessary.

k. DAIMYO YUDONO (大名湯殿 Lord's Bath Room). In this antique bath heated water was poured in from outside the room to reach the bath by conduit. Cold well water adjusted the temperature. A charcoal fire was used to keep the bath water hot. This room is noteworthy for the various forms of tile used in it, as well as for its plaster ceiling, which was inlaid with mother-of-pearl at the corners. The tile was used about three hundred years ahead of its time. The windows of the bath are fitted with fireproof screens.

In the hallway outside the bath room there is a seeming shelf which, when unhooked, lowers to provide a stairway of escape to the concealed upper stories of the building.

l. TOMABUNE-NO-MA (苫船の間 Thatched-Boat Room) or SOTETSU-NO-MA (蘇鉄の間 Cycad Room). This room is built to resemble the interior of a boat. One must step down to enter it as one would step into a boat. The room hangs out over the wall of the grounds, and in former days the schoolyard underneath it was the lower reaches of Shinsen-en's pond, so that water could be brought up by the bucket and pulley outside the west window—as if one were dipping it from a boat. In practical terms the overhang of this room provided a means of emergency escape from the grounds, while the water-dipping was an additional safeguard against fire.

Nearly all the upstairs windows of the *jinya* are fitted with antique fireproofing devices, clay slides to replace the vulnerable paper screens. Many of these windows are built narrow to make them less vulnerable, as well as less noticeable, from the outside.

The second name of this room derives from paintings of cycad palms which were once on its walls.

The room is fragile and can no longer bear much weight.

m. Across the hall from the above, a partition conceals a half-story which can be used for hiding. At its far end is the small triangular opening reached by the hallway escape ladder described in (g) above.

n. This TEAROOM is over the half-story and has a small armory concealed in its east wall. The wide stair to it protects one against being bottled into the room. At its back is another stair that leads to the roof, where there is an eight-mat verandah for moon-viewing and tea.

o. SOUNDPROOF HIDING PLACE for the bodyguard lying over the main downstairs parlor. To make this compartment noiseless, its walls and screens were doubled and its floor specially insulated.

p. THE RED WALL ROOM, named after the former color of its walls. It is 8 mats with an old-style flat tokonoma. The east wall has a four-screen map of the main route between Fukuoka and Edo in which cities are generally represented by pictures of their castles.

In the upper part of the left screen one finds Nagasaki and Fukuoka; in the middle of the second screen is Kyoto; near the top of the fourth (right) one is Mt. Fuji, below it to the right Hakone;

down the right-hand edge are Kanagawa, Totsuka, Kawasaki, and, finally, Edo at the bottom.

q. A narrow HALLWAY with a low ceiling to limit swordplay. Its small fireproof windows let in little light to assist the intruder. It doglegs about a blind staircase in which a person may trap an enemy. Farther on, the flooring can be removed, exposing ankle-breaking beams.

r. KAKOI-NO-MA (囲の間), a tearoom of $4\frac{1}{2}$ mats with an ante-room of 2 mats. The fine bamboo upright of the former, *goma-take,* is said to have lasted more than three centuries in perfect condition because it was "cut at exactly the right moment." The net pattern of the ceiling gave this room its name *kakoi,* "fenced."

s. This HALLWAY can be darkened by closing the fireproof window. The stair leads down to the kitchen.

At the stair there are two cupboards—for hiding purposes there is a third cupboard concealed between them, so both may be opened without revealing a person inside.

t. There is a DUMB-WAITER and a medicine chest from the family's apothecary days here. The wide stairway which leads back down to a point next to the *jinya's* entrance is relatively new. The skylight and round window here are designed so that the lattices of the window can be read as a sundial.

# 清水寺 Kiyomizu-dera
## Clear Water Temple

1. LEGEND AND HISTORY. The history of Kiyomizu recedes into the pre-Kyoto period and falls back on a legend which is told with enough consistency so that one version of it bears repeating here:

"According to the legend, the novice Enchin, having dreamt that he saw a golden stream flowing down into the Yodogawa, went in search of it, and ascending to its source, found there an old man sitting under a tree, who gave his name as Gyoei, and said: 'I have been here for the last two hundred years repeating the invocation to Kannon, and waiting for you to relieve me. Take my place for a while, that I may perform a journey that is required of me. This is a suitable spot for the erection of a hermitage, and the log which you see lying here will supply the material for an image of the Most Compassionate One,' (i.e., Kannon). With these words he disappeared, leaving the novice in charge of the solitude. After a while, finding that the old man did not return, Enchin climbed a neighboring hill, and discovered a pair of shoes lying on its summit, from which he inferred that the mysterious old man was none other than Kannon in human form, who had left the shoes behind on re-ascending to heaven. He now determined to make the image of the god, but found his strength insufficient, and passed several years looking at the log, vainly planning how to overcome the difficulty. Twenty years had elapsed, when one day good luck guided the warrior Saka-no-ue Tamuramaro, who was in pursuit of a stag, to this very spot. While he was resting, Enchin represented his difficulties to the hunter, who was struck with admiration at the untiring devotion of the novice, and subsequently, having taken counsel with his wife, gave his own house to be pulled down and re-erected by the side of the cascade as a temple for the image, which was now at last completed."[1]

1. B. H. Chamberlain and W. B. Mason, *op. cit.,* page 315.

In the person of Saka-no-ue Tamuramaro (758–811), Kiyo-mizu enters history. Tamuramaro's reason for hunting a stag was that his wife was about to give birth, and it was thought that stag's blood would make for an easy delivery. Enchin regarded the killing of a stag as an act against Buddhism and talked Tamu-ramaro out of it. The result was that Tamuramaro became Kiyomizu's first great patron: his house became the temple's first hall, and he himself was named the temple's founder.

Later this same man took part in campaigns against the abo-rigines of northern Japan, and finally in 797 he was given the recently created title *sei-i-tai-shogun* (subjugating-barbarians great general) and sent to conquer them, which he did. When he returned successful, the emperor rewarded him with a build-ing of the former palace at Nagaoka, its Shishin-den. This build-ing, too, Tamuramaro gave to Enchin's temple, in 805, and it was named Tamura-do in his honor. The temple was officially recog-nized the same year and received its own name, Seisui-ji,[2] two years later.

We are not told how Tamuramaro's wife fared in childbirth, but she must have done well, for Kiyomizu has always been as-sociated with pregnancy and childbirth, and to this day prayers for easy delivery are offered here. It is a kind of traditional spe-cialty with the temple.

Tamuramaro is remembered chiefly as the first great bearer of the title *sei-i-tai-shogun*, the same title which, revived some 400 years after him, was used by the Minamoto, Ashikaga, and Toku-gawa families in turn to give them a position from which to impose their wills on Japan.

After his death Tamuramaro was buried near Kyoto. Some say his tomb is the one known as Shogun-zuka, not far from Kiyo-mizu, in which a huge image of a soldier is reputed to have been buried when the city was founded, to serve as its protector.

Always a popular temple, Kiyomizu has been rebuilt many times, for it was repeatedly destroyed or burned in various dis-asters over the centuries. In one 11th-century rebuilding a new main hall was erected, and the Tamura-do was moved to one

2. Kiyomizu-dera is a "Japanese" pronunciation of the temple's original name, Seisui-ji, which is written with the same characters. The former has firmly replaced the latter over the centuries.

side, to its present location. Other halls were added, but the fires continued. By 1633 there had been six major fires, the most recent in 1629, and the shogun Tokugawa Iemitsu ordered the temple rebuilt again. The majority of the temple's buildings now date from 1633; only four survived the fire of 1629. The rebuilt structures, however, are said to reflect the styles of their predecessors.

Kiyomizu is a temple of the Hosso sect of Buddhism, which was brought to Japan from China in 655 and has among its remaining temples Kofuku-ji, Yakushi-ji, and Horyu-ji, all in Nara. In its sect Kiyomizu betrays the length of its history, for the Kyoto temple is rare whose religious roots go back to Nara.

Among the Saikoku San-ju-san Sho—a group of 33 temples in the Kyoto area, all sacred to Kannon, which form a pilgrimage route—Kiyomizu is number 16.

2. THE BUILDINGS. The list of buildings which follows is keyed to map 12. All buildings date from 1633 unless otherwise indicated.

a. TAIZAN-JI (泰産寺 Gentle Delivery Temple). This sub-temple is dedicated to easy childbirth. It consists of two buildings, a main hall and the Koyasu-no-to or Fertility Tower, a small pagoda. Formerly these buildings stood near the Nio-mon in the main compound; they were moved across the valley about 1908–9.

The main hall houses an image of Kannon, Koyasu (easy child[3]) Kannon, that is more than 1200 years old. It is said that the consort of the Emperor Shomu (699–756), Komyo Kogo (701–60), prayed to this image at the time of her delivery in 718. The daughter who was born to her eventually became the Empress Koken.

b. OTOWA-NO-TAKI (音羽の滝 Sound-of-Feathers Waterfall). Springing from an unknown source inside the mountain, this is Enchin's stream. Its water is believed to have purifying qualities, and the deity Fudo Myo-o is worshiped here. Worshipers sometimes stand in the fall, although most just use dippers to get water from it.

3. The Koyasu in the name of the pagoda and the one in the name of the Kannon are different words. The name of the pagoda is written with the character 肥, while that of the Kannon uses the characters 子安.

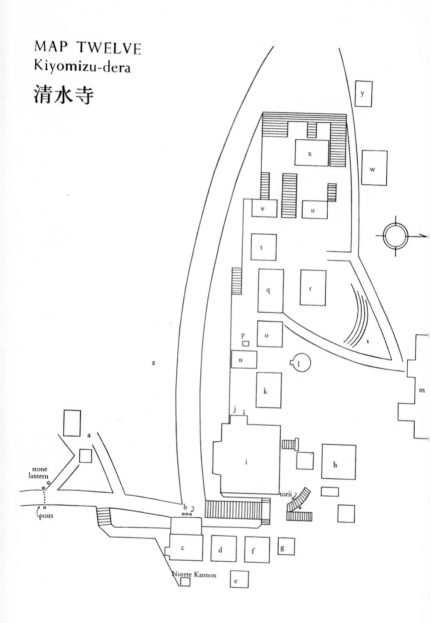

## MAP TWELVE
## Kiyomizu-dera

# 清水寺

y

x

w

v u

t

q r

p o

n s

l

k m

j

stone
lantern

a

i

h

posts

b torii

c

d f g

Nurete Kannon

e

z

c. OKU-NO-IN (奥の院 Innermost Temple). Dedicated to the eleven-faced, thousand-armed Kannon (Ju-ichi-sen Kannon), this hall is reputed to be on the site of Gyo-ei's hut, the place where Enchin first came upon him. By its south wall is a small shrine to Yashajin, a minor deity, and behind the building is a small image of Nurete Kannon—Kannon standing in water. It is a purifying act to dip the water over the image's head.

The large ship painting hanging under the eaves of Oku-no-in dates from 1634. It shows a trading vessel of the house of Sue-yoshi under full sail and was painted by Kitamura Chubei.

Trading ships at that time were known as "red seal ships" after the color of the seal on their license to trade. The Tokugawa were extremely chary of the number of ships they allowed to trade abroad.

d. AMIDA-DO (阿弥陀堂 Amida Hall) of TAKIYAMA-DERA or RYUZAN-JI (滝山寺 Waterfall-Mountain Temple). The main image in this hall is of Amida; it is a restoration of the image that burned in 1629. In 1188 Honen Shonin, founder of the Jodo sect, preached here and inaugurated the practice of the Nembutsu in this hall. This is one instance of Kiyomizu being used for the services of sects other than its own. Nembutsu services have been held here regularly since that first occasion—presently five times a year.

e. A small building containing a hundred stone images of Jizo, protector of travelers and dead children. As is common, many of the images are dressed in miniature clothes.

f. SHAKA-DO (釈迦堂 Shaka Hall). The third of the three large halls facing west, this one is dedicated to Shaka, the historical Buddha.

g. A small shrine called NISHIMUKI JIZO (西向地蔵 West-facing Jizo).

h. JISHU-GONGEN (地主権現), a Shinto shrine which is said to date from the early days of the temple (ca. 798), although it too was last rebuilt in 1633. The principal buildings are the open Hai-den, or Oratory, and the Hon-den, or Main Sanctum, the latter a *gongen*-style hall which is surrounded by a wooden wall. There is a smaller shrine to the east of the Hon-den. The stone *koma-inu* (mythical beasts) that line the steps to Jishu-gongen are the donations of parishioners.

i. HON-DO (本堂 Main Hall). The present Hon-do is on the site of the former Tamura-do, the history of which goes back to the Nagaoka Shishin-den awarded to Tamuramaro by the Emperor Kammu. The Hon-do houses the principal image of Kiyomizu-dera, an eleven-faced, thousand-armed Kannon which is so sacred that it is shown only once every 33 years (the last occasion was to have been the spring of 1962 but this was postponed to 1964 because of typhoon damage and construction work).[4] So tight is this secrecy that even priests of the temple have not seen the image unless they have attended the 33-year festival. The image is in a seated position, about five feet in height, and is at least a successor to the original attributed to Enchin, if not the original itself.

Other images in the Hon-do include those of Kannon's 28 followers. At the east and west sides of the building are images of Bishamonten[5] and Jizo, respectively, the latter work attributed to Enchin. These deities are said to have aided Tamuramaro in his military expeditions. There are also pictures of these two deities, and of Tamuramaro, hanging inside the Hon-do.

The Hon-do is famous for its unique architecture. The huge *hinoki*-shingled roof with its scalloped corners can be examined closely from behind, where the hill under Jishu-gongen comes up to it. In front the large and famous platform hangs out on a scaffolding over the edge of the cliff. It is called *butai* (dancing stage) and is flanked by two wings that run the width of the building, called *gaku-ya* (bandstands). Presumably this platform was created for the presentation of ceremonial dances.

The building is laid out in concentric areas. Inside the outer wings is the *nai-jin* (inner sanctuary), and at the center is the *nai-nai-jin* (innermost sanctuary), where the holy images are kept. The front part of the latter area is sunken and floored in stone.

4. In this manifestation of Kannon, the faces are said to represent the deity's ability and readiness to help man, while the arms hold Kannon's various attributes.

5. Bishamonten: a Buddhist deity adopted as one of the seven Shinto gods of luck, who represents both wealth and war. In Buddhism he is Tamonten, guardian of the north—where Tamuramaro waged his campaigns.

Three more "red ship" paintings hang under the eaves of the Hon-do. Although unsigned, they are dated 1634 and show ships of the houses of Sueyoshi (two) and Suminokura. In addition, the eaves and rafters of the Hon-do are crammed with about thirty large paintings—gifts of parishioners—of which those of strident black horses on gold grounds are the best known. The largest painting of all, dated 1703 and signed Kaiho Yusen, hangs on the outside back wall of the building.

j. "BENKEI'S GETA," a representation of the geta and staffs of the superman-priest Benkei, stalwart companion of the 12th-century hero Minamoto Yoshitsune. These replicas were made and given by a blacksmith in the Meiji era. It is said that, being blind, he prayed for a hundred days at Kiyomizu, and his sight was restored. This was his thank offering, and it always draws a crowd.

Benkei became Yoshitsune's retainer when the latter defeated him in a famous contest at the Gojo Bridge. According to an exaggerated version of the encounter, Benkei's overconfidence led him to use iron *geta* and staffs, which weighed him down so that he lost.

k. ASAKURA-DO (朝倉堂), a hall originally erected by the parishioner Asakura Sadakage in 1510, is dedicated to the eleven-faced, thousand-armed Kannon, and to Jizo. The present hall was built in 1633.

l. BENTEN-JIMA (弁天島), a small man-made island with a shrine on it to the Shinto goddess Benten. It is intended as an imitation of Chikubu-shima in Lake Biwa. Benten shrines are often placed on islands of one kind or another, and similar shrines are found in many Buddhist temples.

m. JOJU-IN (成就院 achievement temple). This temple was founded in the first quarter of the 16th century and is now the priests' quarters. It has an excellent garden from the Momoyama period which contains a stone basin, lanterns, and a stepping stone given by Toyotomi Hideyoshi. The basin is thought to resemble the shape of hanging sleeves. Hideyoshi donated the large stone in the center of the island and the small, squarish, upright one near the building. The latter is said to be from Korea. The garden was first made in the Muromachi period, but its original designer is unknown. Work done on it in the Momoyama period has been attributed to Kobori Enshu (1576–1647).

Originally there were three temples in Kyoto named Joju-in. The first, at Kitano, had fine flowers; so its garden was called *hana* (flower). The second, at Nijo-Horikawa, had a fine view of Mt. Hiei in winter and its garden was called *yuki* (snow). The only survivor of the three is this one at Kiyomizu. Because of its fine moonlight views this garden was called *tsuki* (moon).

n. TODOROKI-MON (轟門 Reverberation Gate)—the middle gate.

o. TAMURA-DO (田村堂), the founder's hall, named after Tamuramaro and moved to its present location in the 11th century. The hall contains statues of Enchin, Gyo-ei, Tamuramaro, and the latter's wife Taka-ko.

p. A DRAGON FOUNTAIN for washing the hands before entering the inner precinct. It was presented in 1861.

q. KYO-DO (経堂 Sutra Hall), where holy scriptures are kept. It contains a trinity of Shaka Nyorai flanked by Monju and Fugen.

r. ZUIGU-DO (随求堂). This sub-temple, which was first built in the Momoyama period, contains images of the eleven-faced Kannon, Dai-Zuigu Bosatsu, and Bishamonten. It also possesses many objects formerly owned by Toyotomi Hideyoshi. Hideyoshi is said to have prayed to this Zuigu Bosatsu before making important decisions.

s. This HILL near Joju-in is covered with small stone images of Jizo, Kannon, Shaka, Amida, Dainichi, etc.

t. THREE-STORIED PAGODA. It was first built in 847 at the instance of the Emperor Saga's consort Tachibana Kachi-ko (787–851). It now dates from 1633 and contains an image of Dainichi Nyorai.

u. SHO-RO (鐘楼 Bell Tower). This tower marks the western limit of the 1629 fire; its western buildings are Kiyomizu's oldest. The present tower probably dates from 1607, but the bell was cast in 1478. The bell has the name "Sugawara Tamenaga" inscribed on it. The elephant heads which decorate the beam-ends of this tower and the West Gate are typical of the Momoyama period; this type of ornamentation is thought to have been brought from Korea.

v. SAI-MON (西門 West Gate). This unusual-looking gate dates from the Momoyama period. The handsome curved gable on its east side is another detail characteristic of this period.

w. HOSHO-IN (宝性院 treasure-like temple). This sub-temple was built in the Edo period and reconstructed on a larger scale about 1920. Its main image is the eleven-faced, thousand-armed Kannon.

x. NIO-MON (仁王門). This gate contains the statues of the two Deva kings, or Nio, who guard temple entrances. It is also called Aka-mon (赤門 Red Gate) because of its color. The gate and its statues date from about 1478; it is the oldest major structure now standing at the temple.

y. UMA-TODOME (馬駐所 Horse Stalls). This final building once provided a place for horses to be kept. It dates from the Muro-machi period.

Between Uma-todome and Nio-mon there are stone lanterns and *koma-inu*, the latter dating from the postwar period. They replaced a former pair, which were of metal and quite ornate and which were taken away during the war to be used for arms.

One of the lanterns near the West Gate is famous for the tiger carved on it by Ganku (1749—1838).

z. The valley of Kiyomizu contains good cherry and maple trees. It has several ponds, which originated long ago as the hill-people's defense from fires in this area.

# PART THREE
Getting There and Back

# General Comments

Kyoto's historic sites are open almost every day of the year, from about 8–9 o'clock in the morning to about 4–5 o'clock in the afternoon. Specific times are listed below, but it should be noted that they may be changed according to seasons or other considerations.

Trains and buses charge fares relative to distance traveled. Bus fares are paid on the bus. Specific fares are also listed below and should, even if superseded, give the reader an idea of the cost involved in a given trip.

All train stations have platform signs in English as well as Japanese. Trains are punctual to the minute. Buses manage to run very close to schedule.

Streetcars charge ¥13 for one ticket (any distance on one car) and ¥25 for two tickets. There are no "transfers" given, but in front of the car barns (*shako-mae* 車庫前, see streetcar guide), where streetcars stop to change their numbers, transfers are given to those wishing to continue on a streetcar of the same number, which are good for that number only.

For example, a number 15 car will arrive in front of the car barn and stop. Schedules are resynchronized, conductors changed, the car number changed. The car number may be left as it is, depending on the schedule. If the car changes its number, transfers good for the next 15 to leave from that platform are handed out to those who desire them, and they get off and await a new 15. Passengers may stay on the car if its new number suits them. After a few minutes, with new personnel and possibly a new number, the old car will start up again and continue on its way.

Directions in this section are given from the Kyoto Hotel not only because it is centrally located but also because I recommend it highly. Its facilities, convenience, and courtesies are all excellent. Its staff is intelligent, helpful, and cheerful. Its location is superior to those of other hotels in the city, being at the center of the best shops, theaters, and all modes of transportation. If one desires to stay at a Japanese inn—something not recommended if he dislikes occasional inconveniences and irritations— the Tawara-ya and Hiiragi-ya, both within two blocks of the Kyoto

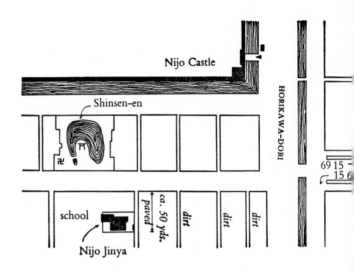

Hotel, are recommended. Arrangements to stay at these places may be made through the Japan Travel Bureau.

For eating outside the hotel, the Bali Grill at Sanjo-Kawaramachi serves good, inexpensive food in attractive surroundings, while Tsubosaka in Gion-Higashiyama is small, special, and more expensive.

Some phrases and place names that may prove useful when traveling are given in appendix III. The greatest freedom for entering buildings, etc. is permitted in winter. In the more crowded seasons—especially at popular places such as Ginkaku-ji and Nijo Castle—valuable rooms are usually roped off and visitors kept at a distance.

## 神泉苑

SHINSEN-EN: As it is more like a small park than anything else, there are no "hours" or admission fee for Shinsen-en. It takes but a few minutes to see and is best combined with a trip to Nijo Castle or Nijo Jinya. All three make a good project for a full half day, or longer if one prefers.

To reach Shinsen-en, Nijo Castle, or Nijo Jinya take bus number 15 or 69 from the stop one block west of Oike-Kawaramachi (see map 13). The fare is ¥15 one way. Going there, one's desti-

## MAP THIRTEEN
Nijo Castle, Shinsen-en, and Nijo Jinya

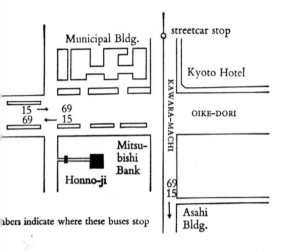

Municipal Bldg.

streetcar stop

Kyoto Hotel

KAWARA-MACHI

OIKE-DORI

15 → 69
69      15

Mitsu-
bishi
Bank

Honno-ji

69
15

Asahi
Bldg.

bers indicate where these buses stop

nation is Oike-Horikawa (御池堀川); returning, it is Oike-Kawaramachi (御池河原町). This should be mentioned or shown to the bus girl when the fare is paid. There are three bus stops between the two mentioned above. Note that, on returning, there are two equally convenient places to disembark (see map).

延暦寺

ENRYAKU-JI: Open from 9 to 4, admission to the precinct is ¥50. To see this temple properly one should allow a whole day; otherwise he will be rushed or have to omit parts of it. The amount of time one spends on the mountain can be used in varied ways. He can see the Eastern and Western Precincts and, if he wishes, can hike beyond them to Yokawa, following the trail back to Sakamoto from there (see map 14). He can hike up the mountain, down it, or both if he enjoys climbing. By using the cable car one saves energy and time, which can be devoted to a closer examination of the halls of the monastery. I recommend that visitors to Enryaku-ji do not limit themselves to the Eastern Precinct but see at least the Western too in order to get a true impression of the monastery's size and former remoteness. A reasonable route, if one is not going to go to Yokawa, is the order in which the halls are discussed in Part II.

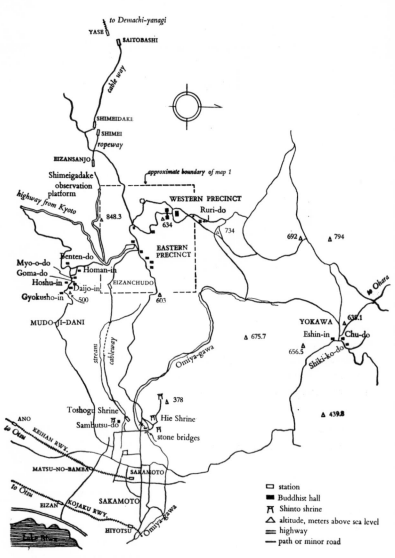

# MAP FOURTEEN
## Mt. Hiei and Vicinity

## 比叡山

### SHOWING ROUTES TO ENRYAKU-JI
### FROM YASE, KYOTO, OTSU, AND SAKAMOTO

## MAP FIFTEEN
## Sanjo Keihan Station

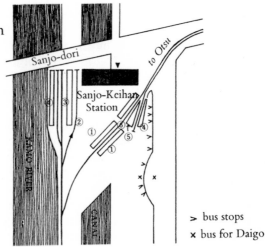

Sanjo-dori

to Otsu

Sanjo-Keihan
Station

> bus stops
× bus for Daigo

Train platforms: 1—to and from Uji
5 & 6—to and from Otsu

## MAP SIXTEEN
## Hama-Otsu Station

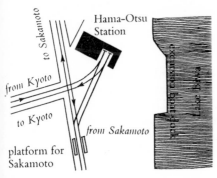

to Sakamoto

Hama-Otsu
Station

from Kyoto

to Kyoto

from Sakamoto

platform for
Sakamoto

Lake Biwa

occasional boat dock

## MAP SEVENTEEN
## Route to Enryaku-ji

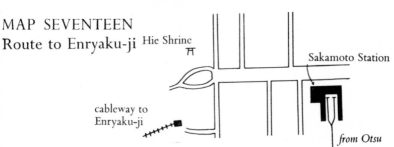

Hie Shrine

Sakamoto Station

cableway to
Enryaku-ji

from Otsu

Eating facilities on the mountain are poor—except at the new observation platform on its west side—but the Kyoto Hotel can provide an excellent box lunch to take along. Mt. Hiei is a good place for a picnic. Good weather is vital to one's enjoyment of the trip—although I have rarely seen a finer sight than Jodo-in enveloped in rain clouds, and thunderstorms on Mt. Hiei are spectacular.

The temperature on the mountain is generally cooler than it is in the city, but large trees and numerous hollows break the wind. In wet or wintry seasons one will need overshoes. The mountain often has snow in winter when Kyoto does not.

The best and most interesting way to reach Enryaku-ji is via train to Sakamoto, thence by cable car to the temple. With good connections, this scenic trip takes less than an hour.

At Sanjo-Keihan Station, located at Sanjo-dori on the east bank of the Kamo River (see map 15), buy a ticket for Sakamoto (坂本), ¥70 one way, and board the train for Hama-Otsu (浜大津) from platform number 5. Trains leave approximately four times per hour (three on Sunday). The express train reaches Hama-Otsu in 21 minutes; the regular, in 27.

At Hama-Otsu make the change indicated on map 16. The small Sakamoto train often pulls up to its platform across the street very shortly after one arrives from Kyoto, and with efficiency a quick change can be effected. The Sakamoto train says "Sakamoto" on its front. Trains leave for Sakamoto about every 15 minutes. Note that you continue to use the ticket purchased in Kyoto. The ride along Lake Biwa to Sakamoto takes 15 minutes.

At Sakamoto walk up to the cable-car station (map 17). The cable car leaves for Enryaku-ji every $\frac{1}{2}$ hour on the hour and $\frac{1}{2}$ hour; in winter, every hour on the hour. The fare is ¥80 one way, ¥160 round trip (*ofuku* 往復). The ascent takes 11 minutes.

Returning, one reverses the course. At Sakamoto Station buy a ticket for Sanjo-Keihan, Kyoto (三条京坂).

If one wishes to see the famous but decrepit giant pine at Karasaki he may walk through Sakamoto to the highway along Lake Biwa and take a bus from there to Karasaki (唐崎), then later another bus the rest of the way to Otsu.

三千院

SANZEN-IN: Open 9:30 to 4:30, admission ¥60. Sanzen-in and Jakko-in should be combined in a single trip to Ohara. It is pleasant to allow a day for a leisurely inspection of both, with lunch in between. A picnic lunch may be taken, or one may sample Japanese country fare at one of the small restaurants near each temple. *Ocha-zuke* (お茶漬)—rice soaked in tea—is the main dish here and has a bitter taste. For the full-course meal, ask for "Ohara shokuji" (大原食事). Good weather is desirable for this trip. Sanzen-in is famous for cherry blossoms (spring); maple leaves (fall).

To get to Sanzen-in, first take streetcar 2 or 12 north from the Kyoto Hotel (the stop nearest the hotel is on Kawaramachi at Nijo) to Kamo O-hashi (streetcar guide); then walk to Demachi-Yanagi Station and take a bus to Ohara (大原) from there (see map 20). The bus may have any of several markings, depending on its ultimate destination (see schematic, map 18); so it is best to query the bus girls of those buses that come to the loading platform (see appendix III). The fare, ¥65 one way, is paid on the bus. The trip takes about 31 minutes. The bus schedule to and from Ohara is somewhat irregular, with departures at intervals varying between 10 and 30 minutes, the intervals being shorter during the morning and evening rush hours. Returning, all buses will go at least as far as Sanjo Station. This takes 40 minutes and costs ¥80.

平等院

BYODO-IN: This temple can be combined with those of Daigo to make a full day's excursion. By itself, it can take 3–4 hours to go down to Uji, see it, and return to Kyoto. Again, one is advised to take a lunch if going for the full day. The hours of Byodo-in are from 8 to 5:30. Admission is ¥20 to the grounds, and an additional ¥50 to see the building, all paid at the gate.

At Sanjo-Keihan Station, buy a ticket for Uji (宇治), ¥60. The train leaves from platform number 1 (see map 15). Departures are at 14, 34, and 54 minutes past the hour. The trip takes 40–43 minutes. Uji is the end of the line, the 19th stop. Note: at Chusho-jima, the 12th stop, the train reverses course (see map 19). No cause for alarm.

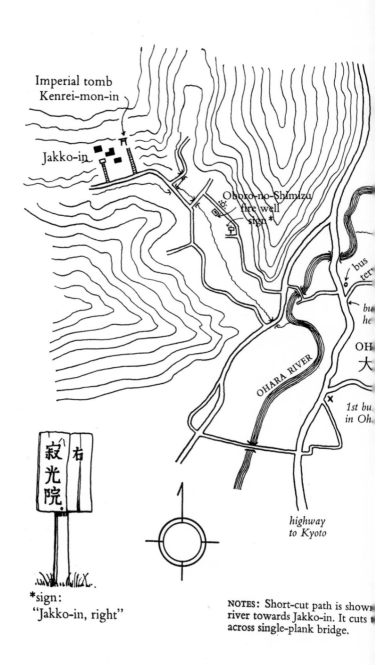

Imperial tomb
Kenrei-mon-in

Jakko-in

Oboro-no-Shimizu
fire well
sign *

bus
ter

bu
he

OH
大

OHARA RIVER

1st bu
in Oh

右
寂光院。

highway
to Kyoto

*sign:
"Jakko-in, right"

NOTES: Short-cut path is show
river towards Jakko-in. It cuts
across single-plank bridge.

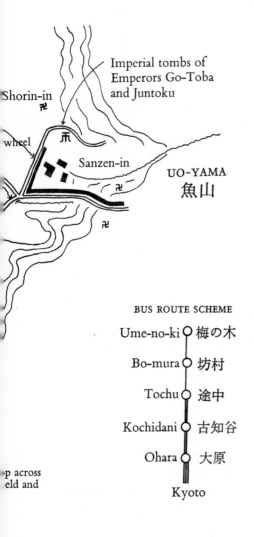

MAP EIGHTEEN
Jakko-in and Sanzen-in

Imperial tombs of
Emperors Go-Toba
and Juntoku

Shorin-in
卍

wheel

卍

Sanzen-in

UO-YAMA
魚山

卍

卍

BUS ROUTE SCHEME

Ume-no-ki ○ 梅の木

Bo-mura ○ 坊村

Tochu ○ 途中

Kochidani ○ 古知谷

Ohara ○ 大原

Kyoto

p across
eld and

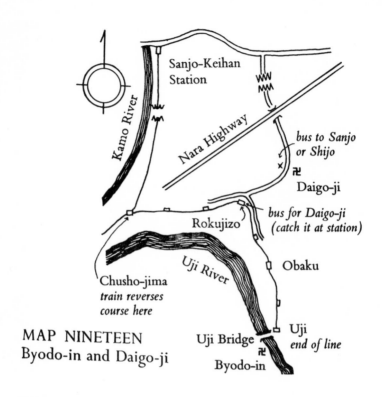

**MAP NINETEEN**
Byodo-in and Daigo-ji

At Uji cross the bridge and take the sharper left turn through the arch with two phoenixes. This street leads to Byodo-in. Returning, buy a ticket for Sanjo-Keihan, or if going to Daigo-ji, for Rokujizo (六地蔵), which is the fourth stop going back. Then refer to Daigo-ji below.

Like every trip in this book, this one can be done with fares and admission fees totaling less than a dollar.

寂光院
JAKKO-IN: See under Sanzen-in above; also streetcar guide and maps 18 and 20. Hours are 9 to 5, admission is ¥60.

法然院、安楽寺、霊鑑寺、冷泉帝陵
HONEN-IN, ANRAKU-JI, REIKAN-JI, REIZEI'S TOMB: There is no admission fee to any of these places. To reach them, take streetcar 2 or 12 north from the Kyoto Hotel and get off at Kinrinshako-

mae, taking the road opposite the platform to reach Reizei's tomb (see streetcar guide and map 5). The streetcar ride is 15–20 minutes. These places can be combined with Ginkaku-ji (see below) to make a full half day or a whole day, depending on one's pace. A reasonable Japanese lunch may be had at the restaurant in front of Ginkaku-ji. If in doubt one can order *nabeyaki* (鍋焼) to get a nourishing bowlful of noodles, meat, fried egg, etc. for about ¥100.

Returning, the streetcar 2 or 12 going west may be caught at Ginkaku-ji-mae (see maps).

If one wishes to make the circuit of Reizei's tomb, show the phrase in appendix III to the guard there, and he will probably allow it. At any of the three temples one makes a donation if he wishes, but this will not be requested and may even be turned down. At Anraku-ji the old lady may ask you to offer incense. In this case put three pinches of the grains in the incense pot after she lights it, put your hands together, rub them, bow, pray.

## 大徳寺、大仙院、高桐院

DAITOKU-JI, DAISEN-IN, KOTO-IN: The hours of Daitoku-ji's Hojo are 8 to 5, admission ¥40. Daisen-in and Koto-in are open 8 to 5 and 9 to 5 respectively, admission ¥50 to each. One can comfortably see all three in a morning or stay longer if he desires, especially if other sub-temples are added to the list.

For Daitoku-ji, take streetcar 5 or 15 north from Kyoto Hotel to Daitoku-ji-mae (see streetcar guide). Note that these cars pass through a car-barn stop (see general comment above). The ride takes about 20 minutes. Daitoku-ji is one block west of the Daitoku-ji-mae stop.

## 銀閣寺、浄土院

GINKAKU-JI, JODO-IN: Ginkaku-ji is open 8 to 5, admission ¥50. Jodo-in, not being a tourist attraction, has neither hours nor fee. Both can be combined with Honen-in, etc. (see above and map 5). For Ginkaku-ji, take streetcar 2 or 12 north from Kyoto Hotel and get off at Ginkaku-ji-mae (15 minutes; streetcar guide and map 5).

## 竜安寺

RYOAN-JI: Open 8 to 5, admission ¥50. The garden is equally well seen in all weathers, and one can spend as little or as much time at the temple and surroundings as he wishes. To avoid crowds and tourists go as early as possible. Ryoan-ji is a good stop if one is headed out towards Arashiyama.

The simplest way to go to Ryoan-ji from the Kyoto Hotel is by city bus 59 from Kawaramachi-Nijo (¥25, 25 minutes). The destination is Ryoan-ji-mae (竜安寺前). The bus stops on the new highway right outside the entrance to the temple. Returning, the destination is Kawaramachi-Nijo (河源町二条). To go to Arashiyama from Ryoan-ji, walk south a block, west a block, and then south again about four blocks to the small railroad station, Ryoan-ji-michi (竜安寺道). Trains pass here every 8 minutes, eastbound for Hakubai-cho, and westbound for Arashiyama.

## 醍醐寺、三宝院

DAIGO-JI, SAMBO-IN: Sambo-in is open from 9 to 4:30, admission ¥50. Daigo-ji has no fee to enter the precinct nor any particular times when it is "open" or "closed." Both are exceptionally crowded when the cherry blossoms are out, at which time one is advised to go as early in the day as possible.

There are two easy ways to get to Daigo. Both originate at the Sanjo-Keihan Station (map 15). By the first method, one buys a ticket to Rokujizo (六地蔵), ¥50, and boards the Uji train (see under Byodo-in above and map 19). Rokujizo is the 16th stop (32–35 minutes). Opposite the station, board a bus to Daigo (醍醐), which is an 8-minute ride costing ¥15.

The second method—especially for connoisseurs of good narrow-road bus driving—is to catch a bus to Daigo direct from Sanjo-Keihan Station (see map 15). The bus may wait away from the platform, near the street. Buy the ticket on the bus, ¥50. The trip takes 29 minutes; it is faster, but the bus leaves less often. Identify Daigo by the temple's long white wall, which runs along the left side of the road. Buses leave Sanjo-Keihan for Daigo at the following times: 7:47, 7:58, 8:10, 8:25, 9:05, 9:23, 9:40, 10:03, 10:23, 10:47, 11:13, 11:40, 12:22, 12:40, 13:13, 13:55, 14:10, 14:21.

Returning, the easiest way is to catch a northbound bus opposite the temple gate. Two kinds go by there. The Keihan bus goes to Sanjo-Keihan (三条京坂), ¥50, while the city bus goes to Shijo-Kawaramachi (四条河原町) and costs ¥65. Either is a reasonable way to get back to the city. Otherwise, the first route outlined above may be reversed (you may have to change trains at Chusho-jima) or used as far as Rokujizo to get a train there for Uji and Byodo-in.

One should allow a good half day for Daigo-ji, and more if he wishes to climb to Upper Daigo and examine it closely. It is good to combine this with Byodo-in for a full day's trip. Dry, cool weather is preferable.

## 二条城

NIJO CASTLE: The castle is open from 9 to 3:30 in winter and to 4 in other seasons. Admission is ¥30 to the grounds and an additional ¥40 to the Ni-no-maru halls, all tickets bought outside the castle walls. Seeing it can take from an hour upwards, depending on how closely one examines the paintings. There is a picnic ground within the walls of the castle, which has been made into a sort of city park. A good place to see in rainy weather, since the tour of the Ni-no-maru is indoors. It is also cool inside on hot days—and restful to tired feet, since you must wear slippers (¥10) inside the Ni-no-maru.

For routes to and from Nijo Castle, see map 13 and under Shinsen-en above.

## 修学院離宮

SHUGAKU-IN RIKYU: This villa may be seen only by appointment after gaining permission from the Imperial Household Agency. To obtain permission, get an application at the hotel and then go to the Imperial Household Agency, located inside the west entrance to the grounds of the Imperial Palace. Application must be made a day in advance. There is no fee to see the villa.

Weekdays there are four times when one may go: 9 and 11:00 a.m.; 1:30 and 3:00 p.m. Saturdays, 9 and 11:00; Sundays and holidays, closed. The time and date are specified on the permit, and one is advised to be prompt. Interpreters are provided at the two middle hours, and foreigners are supposed to go at these times. However, it is possible to see more by going at nine and

343

# MAP TWENTY
## Route to Shugaku-in

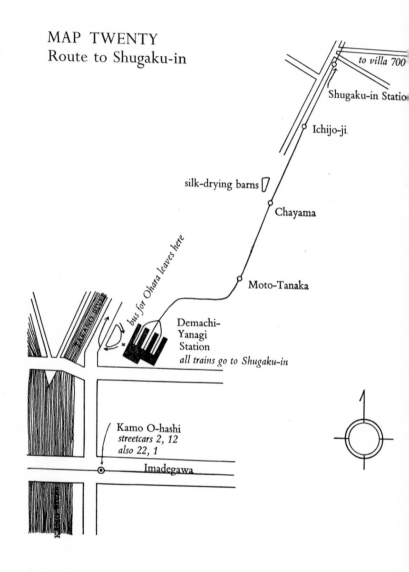

to villa 700

Shugaku-in Station

Ichijo-ji

silk-drying barns

Chayama

*bus for Ohara leaves here*

Moto-Tanaka

Demachi-
Yanagi
Station
*all trains go to Shugaku-in*

Kamo O-hashi
*streetcars 2, 12
also 22, 1*

Imadegawa

trailing behind the Japanese crowd, using this book and the booklet for sale at the grounds to inform oneself. This way one's activities are not so closely supervised. It may be necessary to take a Japanese acquaintance along in the capacity of "guide" in order to get permission to go at a "Japanese" hour.

The tour takes about one hour and fifteen minutes.

Shugaku-in is reached by train from Demachi-Yanagi Station (see map 20). Take streetcar 2 or 12 north from the Kyoto Hotel and get off at Kamo O-hashi (streetcar guide); at Demachi-Yanagi Station buy a train ticket for Shugaku-in (修学院), ¥15 one way. Trains leave at frequent intervals and all of them go to Shugaku-in Station. The trip takes 6 minutes. It is a walk of 10–15 minutes from the station to the villa (see map 20). Once on the road from the station simply follow it to the end. Mt. Hiei is dead ahead as one approaches the villa.

To calculate the whole trip in order to arrive on time, it is sufficient to allow 45–50 minutes for the trip by streetcar, train, and foot from the Kyoto Hotel to the villa.

## 二条陣屋

NIJO JINYA: This is a privately owned building and is shown by appointment only. The Kyoto Hotel can phone the *jinya* and make arrangements—the phone number is 84–0972. There is no set fee, but a donation (¥100 is reasonably generous) is generally asked. There is usually a student guide in residence who speaks some English. The tour can take an hour or more. The *jinya* is a good place to see in rainy weather.

For the route to Nijo Jinya see under Shinsen-en and map 13.

## 清水寺

KIYOMIZU-DERA: Open from 7 a.m. to 6 p.m., admission to the inner sector ¥20. Actually the temple is never "closed"—one can go any time or at night, the only thing closing at 6 being the booths where they sell tickets. There is a refreshment house on the grounds that sells noodles and beverages.

Take any streetcar south from the Kyoto Hotel to Shijo-Kawaramachi—or walk—and there take streetcar 7 to either Kiyomizu-michi or Uma-machi (see streetcar guide and map 21), depending on how you wish to go to the temple. To take the route recommended in chapter 15, get off at Uma-machi

345

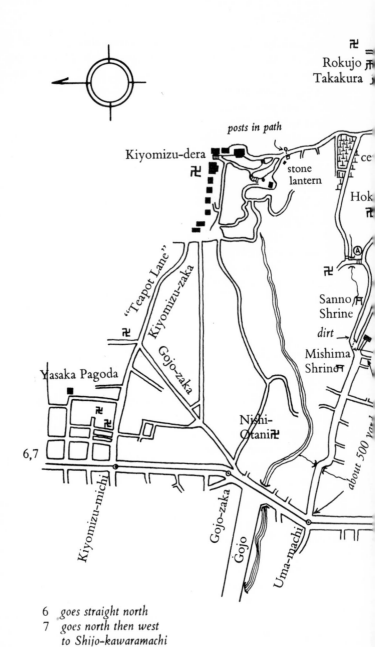

Rokujo 卍
Takakura

posts in path

Kiyomizu-dera
卍
stone
lantern

ce

Hok
卍

"Teapot Lane"

Kiyomizu-zaka

卍

Gojo-zaka

Sanno 🏮
Shrine

dirt →

Mishima
Shrine 🏮

Yasaka Pagoda

卍
卍

Nishi-
Otani 卍

about 500 yards

6,7

Kiyomizu-michi

Gojo-zaka

Gojo

Uma-machi

6  goes straight north
7  goes north then west
   to Shijo-kawaramachi

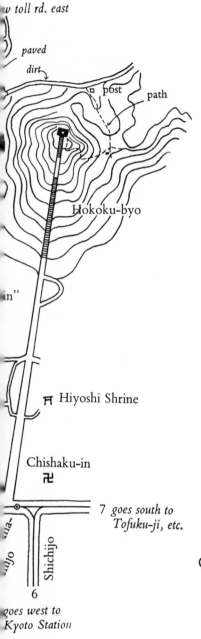

w toll rd. east

*paved*

*dirt*

post

path

## MAP TWENTY-ONE
### Kiyomizu and Its Environs

卍 Imperial tomb
卍 Buddhist temple
卍 Shinto shrine

Hokoku-byo

"in"

卍 Hiyoshi Shrine

Chishaku-in
卍

7 *goes south to*
*Tofuku-ji, etc.*

Shichijo

6

*goes west to*
*Kyoto Station*

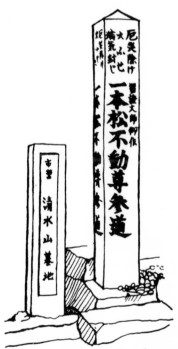

Ⓐ One turns off the road and goes down the steps here to the path leading to Kiyomizu. The stone post says: "Mt. Kiyomizu Cemetery."

and take the uphill street to the left as shown on map 15. For this route, overshoes are recommended in bad weather. If possible, however, see Kiyomizu in fine weather, as its appeal is largely exterior. One can go and be back in less than two hours or take longer as he wishes.

Map 21 also shows a little-known path up the Hokoku-byo, Toyotomi Hideyoshi's tomb on Amida-ga-mine, for those who want some exercise, a change of pace, a good view. For this climb take a city map and binoculars for identifying different sights. The top is a good place to picnic in warm weather, but avoid climbing up on hazy or particularly hot days. Clear cool ones are the best.

For the path, turn off the dirt road at the white sign post (it says, "Amida-ga-mine National Forest; don't disturb the trees; stake 20 第二十号.") Stick to the bigger path, and in the early going keep right; later take the upper route when offered a choice. The climb takes 20–25 minutes. From Hokoku-byo there is a fine view of Kiyomizu, as well as (NW to W): Nishi-Otani Cemetery, Yasaka Pagoda, Imperial Palace (beyond Kyoto Hotel), Kennin-ji, Nijo Castle, Chorin-ji, Nishi and Higashi Hongan-ji, etc.

One can come down by the long flight of steps (there is a fine Momoyama gate), which are dull to climb. Besides, opportunists often station themselves at the foot of the steps and charge you ¥10 for the privilege of climbing them!

# APPENDICES

# Appendix I: Japanese Art Periods

*The following is the generally accepted breakdown of the major periods of Japanese art:*

| | | |
|---|---|---|
| Archaic | –552 | Pre-Buddhist, native |
| Asuka | 552–645 | Buddhism arrives, Korean influences |
| Nara | 645–794 | Capital at or near Nara, Buddhism establishes itself |
| Early Heian | 794–897 | Chinese influences ⎤ Buddhism |
| Later Heian | 897–1185 | National styles emerge ⎦ now Supreme |
| Kamakura | 1185–1392 | The Minamoto shoguns, etc. |
| Muromachi | 1392–1573 | Ashikaga shoguns, civil war |
| Momoyama | 1573–1615 | Nobunaga and the Toyotomi |
| Edo | 1615–1868 | Tokugawa shoguns |
| Meiji-Taisho | 1868–1926 | Post-restoration, "pure" Shinto revived |
| Present | 1926– | Present reign |

Note: The Nambokucho, or period of imperial schism (1336–92), is assigned to either the Kamakura or the Muromachi period and sometimes is separated from them both.

# Appendix II: Glossary

a. JAPANESE WORDS USED IN THE TEXT.

*biwa:* a large musical instrument like a lute which is played while it lies flat on the floor

*chigai-dana:* a set of offset or fancy shelves in an alcove

*daimyo:* a feudal lord or baron

*fusuma:* heavier sliding screens papered on both sides and usually decorated or painted; cf. *shoji*

*geta:* wooden clogs worn on the feet

*ho-o:* a title given to an emperor who becomes a Buddhist priest after abdicating

*horai:* a mythical paradise, usually imagined as a distant island—an idea originally from China

*hyotan:* a gourd or gourd shape, often used as a symbol

*ihai:* a memorial tablet to a dead person, which is thought to be inhabited by his spirit

# Appendices

*jingu:* a Shinto shrine of national importance, a great shrine, such as Heian Jingu, Kyoto; Meiji Jingu, Tokyo; and the shrines at Ise

*jinja:* a Shinto shrine not belonging to the above group

*jinya:* an "encampment house," or sub-castle, e.g., Nijo Jinya

*karesansui:* "lacking mountain and water"—a flat dry garden, usually of raked gravel or sand and rocks

*ko-an:* a phrase or snatch of dialogue used as a subject of meditation by Zen Buddhists

*kohai:* the "halo" placed behind a Buddhist image, usually in the shape of a rising flame and gilded; often very intricate and covered with minor Buddhas

*koma-inu:* lit., Korean dog, a general term for "Korean dogs and Chinese lions," mythical beasts whose images guard the access routes to temples and shrines

*mandala:* (Sk., Jap. is *mandara*) an intricate schematic painting of a Buddhist afterworld which attempts in a formal way to portray all aspects of the subject; prominent in the Shingon sect, and common in those sects worshiping Amida

*mikoshi:* a portable shrine of the type carried through the streets by crowds during festivals

*mokugyo:* a wooden gong, usually in the shape of a curled fat fish, sounded during Buddhist services

*monzeki:* a temple having an imperial abbot or an imperial person in residence; also applied to nunneries with imperial women *(ama-monzeki)*

*Nembutsu:* the phrase *"Namu Amida Butsu,"* repeated by worshipers of the Amidist sects as the principal part of their worship (see chapter 3)

*nijiri-guchi:* the "wriggling-in" or "humble" entrance, a small demeaning hole through which people enter a teahouse

*Noh:* a form of drama characterized by the use of masks and by dance and song accompanied by instrumental music

*Ojo:* in the Jodo and Shin sects, birth into Amida's Paradise immediately after death; in the Shin sect, including immediate perfect enlightenment, but not in the Jodo, where enlightenment is not achieved until long after Ojo

*rikyu:* a detached palace, or imperial villa

*samurai:* a warrior or his class, esp. of the 12th to 18th centuries, during which time the class was most powerful

*satori:* a religious awakening or insight which is a prominent part of Zen worship and which, if achieved, comes suddenly and intuitively

*sei-i-tai-shogun:* "barbarian-quelling great general," a title originally conferred by the emperor upon his generals who led expeditions against the northern aborigines around A.D. 800; later assumed by generals of the Minamoto, Ashikaga, and Tokugawa families in establishing their military regimes

*shiro:* a castle

*shogun:* an abbreviation of *sei-i-tai-shogun,* q.v.

*shoji:* lightweight sliding screens usually papered with plain white paper on one side only; cf. *fusuma*

*sorin:* the metal spire of a pagoda

*sugoroku:* a sort of backgammon game played with dice, popular during the middle ages

*tana:* shelf

*tatami:* mats which cover the floor of a Japanese room

*tokonoma:* an alcove, often decorated with a flower arrangement and hanging scroll, found in Japanese rooms

*tsukubai:* a stone basin for water usually found near teahouses

b. SOME COMMON SUFFIXES. *Japanese suffixes are numerous and are often a quick key to the character of an object described by a word. Note that their initial sounds are often hardened when they are attached to words.*

| | | | | |
|---|---|---|---|---|
| *-an* 庵 | cottage, arbor | *-gawa* 川 | (*-kawa*) |
| *-bashi* 橋 | (*-hashi*) | *-gu* 宮 | (*kyu*) shrine, palace |
| *-chi* 池 | pond | *-guchi* 口 | (*kuchi*) entrance |
| *-cho* 町 | street, area | *-hashi* 橋 | bridge |
| *-dai* 臺 or 台 | (*tai*) stand, stage | *-ike* 池 | pond |
| *-daki* 滝 | (*-taki*) | *-in* 院 | temple |
| *-dan* 段 | degree, step | *-ishi* 石 | rock, stone |
| *-dana* 棚 | (*tana*) shelf | *-ji* 寺 | temple |
| *-dani* 谷 | (*-tani*) | *-jima* 島 | (*-shima*) |
| *-den* 殿 | (*ten*) palace, temple | *-kai* 海 | sea |
| *-dera* 寺 | (*tera*) temple | *-kaku* 閣 | pavilion |
| *-do* 堂 | (*to*) hall | *-kawa* 川 | river |
| *-dono* 殿 | Mr., lord of ...; *also* palace, temple | *-ken* 軒 | house, eaves |
| | | *-ki* 木 | tree, wood |
| *-dori* 道 | street | *-ma* 間 | space, room |
| *-e* 絵 | picture | *-machi* 町 | street, area |
| *-en* 苑 | garden | *-michi* 道 | way, street |
| *-gata* 形 | shape | *-miya* 宮 | shrine, palace |

| | | | | |
|---|---|---|---|---|
| -*mon* 門 | gate | -*to* 塔 | tower, pagoda |
| -*ro* 楼 | belvedere, high structure | -*tsukuri* 作 | construction, architectural style |
| -*san* 山 | mountain, hill | | |
| -*seki* 石 | rock | -*ya* 屋 | house, shop |
| -*shima* 島 | island | -*yama* 山 | mountain |
| -*taki* 滝 | waterfall | -*za* 座 | theater |
| -*tani* 谷 | valley | -*zan* 山 | (-*san*) |
| -*tei* 亭 | arbor, teahouse | -*zukuri* 作 | (-*tsukuri*) |

# Appendix III: Useful Phrases

At Honen-in, Reikan-ji, Kiyomizu-dera, etc.:

May I see the garden?

*Niwa o mite yoroshii desu ka?*

庭を見てよろしいですか。

At Reizei's Tomb:

I wish to follow the path around the tomb. I shall not attempt to enter the tomb.

*Ohaka no mawari o arukitai no desu. Ohaka no naka ni wa hairimasen.*

お墓の廻りを歩きたいのです。お墓の中にははいりません。

At Sanjo-Keihan Station, etc.:

What is the number of the platform where I board the train to _____ ?

_____ *yuki wa namban sen kara hassha shimasu ka?*

_____ 行は何番線から発車しますか。

I wish to buy one (two, three, four, five) ticket(s) for _____ .

_____ *made no kippu o ichimai (nimai, sammai, yommai, gomai) kudasai.**

_____ までの切符を一枚（二枚、三枚、四枚、五枚）下さい。

   * The name of the destination and a given number of fingers will be equally effective.

I wish to get off at _____ .

_____ *de oritai no desu.*

_____ で下りたいのです。

Does this train (bus, streetcar) go to _____ ?

*Kono ressha (basu, densha) wa _____ e ikimasu ka?*

この列車（バス、電車）は _____ へ行きますか。

At Ryoan-ji:

Please show me the altar room.

*Dozo saidan-shitsu o misete kudasaimasen ka?*

どうぞ祭壇室を見せて下さいませんか。

At Anraku-ji:

May I enter the Hon-do, please?

*Hondo e haitte yoroshii desu ka?*

本堂へはいってよろしいですか。

(If no one is around, go to the door of the priest's quarters—on the right of the Hon-do—open it, and make a noise or call inside until someone comes.)

Destinations for which the above "transportation" phrases can be used:

| | |
|---|---|
| Daigo-ji 醍醐寺 | Nijo-Horikawa 二条堀川 |
| Daitoku-ji-mae 大徳寺前 | Ohara 大原 |
| Demachi-Yanagi 出町柳 | Oike-Horikawa 御池堀川 |
| Enryaku-ji 延暦寺 | Oike-Kawaramachi (Kyoto Hotel) |
| Ginkaku-ji-mae 銀閣寺前 | 御池河原町 (京都ホテル) |
| Hakubai-cho 白梅町 | Otsu 大津 |
| Imadegawa 今出川 | Rokujizo 六地蔵 |
| Kawaramachi-nijo 河原町二条 | Ryoan-ji-mae 竜安寺前 |
| Kawaramachi-sanjo 河原町三条 | Sakamoto 坂本 |
| Kawaramachi-shijo 河原町四条 | Sanjo-Keihan 三条京阪 |
| Kinrinshako-mae 錦林車庫前 | Shijo 四条 |
| Kiyomizu-michi 清水道 | Shugaku-in (station or villa) 修学院 |
| Maruta-machi 丸太町 | Uji 宇治 |
| Nijo 二条 | Uma-machi 馬町 |

# Acknowledgments

I WISH to acknowledge the generous efforts of the following persons, all of whom contributed markedly to the possibility of this book's being written: Ishida Eiji, professor at Kyoto Prefectural University; Shimojima Masao; Okubo Hiromasa; Fujitani Kiyoshi; Terasoma Shigeo; Sakabe Hiroshi. Among the priests and personnel of many temples who gave me their patient assistance, I owe special thanks to Matsumoto Daien of Kiyomizu-dera, Akamatsu Enzui of Enryaku-ji, and my good friends Kodama Kogetsu of Eifuku-ji in Osaka and Okamoto Ryuen of Enryaku-ji. For hours of work and helpful suggestions I wish to thank John Philip Emerson and Austin M. Francis, Jr. I have a particular debt to Philip Yampolsky, whose translation of Daitoku-ji's own guide forms the backbone of the information on that temple appearing in Part II, and to Nagai Atsuko, who sacrificed much of her free time to my research for this book and provided many good ideas. Finally, I wish to thank Ralph Friedrich for editing the book with tireless patience, energy, and interest.

In the realm of printed sources, I wish to acknowledge the special help provided by the following, especially as indicated:

A. Akiyama: *Pagodas in Surprise Land,* Tokyo, 1915 (Enryaku-ji)

C. R. Boxer: "Hosokawa Tadaoki and the Jesuits, 1587—1645," *Transactions and Proceedings,* Japan Society, London, Vol. XXXII, 1934–35 (Daitoku-ji)

H. H. Coates and R. Ishizuka: *Honen the Buddhist Saint,* Kyoto, 1949 (Enryaku-ji, Sanzen-in, Anraku-ji and Honen-in, Daigo-ji, and others)

R. T. Paine and A. Soper: *The Art and Architecture of Japan,* London, 1960 (Enryaku-ji, Daigo-ji, Nijo-jo)

E. Papinot: *Historical and Geographical Dictionary of Japan,* Yokohama, 1909 (nearly all subjects, especially personalities)

R. A. B. Ponsonby-Fane: *The Imperial House of Japan,* Kyoto, 1959 (Shugaku-in Rikyu)

————: *Kyoto, the Old Capital of Japan,* Kyoto, 1956 (Shinsen-en, Ginkaku-ji, Nijo-jo, Shugaku-in Rikyu, Nijo Jinya [Temmei Fire], and others)

# Acknowledgments

A. L. Sadler: *The Ten Foot Square Hut and Tales of the Heike*, Sydney, 1928 (Uji, Jakko-in)

G. B. Sansom: *Japan, A Short Cultural History*, New York, 1943 (Daigo-ji)

R. F. Sasaki: *Rinzai Zen Study for Foreigners in Japan*, Kyoto, 1960 (Daitoku-ji)

————: *Zen: A Religion*, Kyoto, 1958 (Daitoku-ji)

D. T. Suzuki: *Japanese Buddhism*, Tokyo, 1938 (Daitoku-ji)

M. Tatsui: *Japanese Gardens*, Tokyo, 1936 (Ginkaku-ji)

W. Watson: *Sculpture of Japan*, New York, 1959 (Enryaku-ji, Byodo-in, Daigo-ji)

I made use of pamphlets and other materials provided by the following places: Enryaku-ji, Sanzen-in, Byodo-in, Daitoku-ji, Jodo-in, Ryoan-ji, Daigo-ji, Nijo-jo, Shugaku-in Rikyu, Nijo Jinya, Kiyomizu-dera. Shugaku-in's new booklet in English is an outstanding contribution; most of the others are in Japanese.

# Index

*Page numbers in italics refer to sources of more detailed information. The more important buildings, gardens, and other identifiable parts of the places discussed in this book are listed* under the name of the place.

# Index

# Index

# Index

# Index

# Index

# Index